BLACK SHEEP, SCOUNDRELS AND WEIRDOS, PETER QUILL, A.K.A. STAR-LORD, DRAX THE DESTROYER, GAMORA, ROCKET RACCOON AND GROOT LEARNED TO LOOK AFTER THEIR OWN INTERESTS, THEN DISCOVERED THEY COULD NOT STAND BY WHEN THE UNIVERSE WAS IN PERIL. THEY HAVE NO OFFICIAL JURISDICTION, BUT IF YOU'RE IN TROUBLE (OR YOU'VE GOT A LINE ON A SCORE) IN THE MILKY WAY, YOU CAN CALL THE...

All New GUARDIANS of the GALAXY

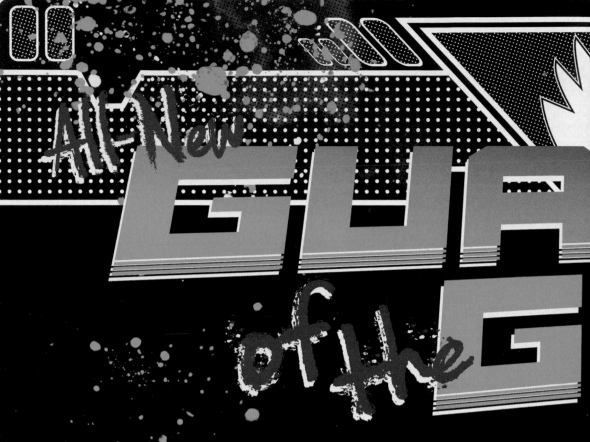

THE GUARDIANS ARE CAUGHT BETWEEN TWO ELDERS OF THE UNIVERSE – STEALING FROM THE COLLECTOR FOR THE GRANDMASTER – PARTLY FOR MONETARY GAIN, BUT PARTLY FOR REASONS GAMORA IS KEEPING TO HERSELF. SHE'S SEEKING SOMETHING – SOME INFORMATION, SECRET OR ARTIFACT – AND THE QUEST HAS OCCUPIED HER TO THE POINT OF OBSESSION.

MEANWHILE, THE *MILANO* WAS BOARDED BY A MYSTERIOUS GROUP OF SHI'AR WARRIORS KNOWN AS THE FRATERNITY OF THE RAPTORS, WHOSE LEADER, TALONAR, WAS HELL-BENT ON RETRIEVING THE NEGA-BANDS THE GUARDIANS WERE TRANSPORTING. TO DRIVE THE INTRUDERS OFF, DRAX WAS REQUIRED TO BREAK HIS VOW OF NONVIOLENCE. ROCKET WAS LETHALLY POISONED DURING THE RAID, AND QUILL RACED TO SECURE AN ANTIDOTE – UNFORTUNATELY LOSING THE SET OF NEGA-BANDS IN THE PROCESS. GROOT STOOD ASIDE HELPLESSLY, HIS SMALL SIZE BECOMING MORE AND MORE OF A HINDRANCE. WHILE NO ONE CAN FIGURE OUT WHY GROOT ISN'T GROWING, ACROSS THE GALAXY A STRANGE HOODED FIGURE MAY HAVE THE ANSWER.

COLLECTION EDITOR JENNIFER GRÜNWALD ASSISTANT EDITOR CAITLIN O'CONNELL ASSOCIATE MANAGING EDITOR KATERI WOODY
EDITOR, SPECIAL PROJECTS MARK D. BEAZLEY VP PRODUCTION & SPECIAL PROJECTS JEFF YOUNGQUIST SVP PRINT, SALES & MARKETING DAVID GABRIEL
BOOK DESIGNERS JAY BOWEN & MANNY MEDEROS

EDITOR IN CHIEF AXEL ALONSO CHIEF CREATIVE OFFICER JOE QUESADA PRESIDENT DAN BUCKLEY EXECUTIVE PRODUCER ALAN FINE

ALL-NEW GUARDIANS OF THE GALAXY VOL. 2: RIDERS IN THE SKY. Contains material originally published in magazine form as ALL-NEW GUARDIANS OF THE GALAXY #3, #5, #7, #9 and #11-12. First printing 2017. ISBN# 978-1-302-90545-3. Published by MARVEL WORLDWIDE, INC., a subsidiary of MARVEL ENTERTAINMENT, LLC. OFFICE OF PUBLICATION: 135 West 50th Street, New York, NY 10020. **Printed in Canada.** DAN BUCKLEY, President, Marvel Entertainment; JOE QUESADA, Chief Creative Officer; TOM BREVOORT, SVP of Publishing; DAVID BOGART, SVP of Business Affairs & Operations, Publishing & Partnership; C.B. CEBULSKI, VP of Brand Management & Development, Asia; DAVID GABRIEL, SVP of Sales & Marketing, Publishing; JEFF YOUNGQUIST, VP of Production & Special Projects; DAN CARR, Executive Director of Publishing Technology; ALEX MORALES, Director of Publishing Operations; SUSAN CRESPI, Production Manager; STAN LEE, Chairman Emeritus. For information regarding advertising in Marvel Comics or on Marvel.com, please contact Jonathan Parkhideh, VP of Digital Media & Marketing Solutions, at jparkhideh@marvel.com. For Marvel subscription inquiries, please call 888-511-5480. **Manufactured between 10/27/2017 and 11/28/2017 by SOLISCO PRINTERS, SCOTT, QC, CANADA.**

10 9 8 7 6 5 4 3 2 1

RDIANS ALAXY

RIDERS IN THE SKY

WRITER GERRY DUGGAN

ARTISTS FRAZER IRVING [#3], CHRIS SAMNEE [#5],
GREG SMALLWOOD [#7], MIKE HAWTHORNE & TERRY PALLOT [#9],
ROLAND BOSCHI [#11] AND ROD REIS [#12]

COLOR ARTISTS FRAZER IRVING [#3], MATTHEW WILSON [#5],
GREG SMALLWOOD [#7], JORDIE BELLAIRE [#9],
DAN BROWN [#11] AND ROD REIS [#12]

LETTERER VC's CORY PETIT

COVER ART AARON KUDER & IVE SVORCINA [#3, #5, #7, #9],
FRANCESCO MATTINA [#11] AND ROD REIS [#12]

ASSISTANT EDITORS KATHLEEN WISNESKI & CHARLES BEACHAM
ASSOCIATE EDITOR DARREN SHAN   EDITOR JORDAN D. WHITE

3

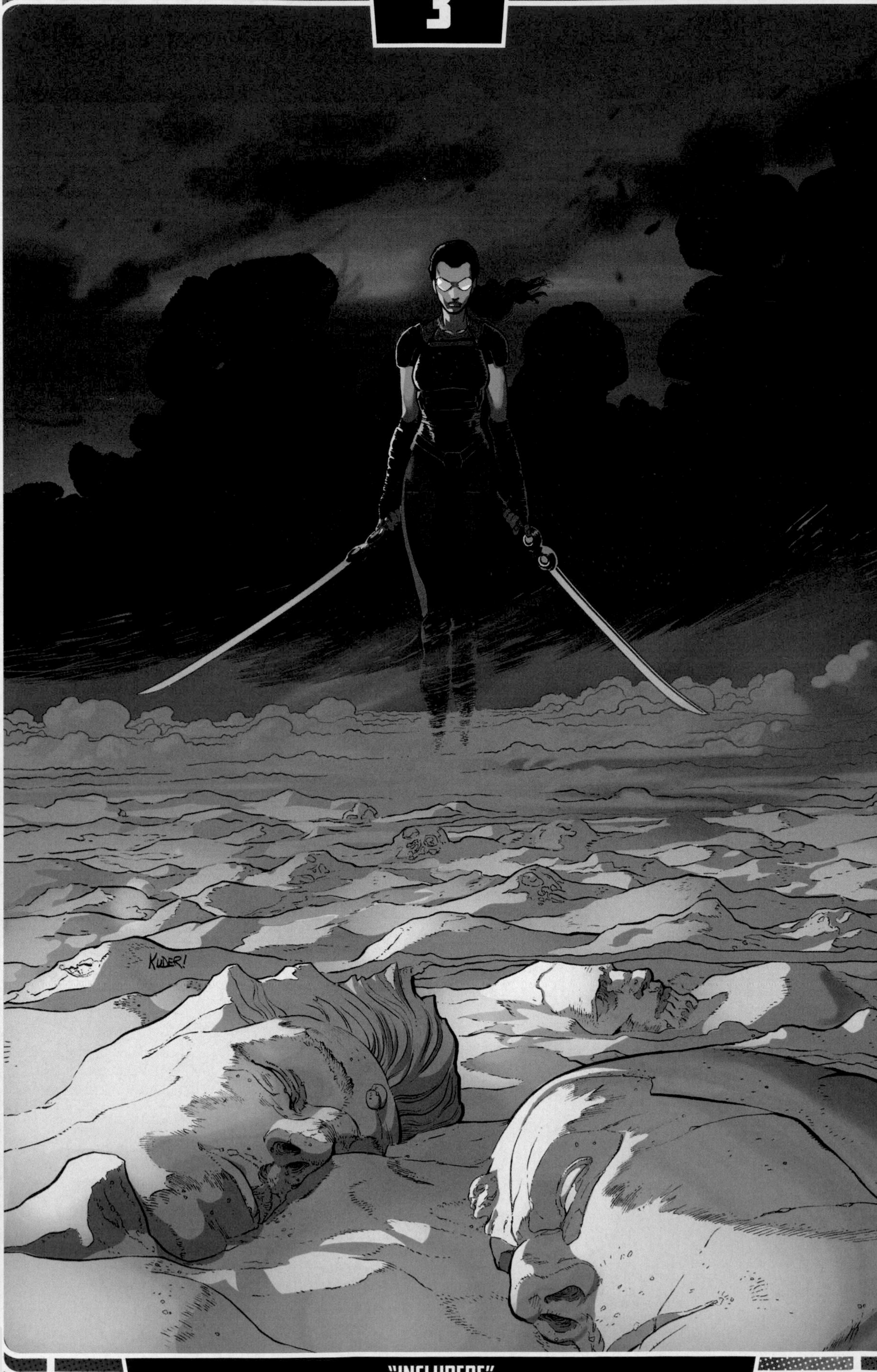
KUDER!

"INCLUDERE"

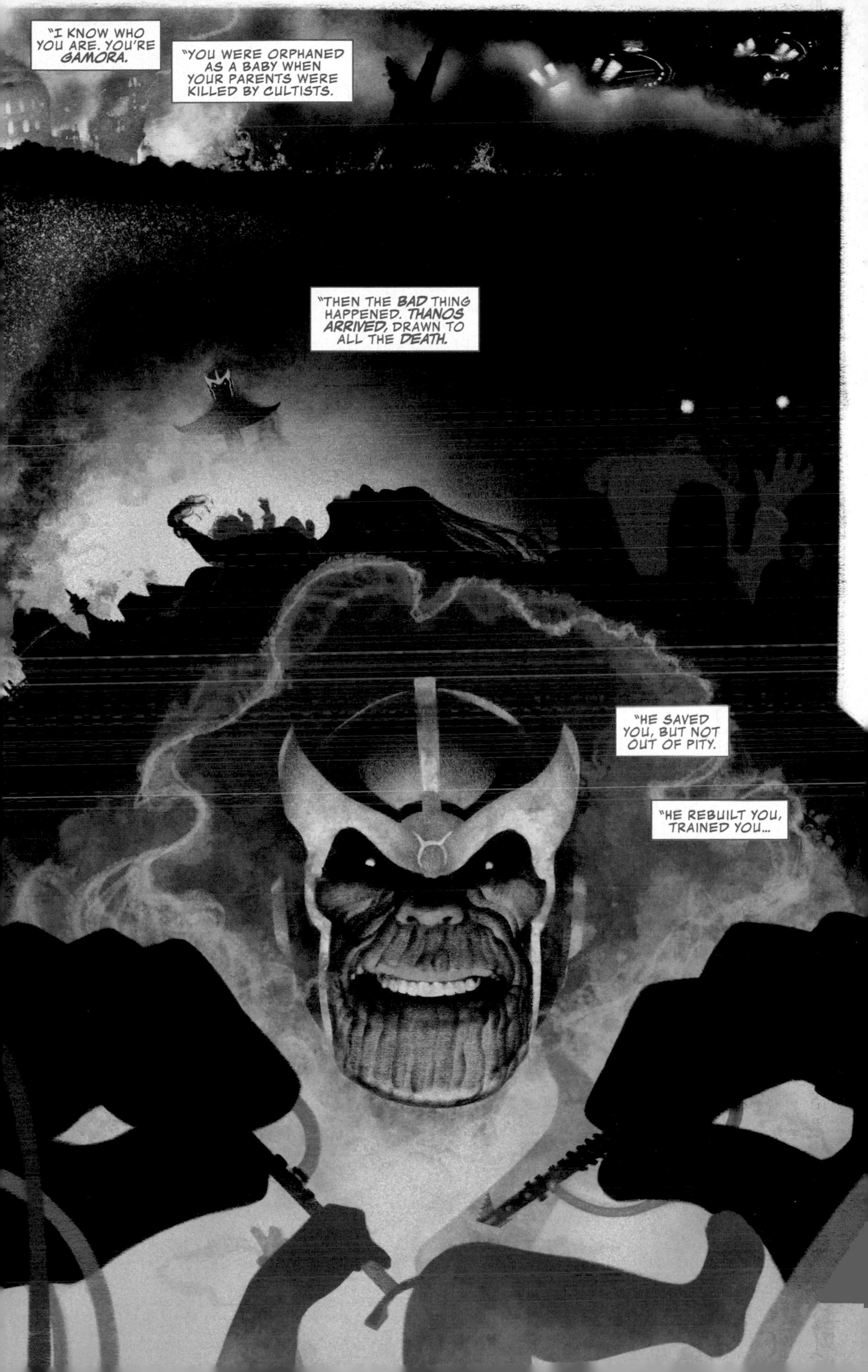
"I KNOW WHO YOU ARE. YOU'RE GAMORA.
"YOU WERE ORPHANED AS A BABY WHEN YOUR PARENTS WERE KILLED BY CULTISTS.
"THEN THE BAD THING HAPPENED. THANOS ARRIVED, DRAWN TO ALL THE DEATH.
"HE SAVED YOU, BUT NOT OUT OF PITY.
"HE REBUILT YOU, TRAINED YOU...

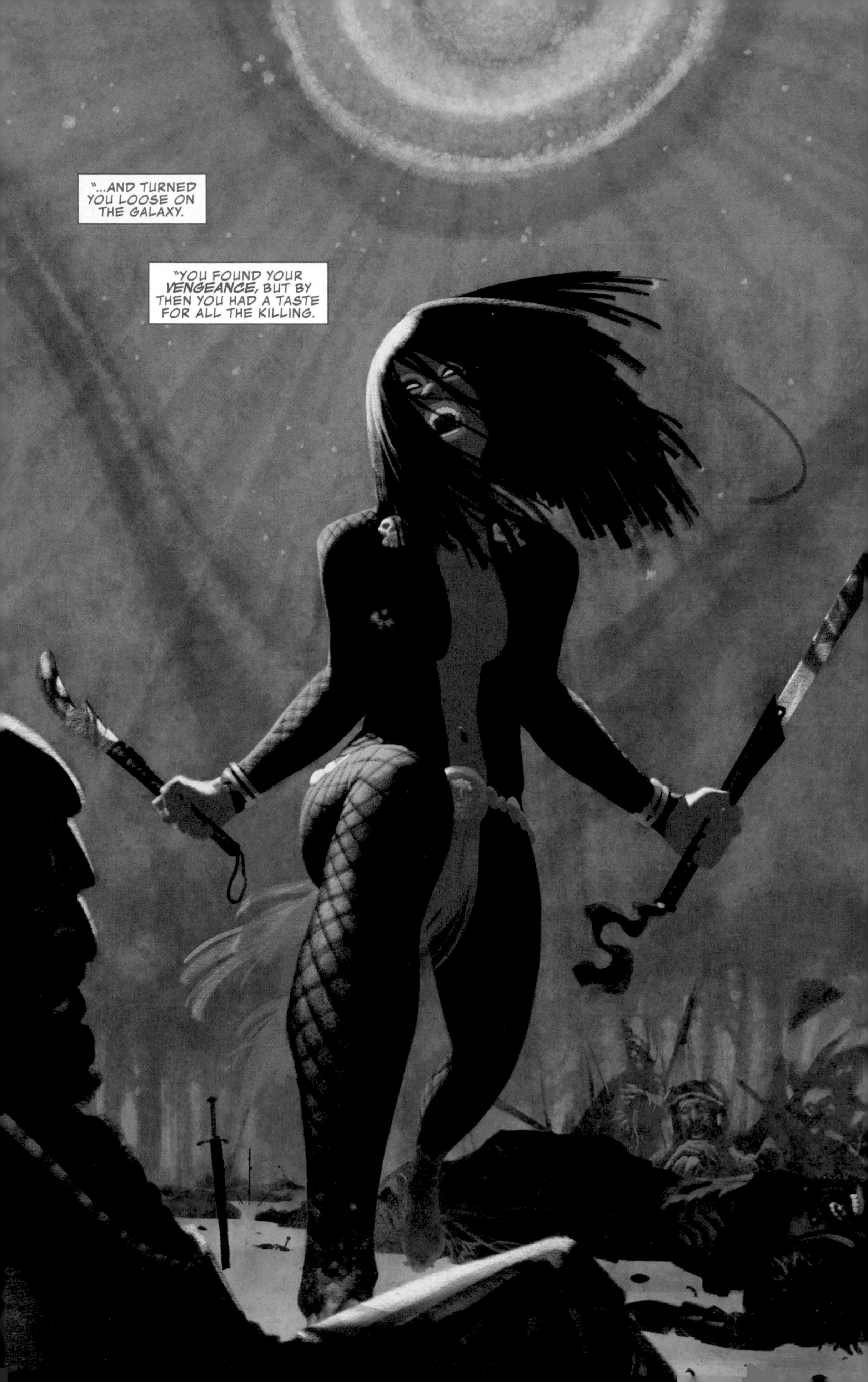
"...AND TURNED YOU LOOSE ON THE GALAXY.
"YOU FOUND YOUR VENGEANCE, BUT BY THEN YOU HAD A TASTE FOR ALL THE KILLING.

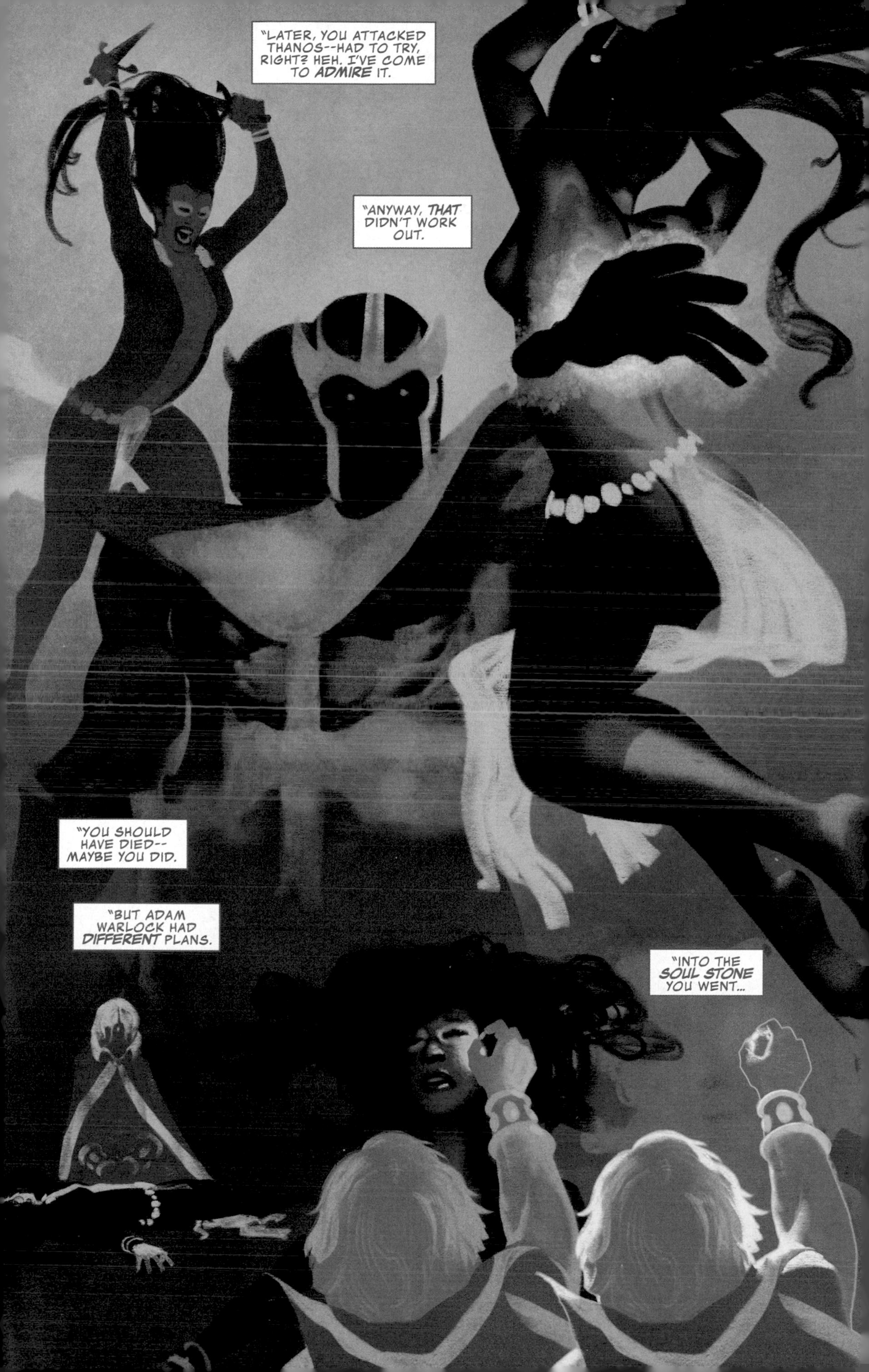
"LATER, YOU ATTACKED THANOS--HAD TO TRY, RIGHT? HEH. I'VE COME TO ADMIRE IT.
"ANYWAY, THAT DIDN'T WORK OUT.
"YOU SHOULD HAVE DIED-- MAYBE YOU DID.
"BUT ADAM WARLOCK HAD DIFFERENT PLANS.
"INTO THE SOUL STONE YOU WENT...

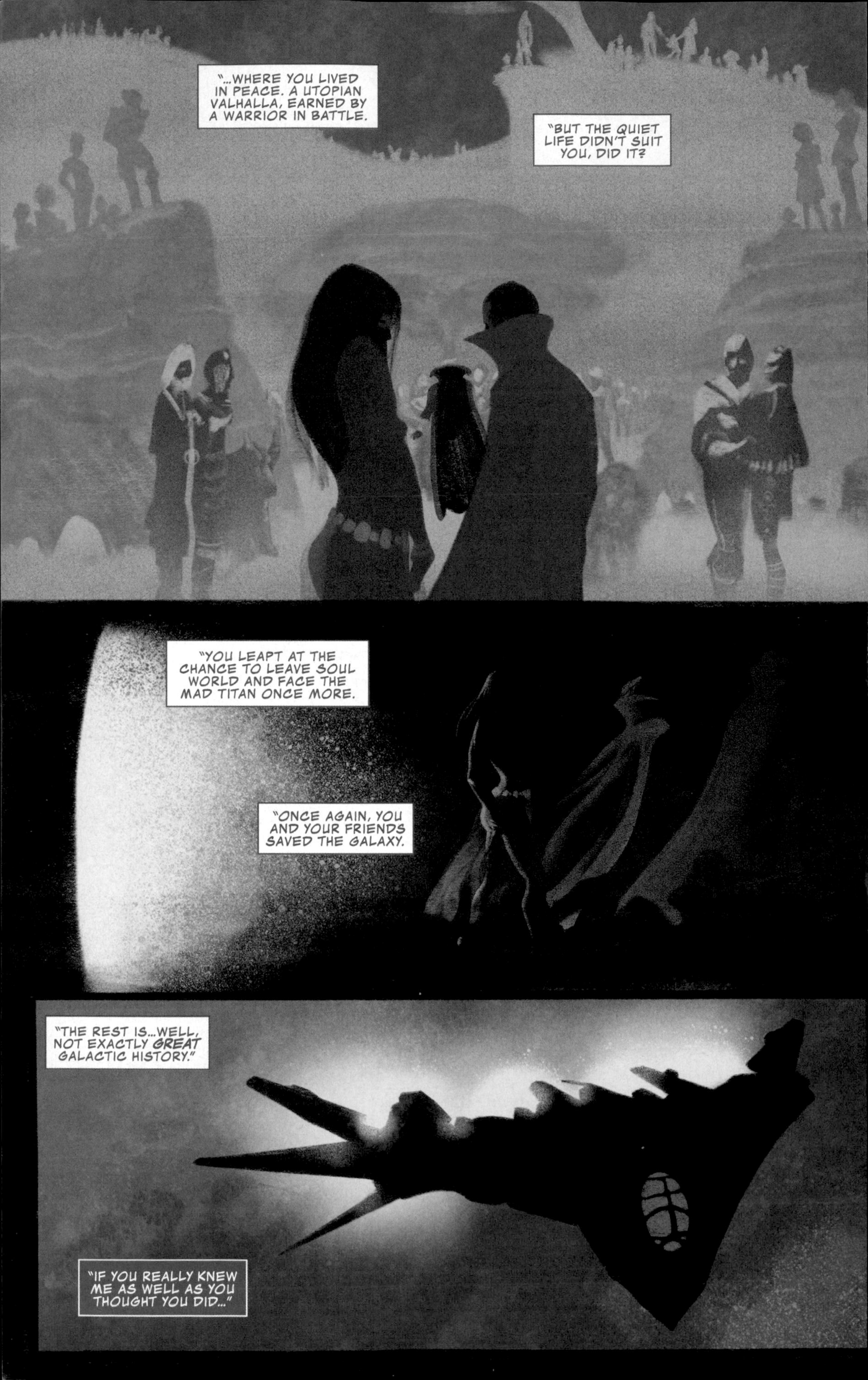
"...WHERE YOU LIVED IN PEACE. A UTOPIAN VALHALLA, EARNED BY A WARRIOR IN BATTLE.
"BUT THE QUIET LIFE DIDN'T SUIT YOU, DID IT?
"YOU LEAPT AT THE CHANCE TO LEAVE SOUL WORLD AND FACE THE MAD TITAN ONCE MORE.
"ONCE AGAIN, YOU AND YOUR FRIENDS SAVED THE GALAXY.
"THE REST IS...WELL, NOT EXACTLY *GREAT* GALACTIC HISTORY."
"IF YOU REALLY KNEW ME AS WELL AS YOU THOUGHT YOU DID..."

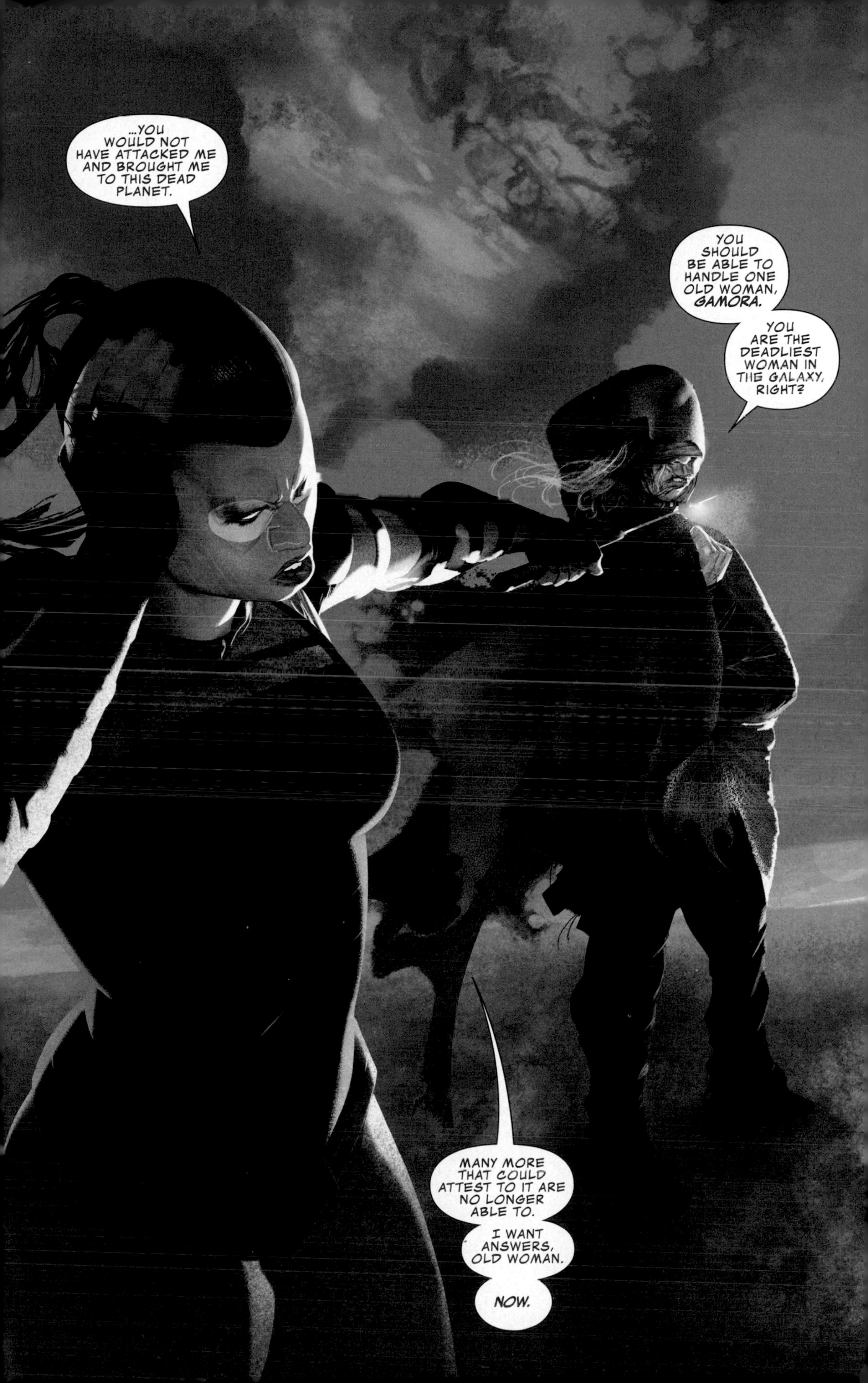
...YOU WOULD NOT HAVE ATTACKED ME AND BROUGHT ME TO THIS DEAD PLANET.
YOU SHOULD BE ABLE TO HANDLE ONE OLD WOMAN, GAMORA.
YOU ARE THE DEADLIEST WOMAN IN THE GALAXY, RIGHT?
MANY MORE THAT COULD ATTEST TO IT ARE NO LONGER ABLE TO.
I WANT ANSWERS, OLD WOMAN.
NOW.

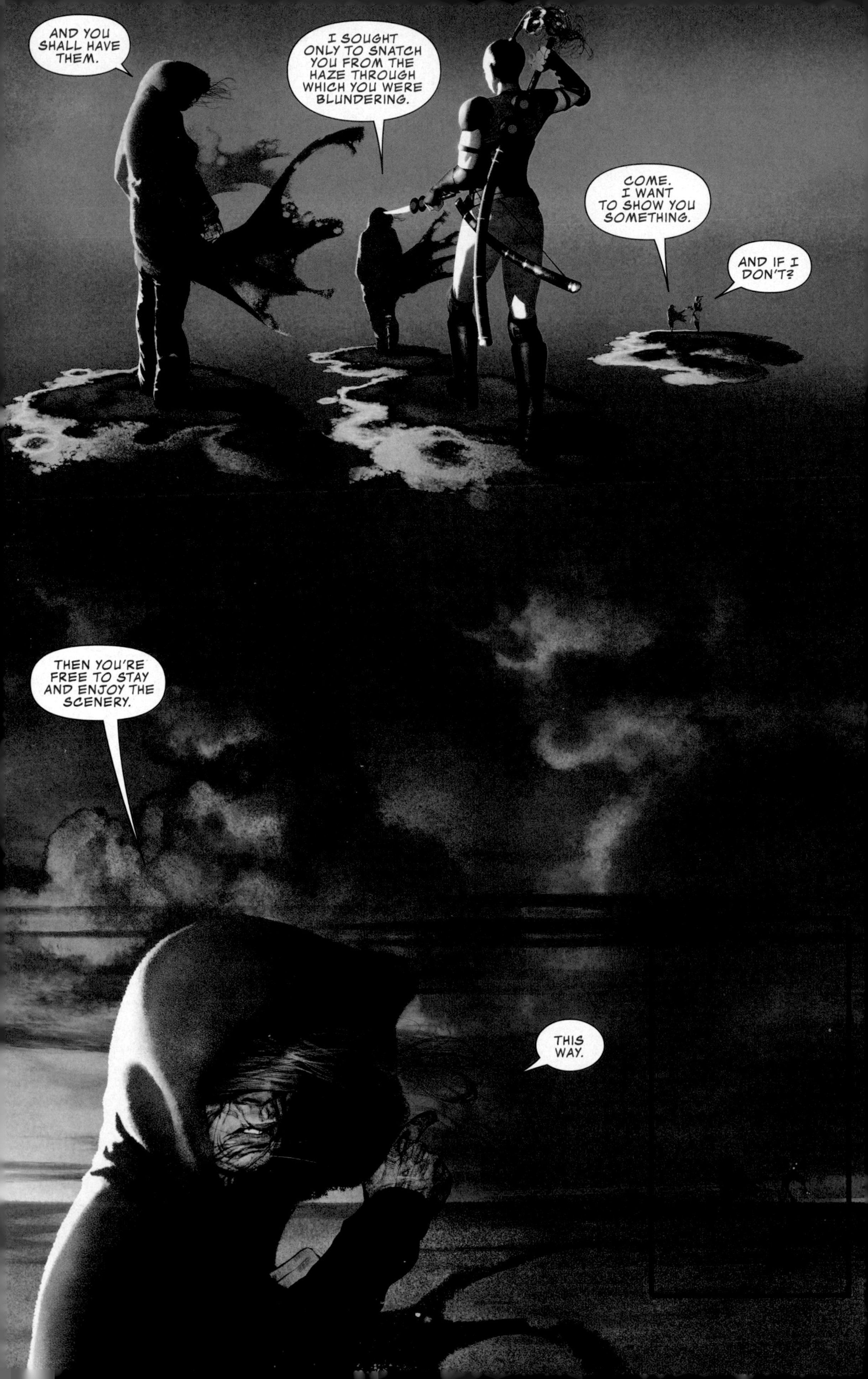
AND YOU SHALL HAVE THEM.
I SOUGHT ONLY TO SNATCH YOU FROM THE HAZE THROUGH WHICH YOU WERE BLUNDERING.
COME. I WANT TO SHOW YOU SOMETHING.
AND IF I DON'T?
THEN YOU'RE FREE TO STAY AND ENJOY THE SCENERY.
THIS WAY.

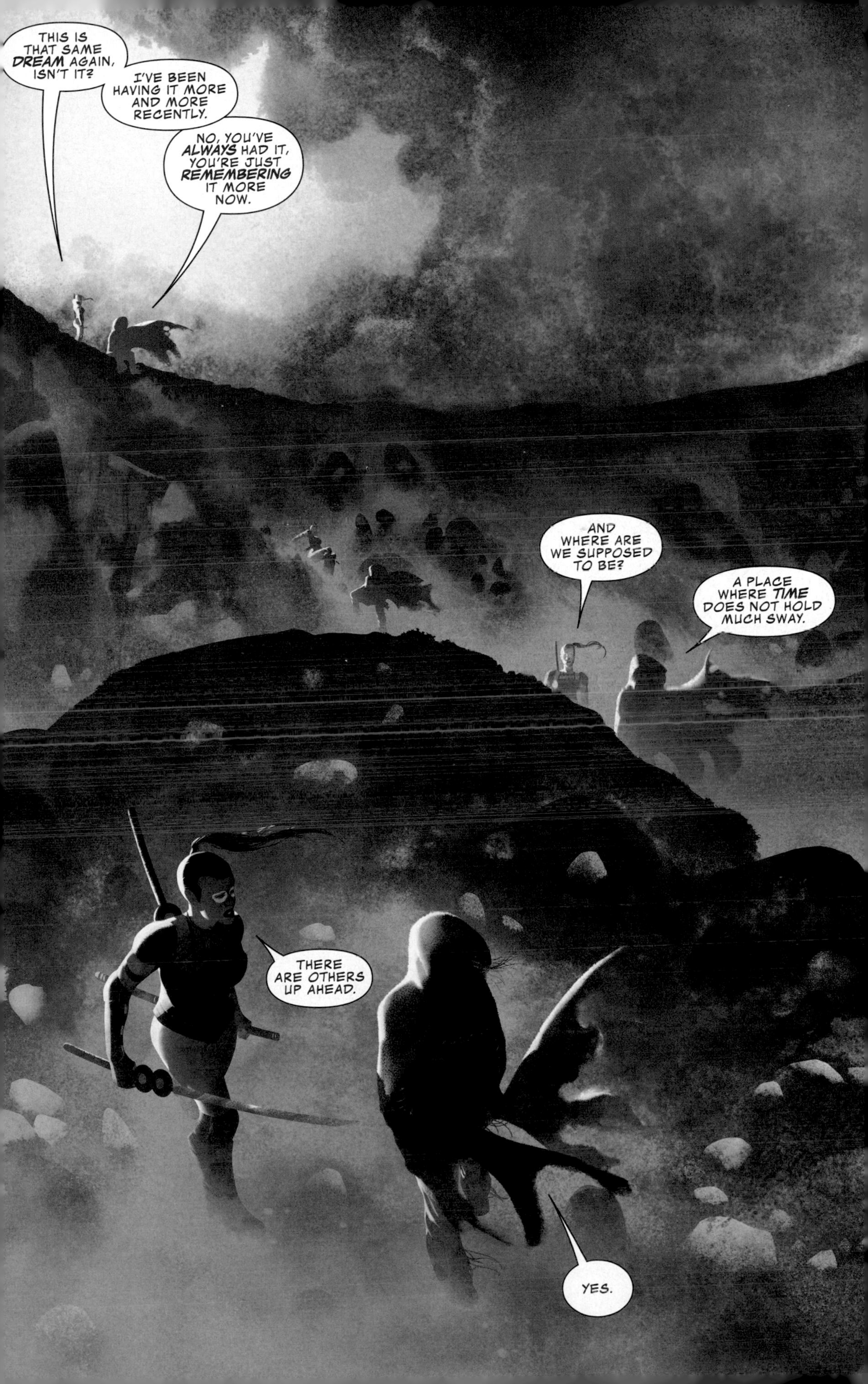
THIS IS THAT SAME DREAM AGAIN, ISN'T IT?
I'VE BEEN HAVING IT MORE AND MORE RECENTLY.
NO, YOU'VE ALWAYS HAD IT, YOU'RE JUST REMEMBERING IT MORE NOW.
AND WHERE ARE WE SUPPOSED TO BE?
A PLACE WHERE TIME DOES NOT HOLD MUCH SWAY.
THERE ARE OTHERS UP AHEAD.
YES.

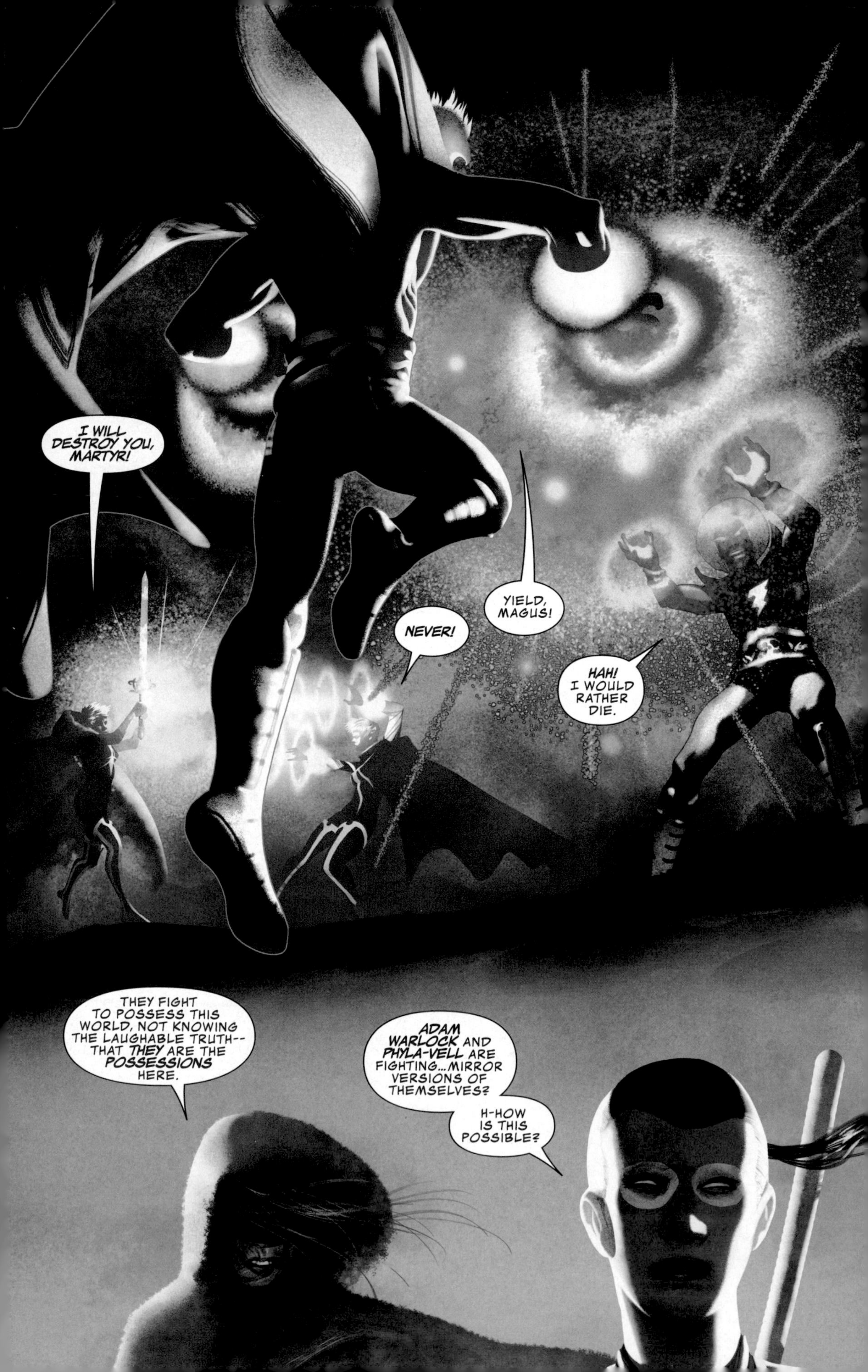
I WILL DESTROY YOU, MARTYR!
YIELD, MAGUS!
NEVER!
HAH! I WOULD RATHER DIE.
THEY FIGHT TO POSSESS THIS WORLD, NOT KNOWING THE LAUGHABLE TRUTH-- THAT THEY ARE THE POSSESSIONS HERE.
ADAM WARLOCK AND PHYLA-VELL ARE FIGHTING... MIRROR VERSIONS OF THEMSELVES?
H-HOW IS THIS POSSIBLE?

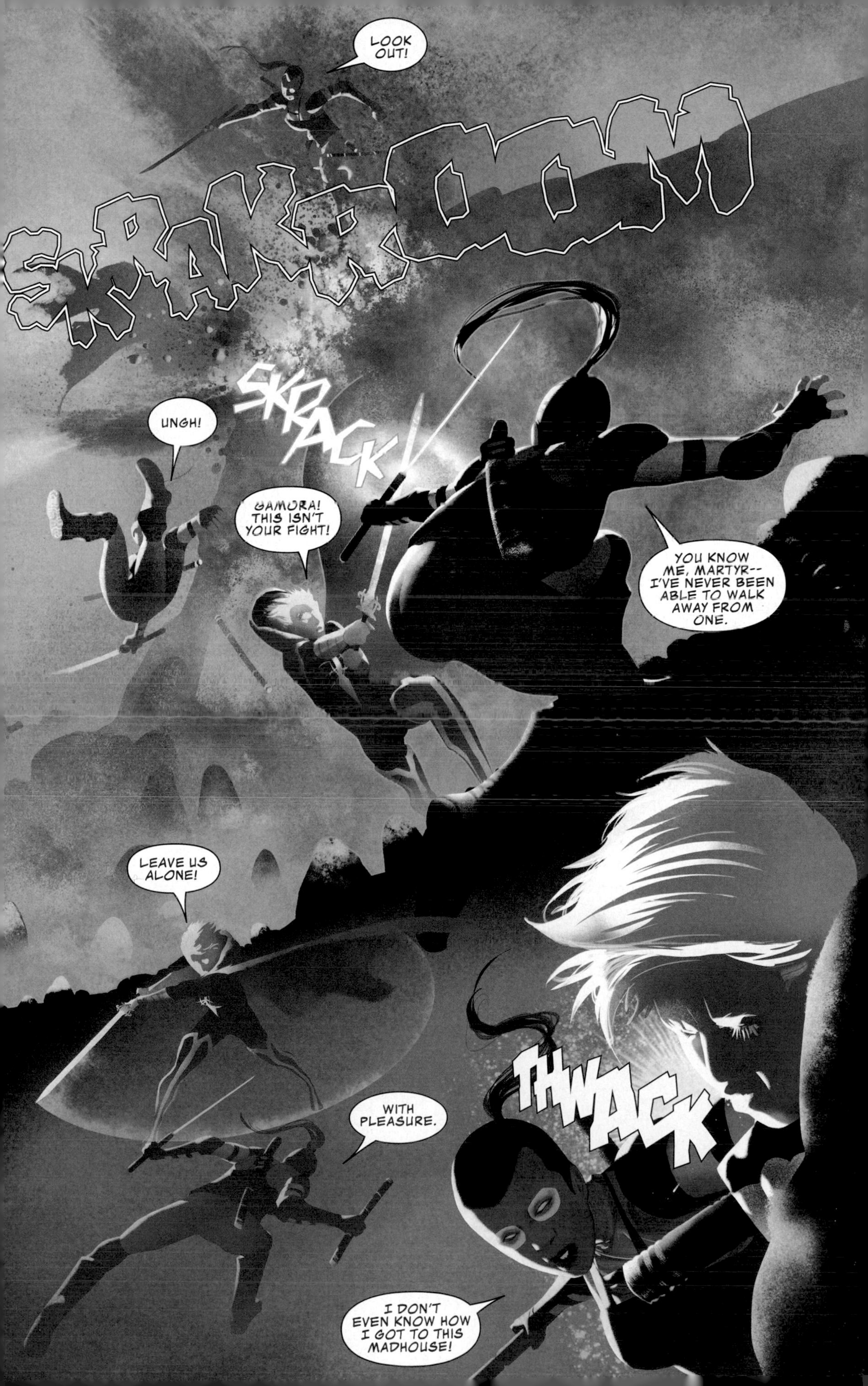
LOOK OUT!
SRAKADOOM
UNGH!
SKRACK
GAMORA! THIS ISN'T YOUR FIGHT!
YOU KNOW ME, MARTYR-- I'VE NEVER BEEN ABLE TO WALK AWAY FROM ONE.
LEAVE US ALONE!
WITH PLEASURE.
THWACK
I DON'T EVEN KNOW HOW I GOT TO THIS MADHOUSE!

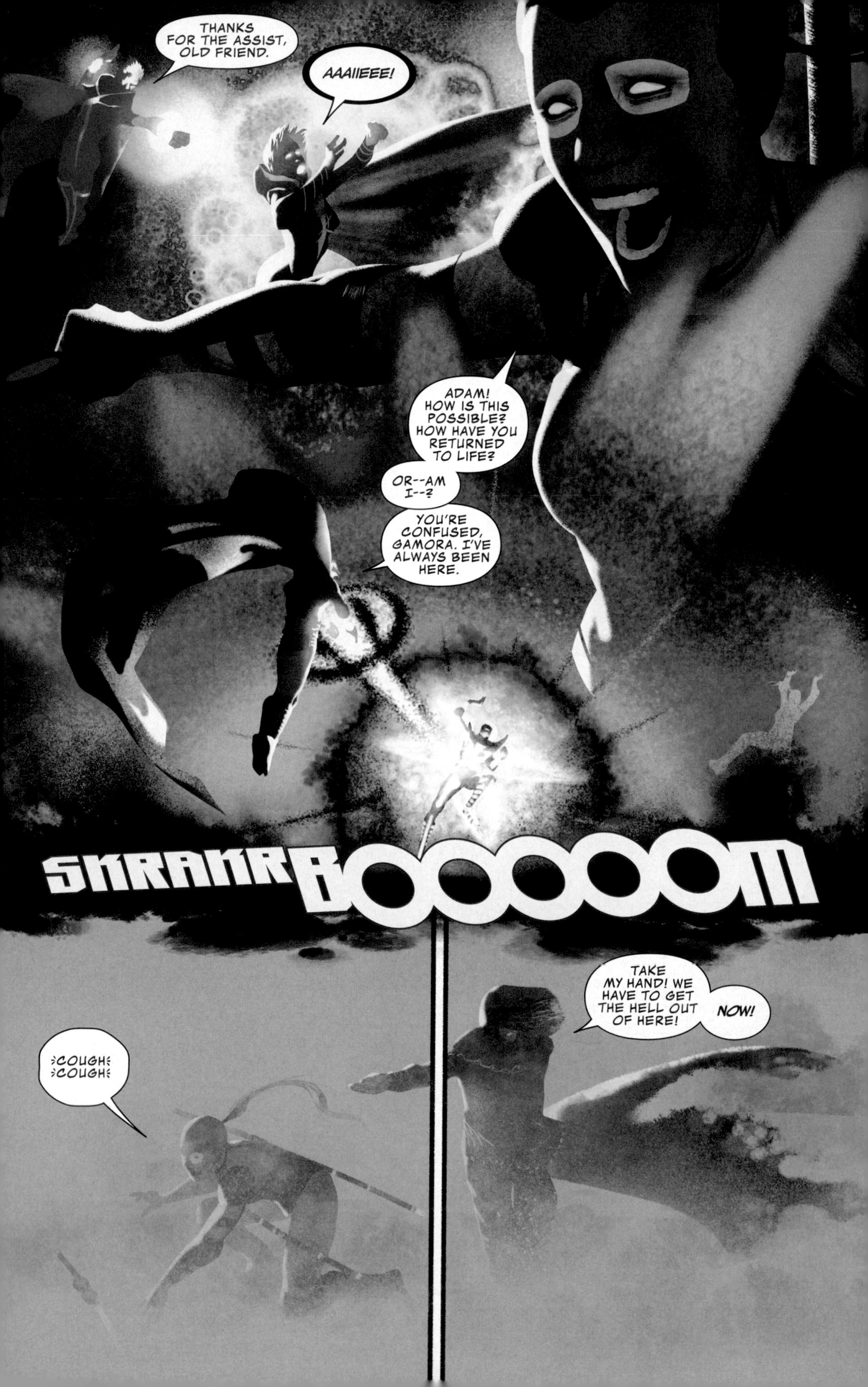
THANKS FOR THE ASSIST, OLD FRIEND.
AAAIIEEE!
ADAM! HOW IS THIS POSSIBLE? HOW HAVE YOU RETURNED TO LIFE?
OR--AM I--?
YOU'RE CONFUSED, GAMORA. I'VE ALWAYS BEEN HERE.
SKRAKRBOOOOOOM
COUGH *COUGH*
TAKE MY HAND! WE HAVE TO GET THE HELL OUT OF HERE!
NOW!

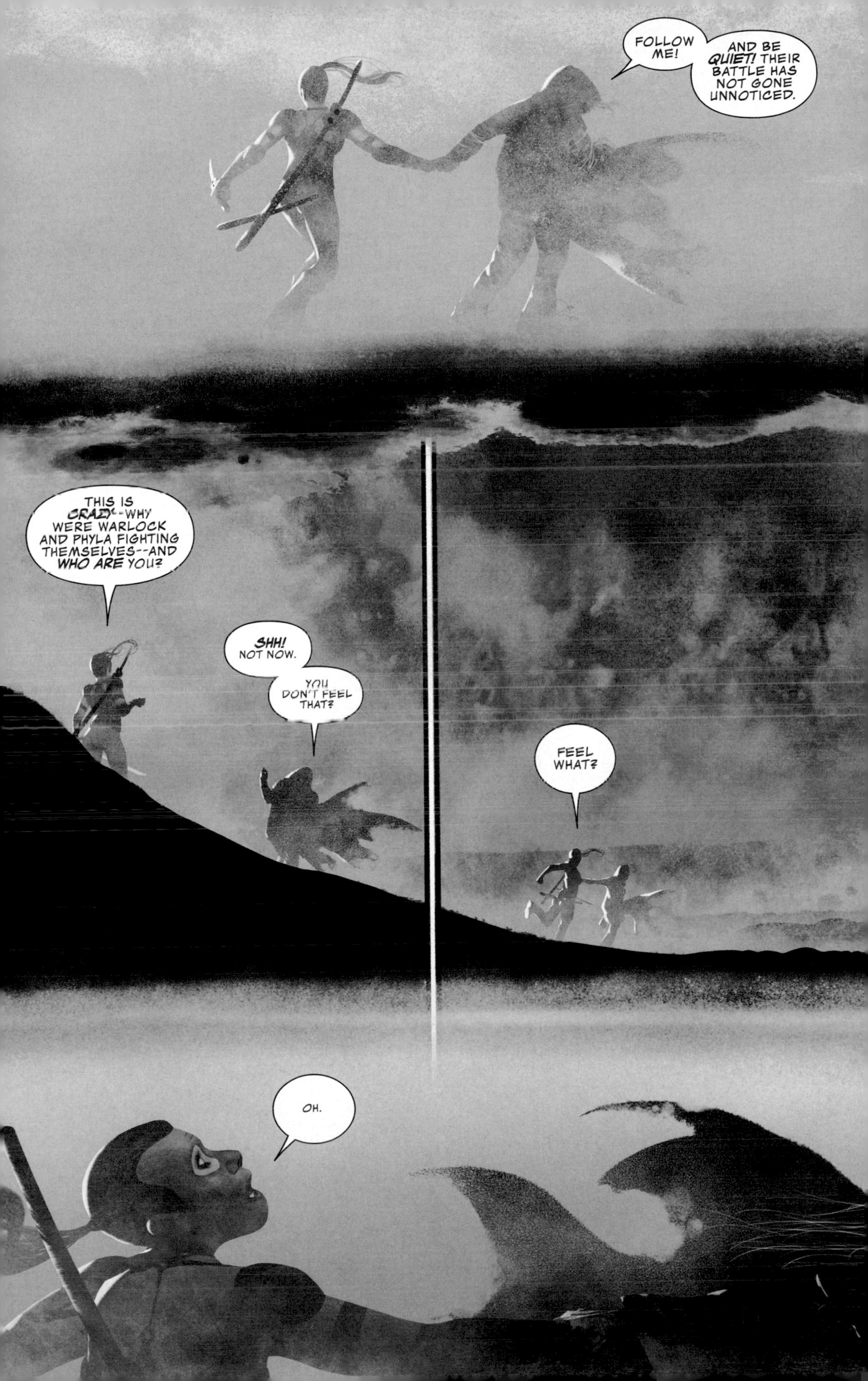
FOLLOW ME!
AND BE QUIET! THEIR BATTLE HAS NOT GONE UNNOTICED.
THIS IS CRAZY--WHY WERE WARLOCK AND PHYLA FIGHTING THEMSELVES--AND WHO ARE YOU?
SHH! NOT NOW.
YOU DON'T FEEL THAT?
FEEL WHAT?
OH.

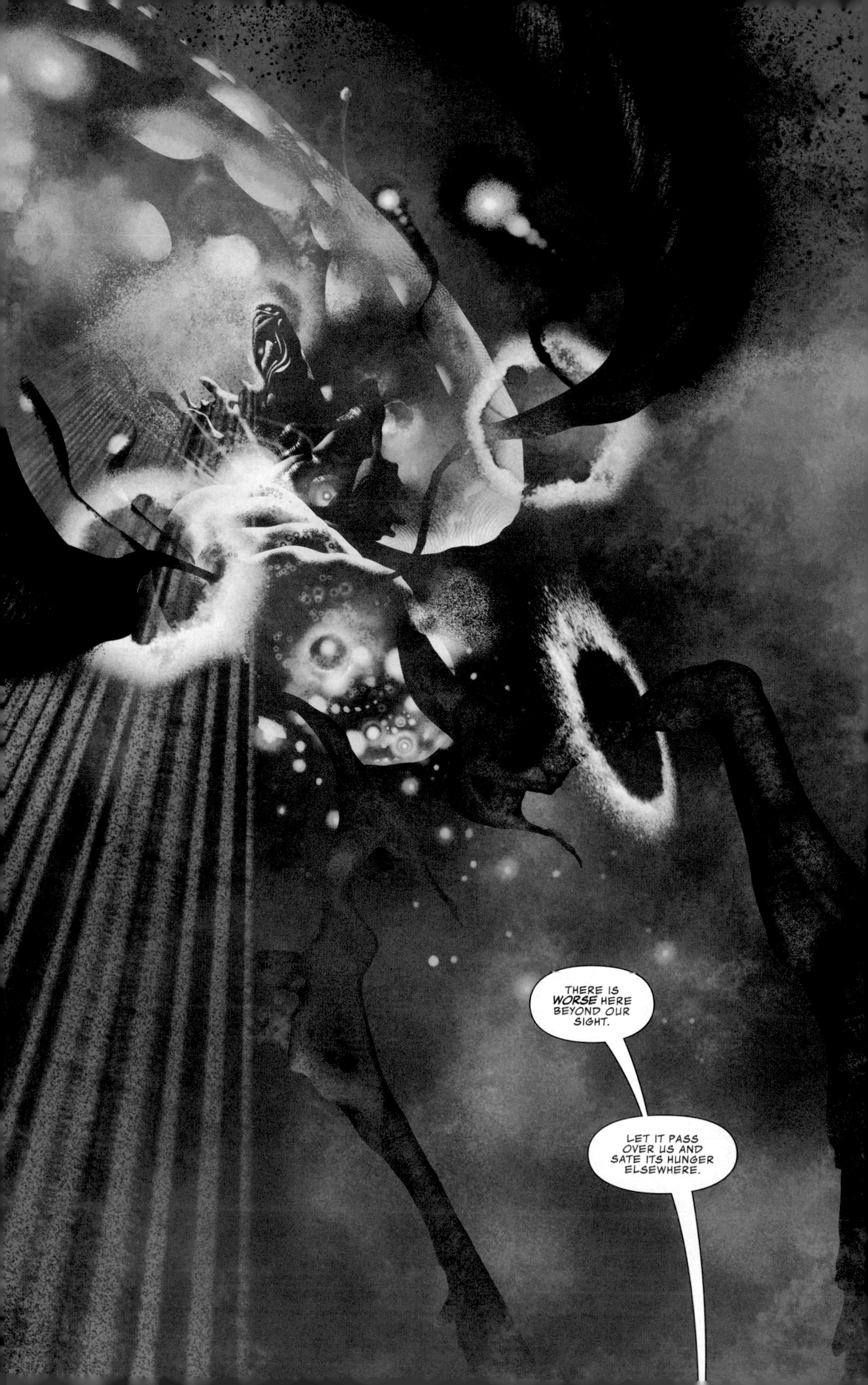
THERE IS WORSE HERE BEYOND OUR SIGHT.
LET IT PASS OVER US AND SATE ITS HUNGER ELSEWHERE.

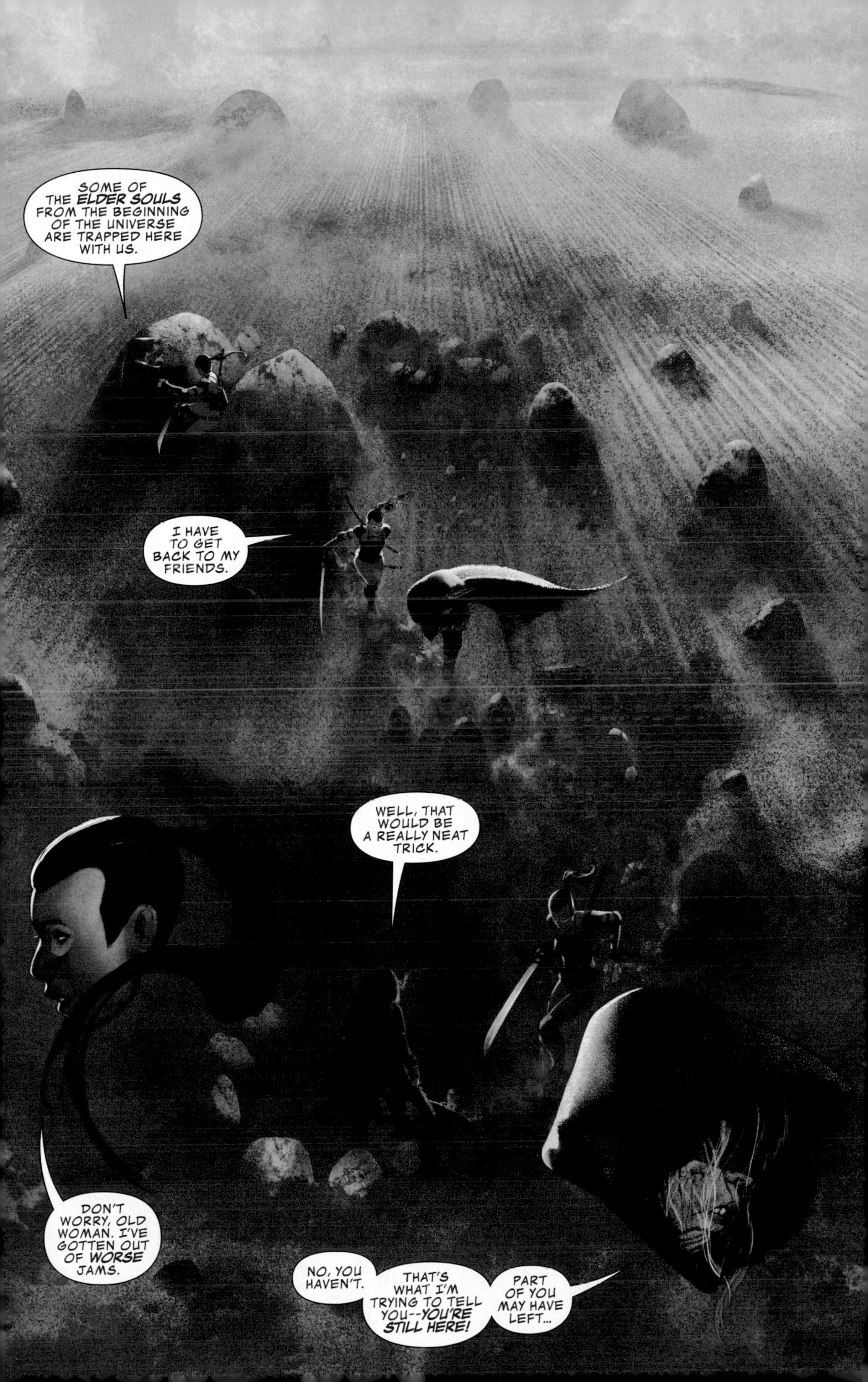

SOME OF THE ELDER SOULS FROM THE BEGINNING OF THE UNIVERSE ARE TRAPPED HERE WITH US.
I HAVE TO GET BACK TO MY FRIENDS.
WELL, THAT WOULD BE A REALLY NEAT TRICK.
DON'T WORRY, OLD WOMAN. I'VE GOTTEN OUT OF WORSE JAMS.
NO, YOU HAVEN'T.
THAT'S WHAT I'M TRYING TO TELL YOU--YOU'RE STILL HERE!
PART OF YOU MAY HAVE LEFT...

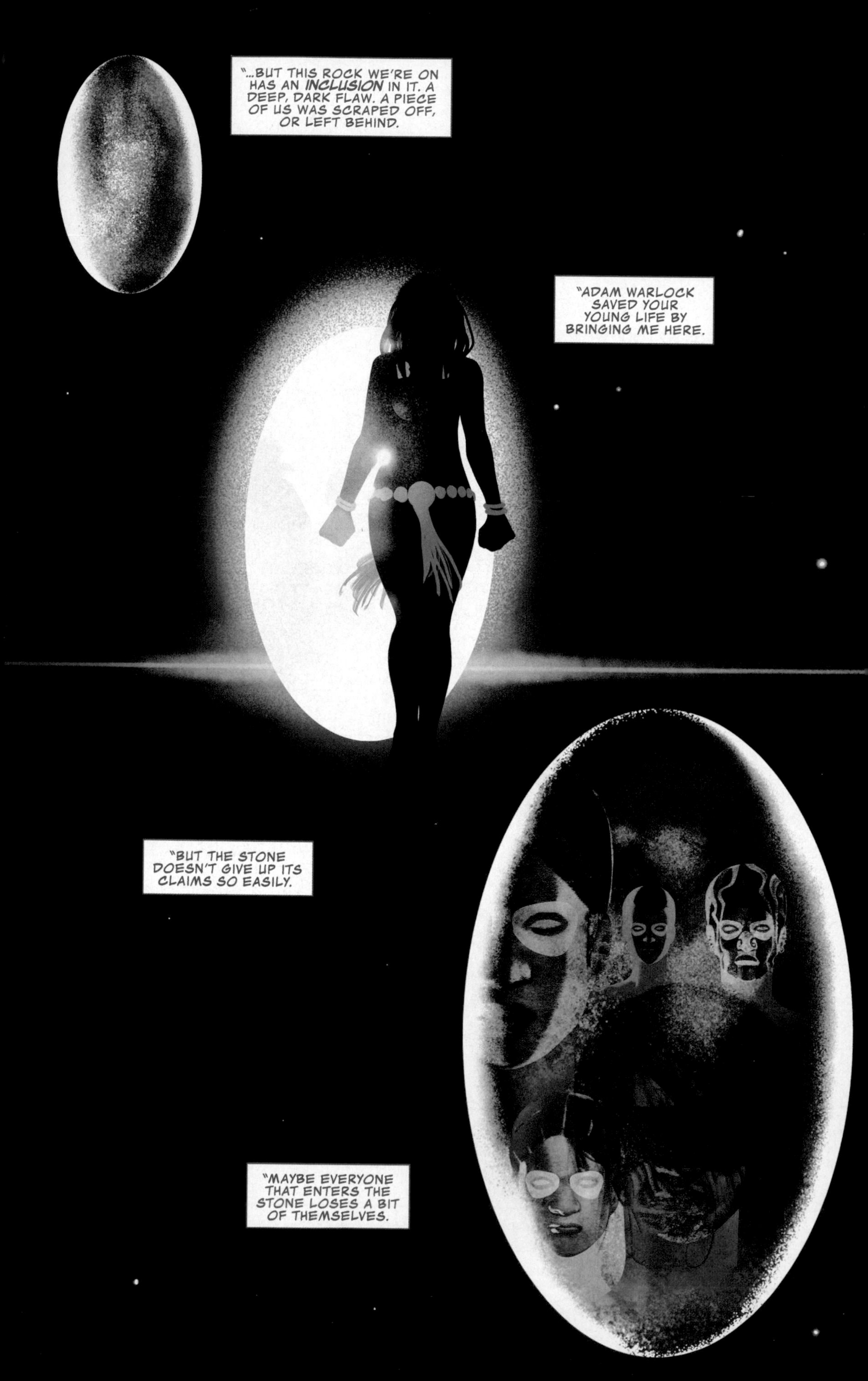
"...BUT THIS ROCK WE'RE ON HAS AN INCLUSION IN IT. A DEEP, DARK FLAW. A PIECE OF US WAS SCRAPED OFF, OR LEFT BEHIND.
"ADAM WARLOCK SAVED YOUR YOUNG LIFE BY BRINGING ME HERE.
"BUT THE STONE DOESN'T GIVE UP ITS CLAIMS SO EASILY.
"MAYBE EVERYONE THAT ENTERS THE STONE LOSES A BIT OF THEMSELVES.

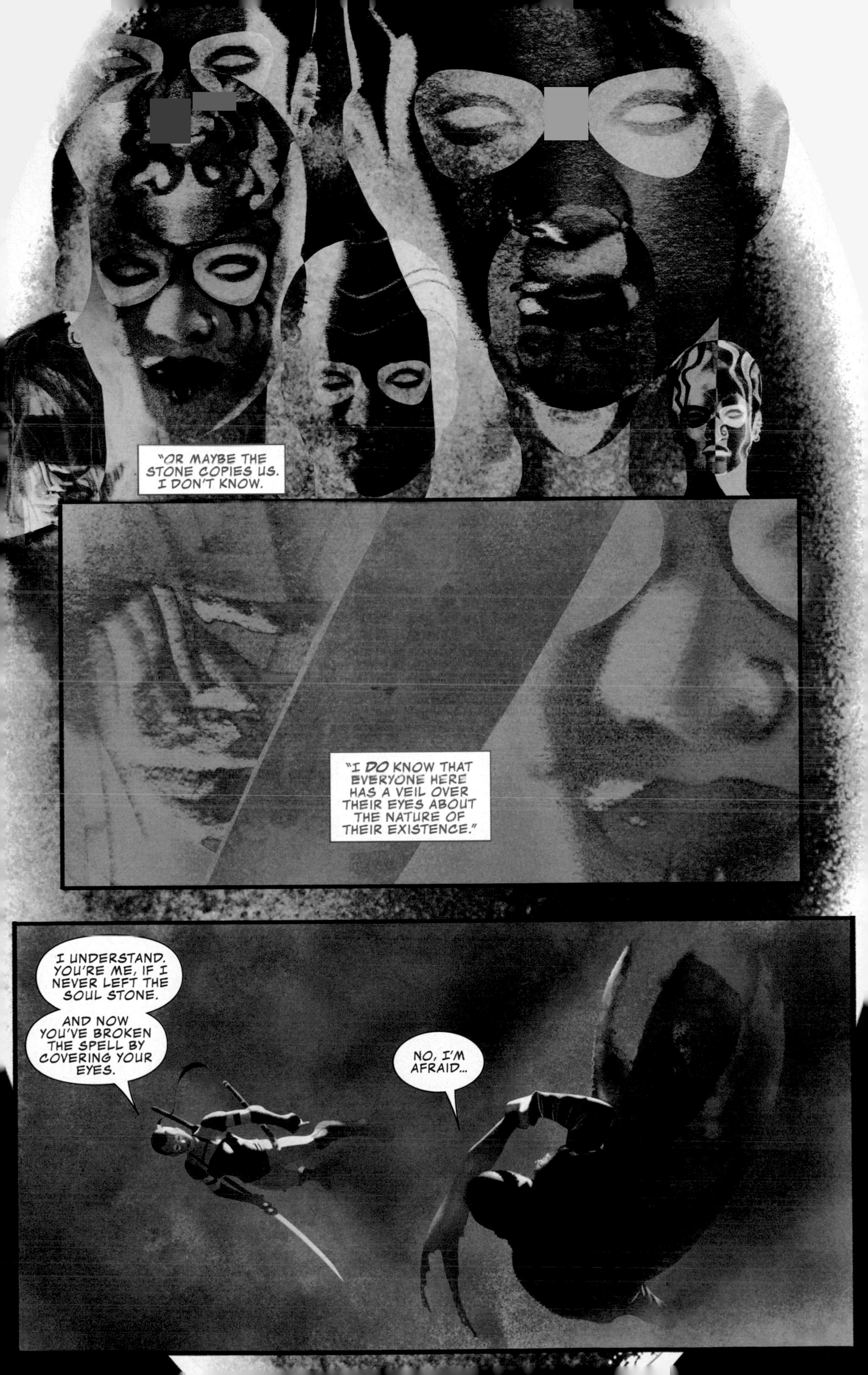
"OR MAYBE THE STONE COPIES US. I DON'T KNOW.
"I DO KNOW THAT EVERYONE HERE HAS A VEIL OVER THEIR EYES ABOUT THE NATURE OF THEIR EXISTENCE."
I UNDERSTAND. YOU'RE ME, IF I NEVER LEFT THE SOUL STONE.
AND NOW YOU'VE BROKEN THE SPELL BY COVERING YOUR EYES.
NO, I'M AFRAID...

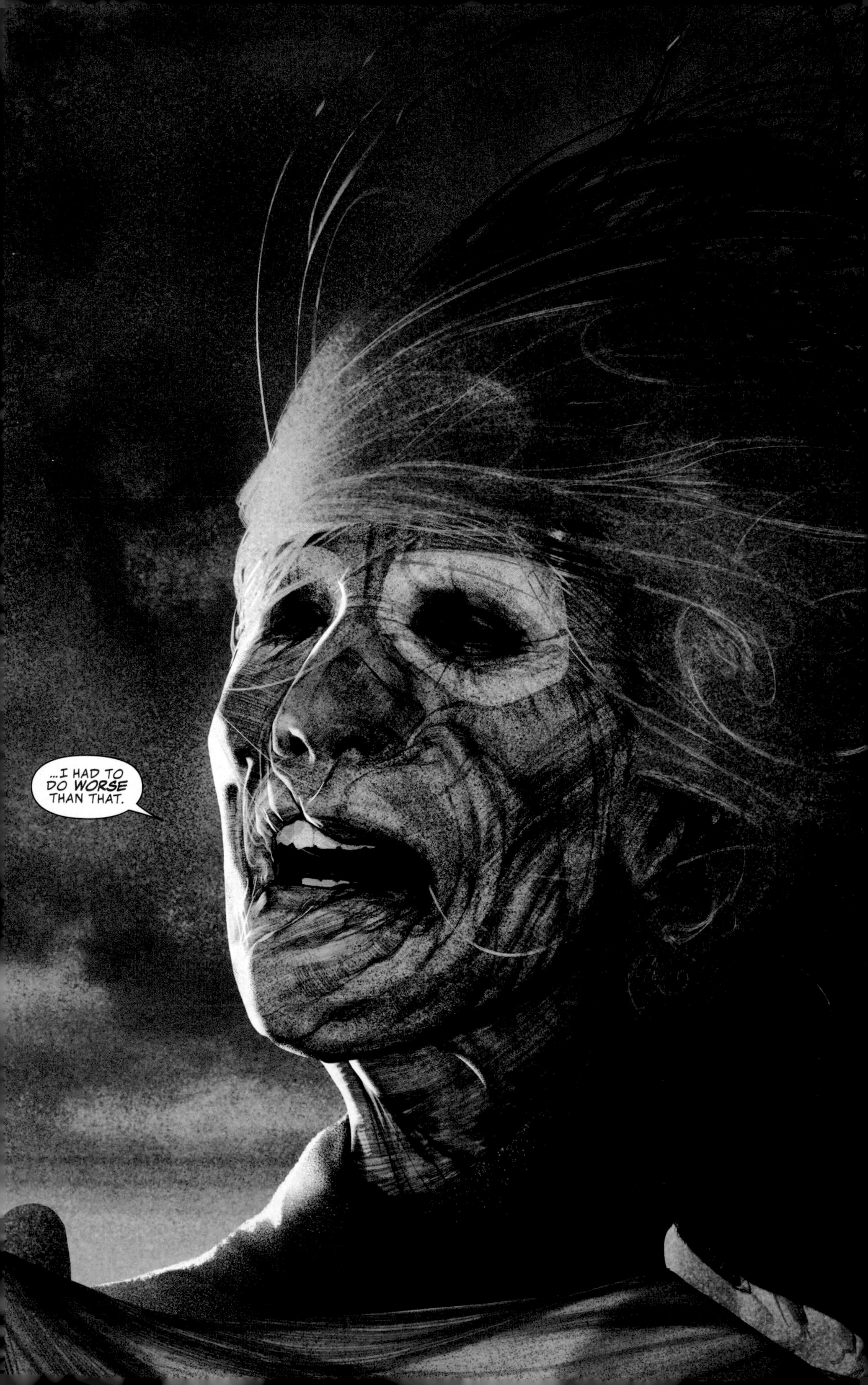
...I HAD TO DO WORSE THAN THAT.

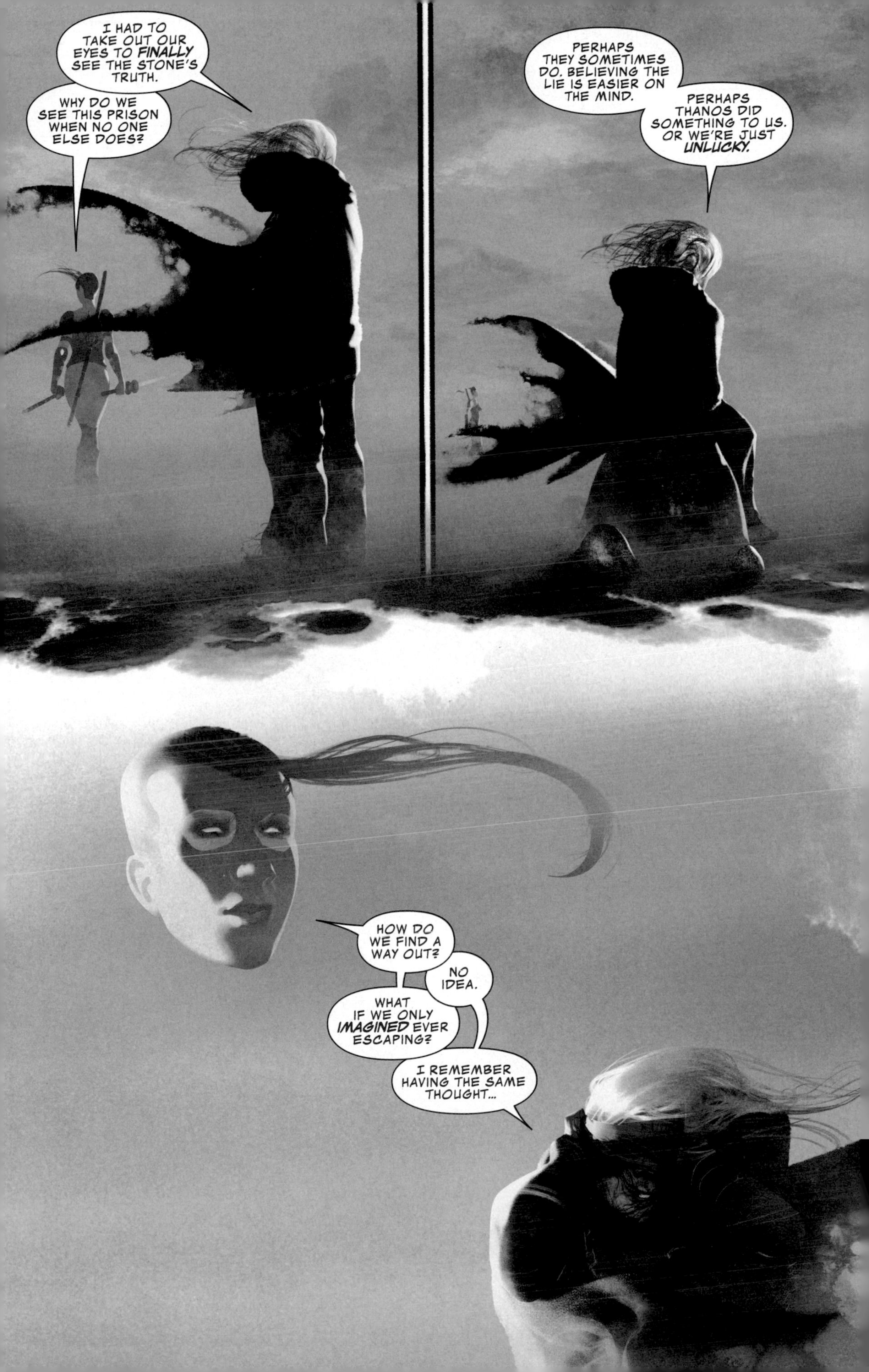
I HAD TO TAKE OUT OUR EYES TO **FINALLY** SEE THE STONE'S TRUTH.
WHY DO WE SEE THIS PRISON WHEN NO ONE ELSE DOES?
PERHAPS THEY SOMETIMES DO. BELIEVING THE LIE IS EASIER ON THE MIND.
PERHAPS THANOS DID SOMETHING TO US. OR WE'RE JUST **UNLUCKY.**
HOW DO WE FIND A WAY OUT?
NO IDEA.
WHAT IF WE ONLY **IMAGINED** EVER ESCAPING?
I REMEMBER HAVING THE SAME THOUGHT...

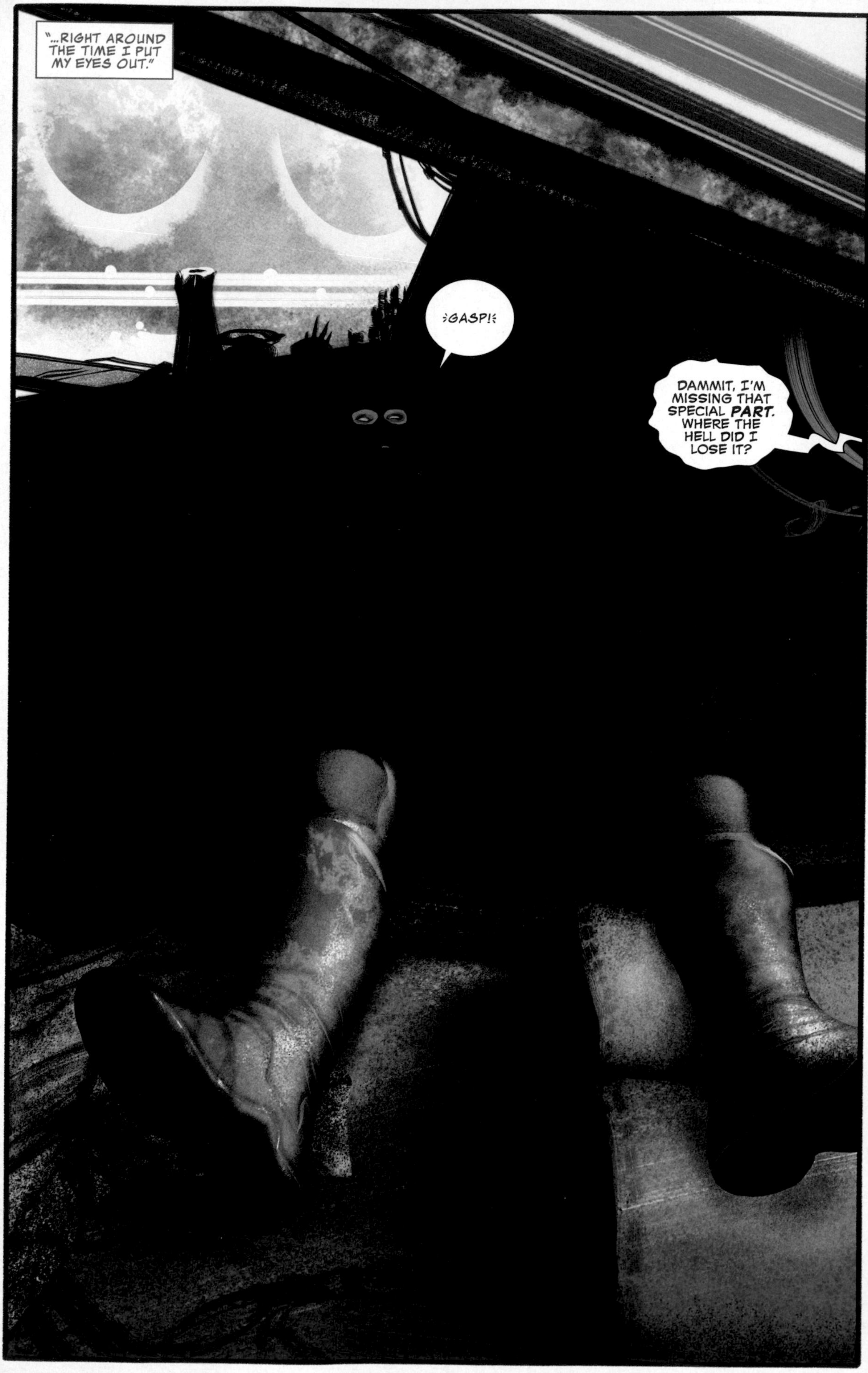
"...RIGHT AROUND THE TIME I PUT MY EYES OUT."
>GASP!<
DAMMIT, I'M MISSING THAT SPECIAL PART. WHERE THE HELL DID I LOSE IT?

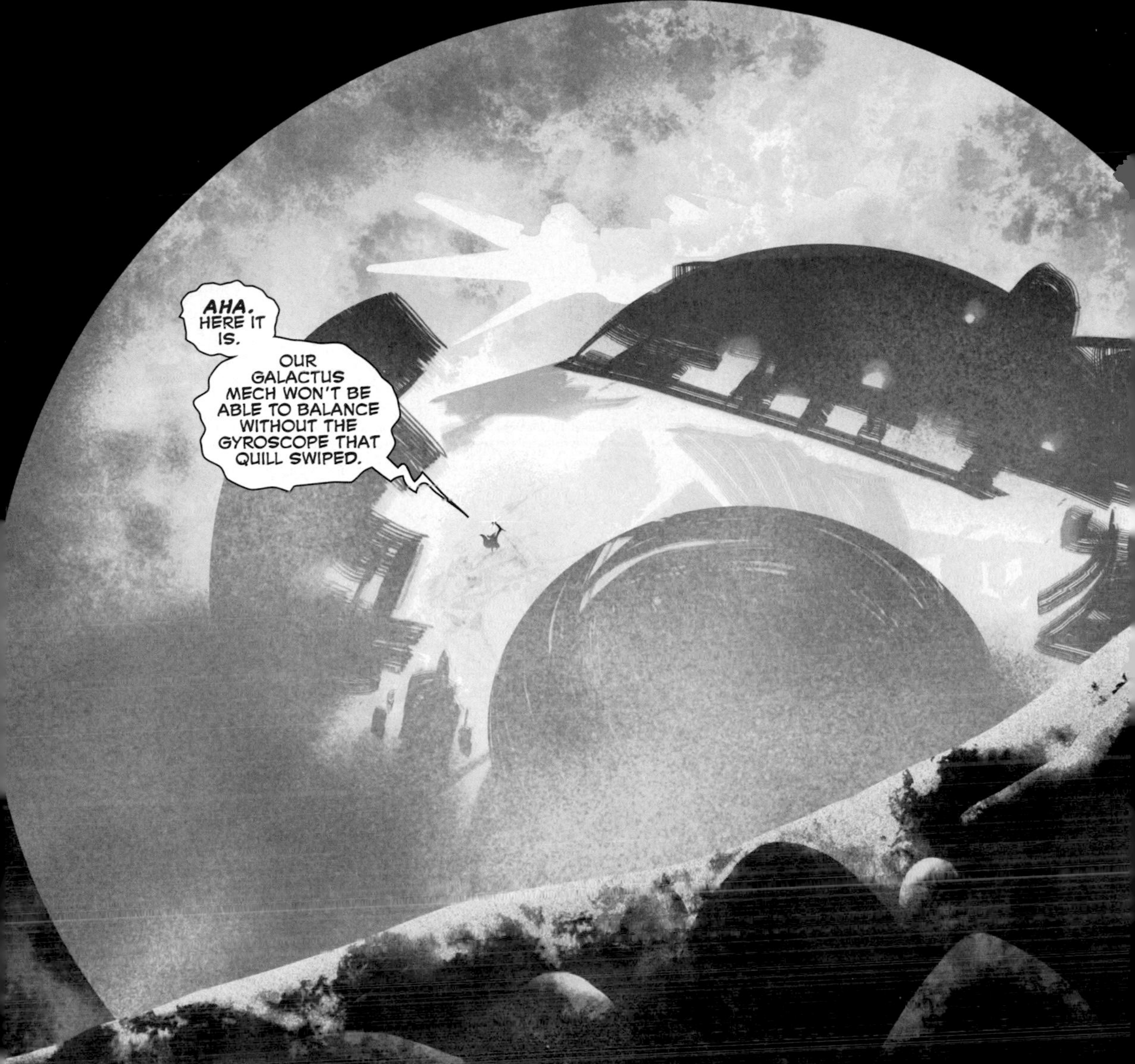
AHA. HERE IT IS.
OUR GALACTUS MECH WON'T BE ABLE TO BALANCE WITHOUT THE GYROSCOPE THAT QUILL SWIPED.

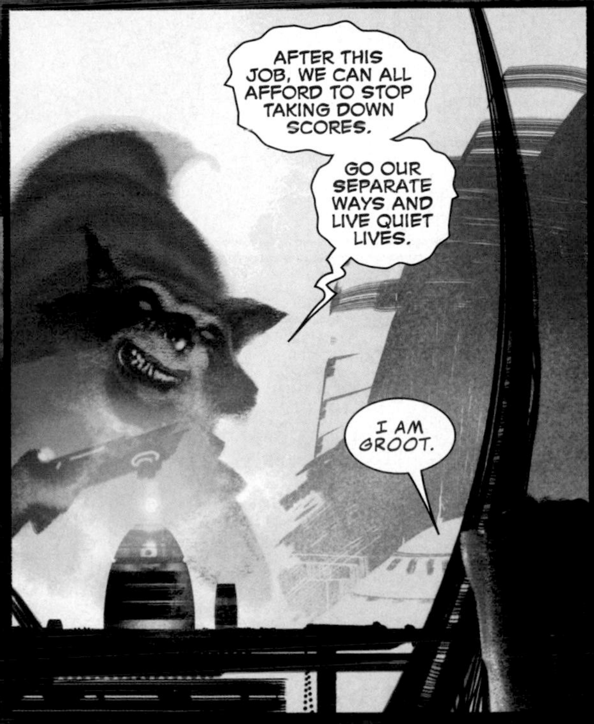
AFTER THIS JOB, WE CAN ALL AFFORD TO STOP TAKING DOWN SCORES.
GO OUR SEPARATE WAYS AND LIVE QUIET LIVES.
I AM GROOT.

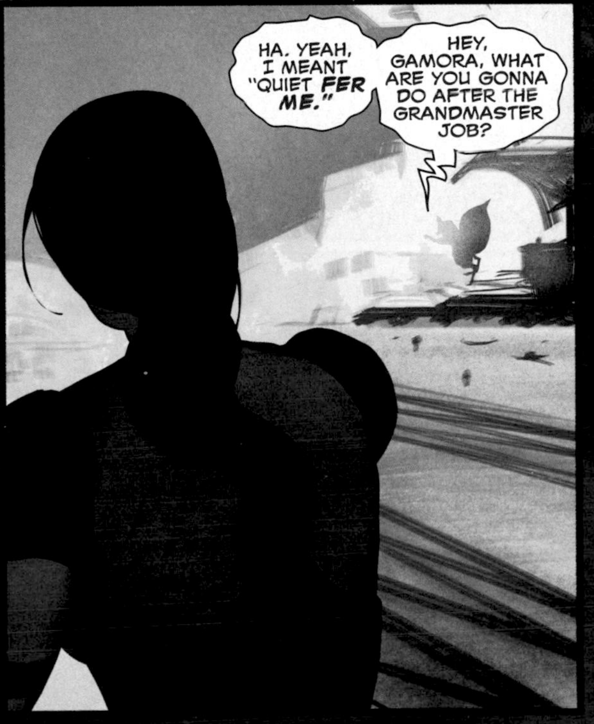
HA. YEAH, I MEANT "QUIET FER ME."
HEY, GAMORA, WHAT ARE YOU GONNA DO AFTER THE GRANDMASTER JOB?

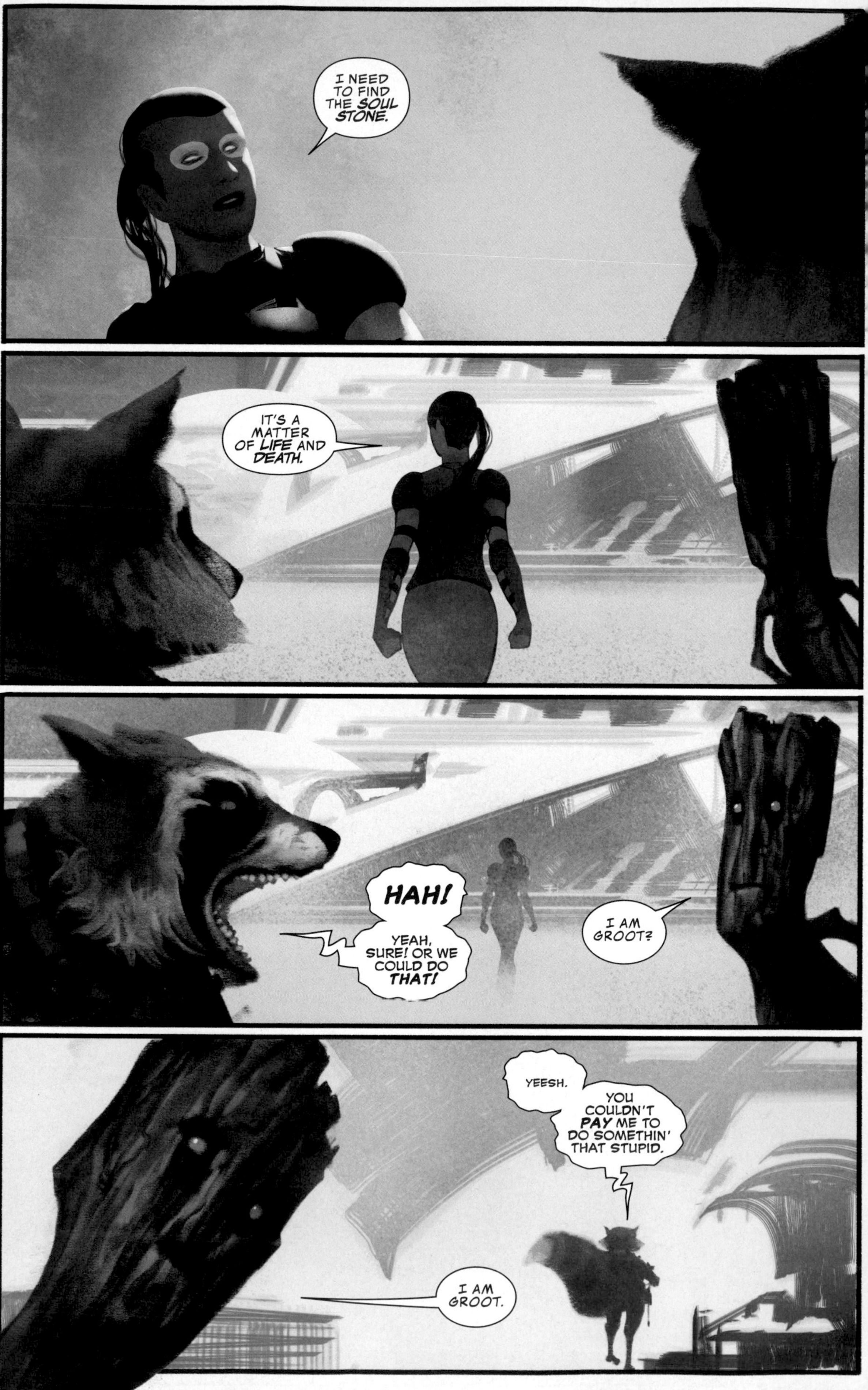
I NEED TO FIND THE SOUL STONE.
IT'S A MATTER OF LIFE AND DEATH.
HAH!
YEAH, SURE! OR WE COULD DO THAT!
I AM GROOT?
YEESH.
YOU COULDN'T PAY ME TO DO SOMETHIN' THAT STUPID.
I AM GROOT.

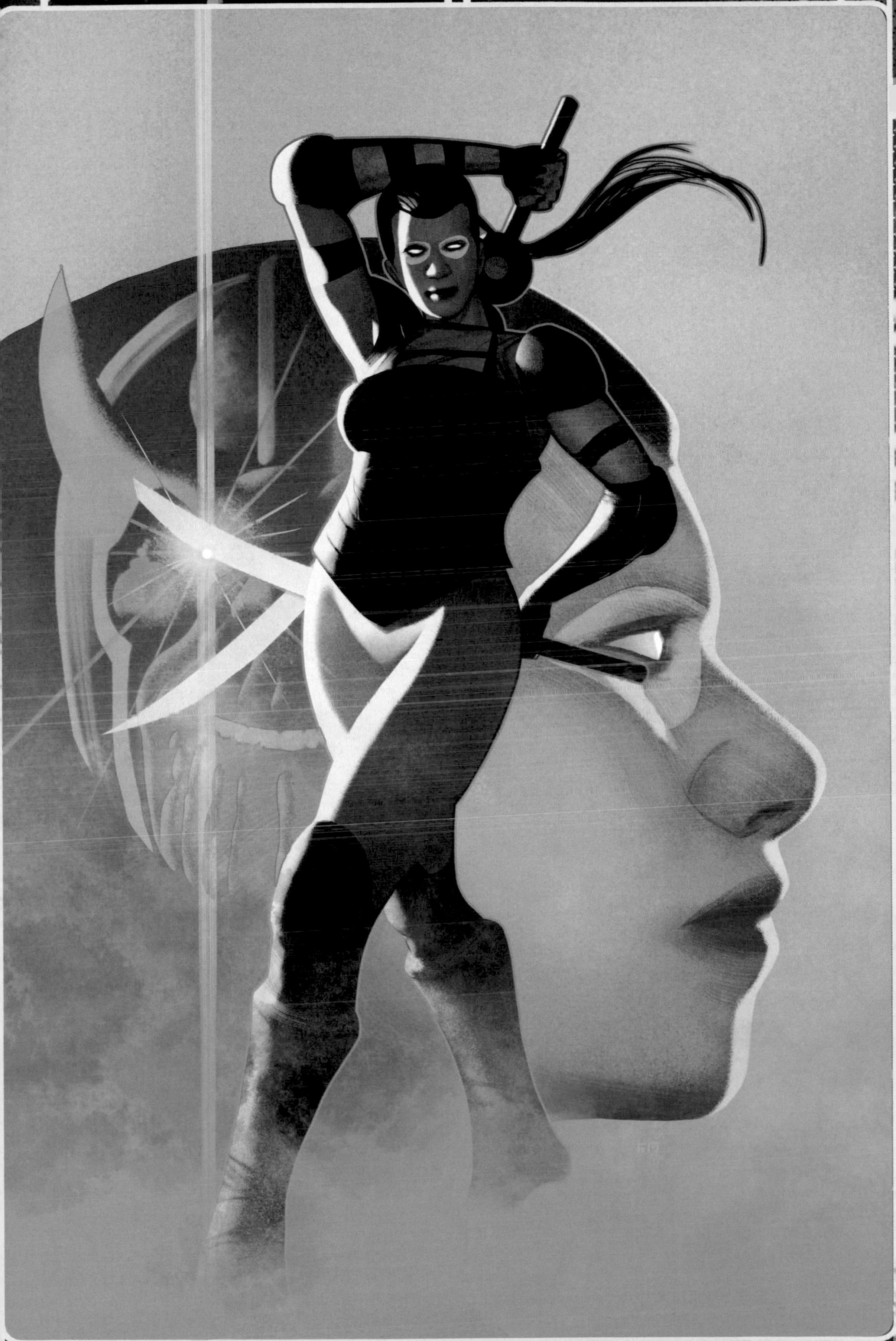

#3 VARIANT BY **FRAZER IRVING**

5

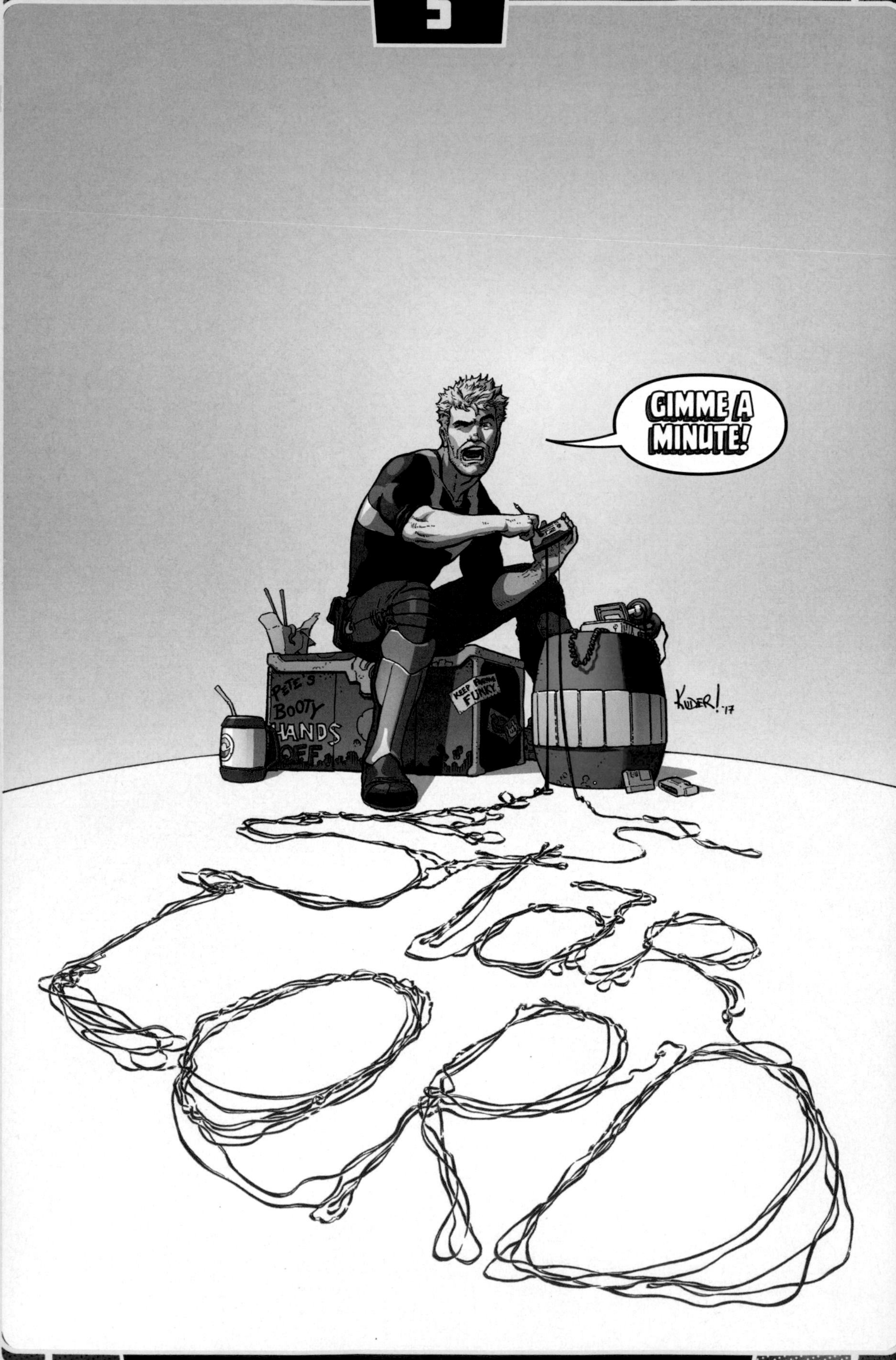
GIMME A MINUTE!
PETE'S BOOTY HANDS OFF
KEEP FUNKY

"ACROSS THE UNIVERSE"

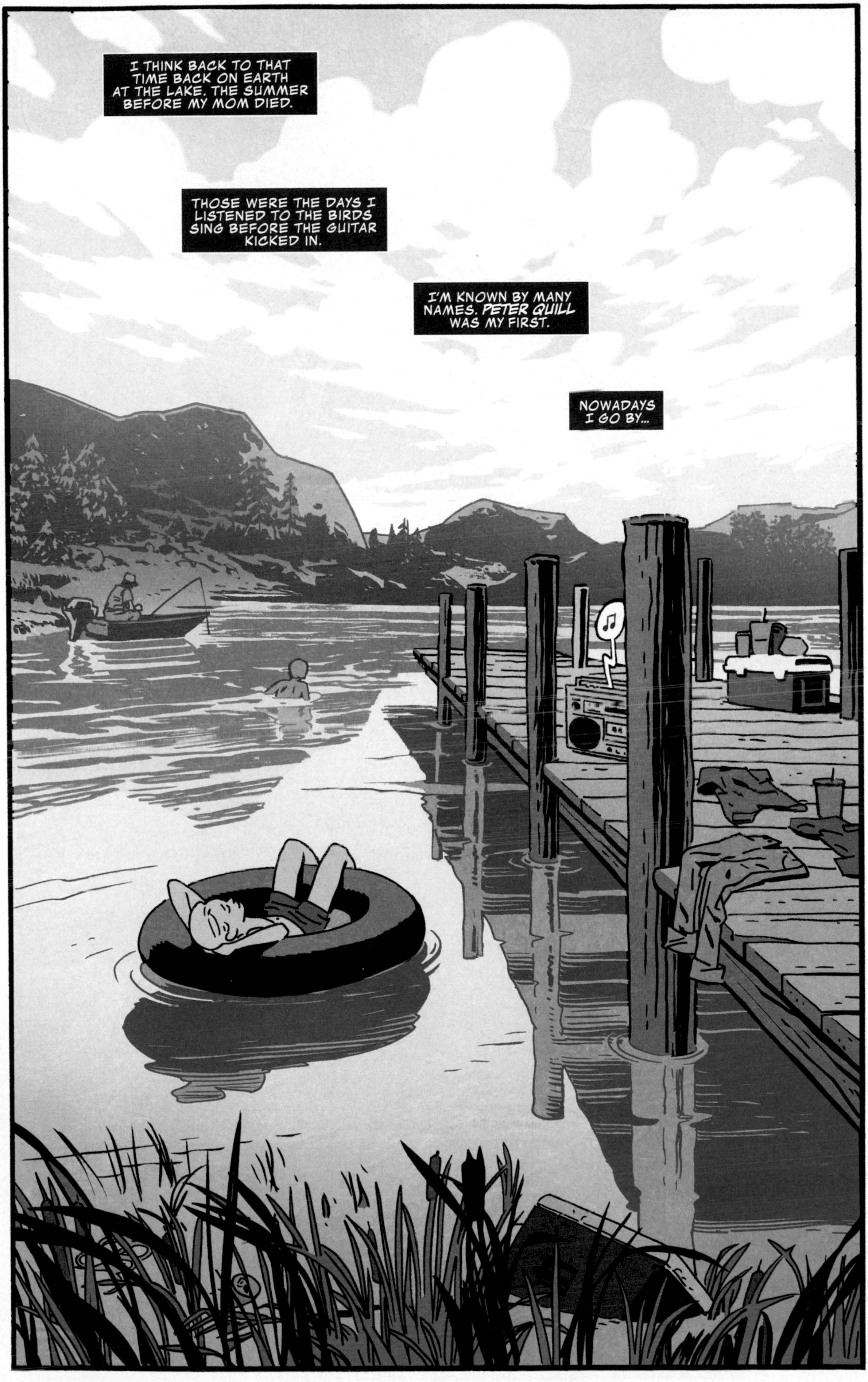
I THINK BACK TO THAT TIME BACK ON EARTH AT THE LAKE. THE SUMMER BEFORE MY MOM DIED.
THOSE WERE THE DAYS I LISTENED TO THE BIRDS SING BEFORE THE GUITAR KICKED IN.
I'M KNOWN BY MANY NAMES. PETER QUILL WAS MY FIRST.
NOWADAYS I GO BY...

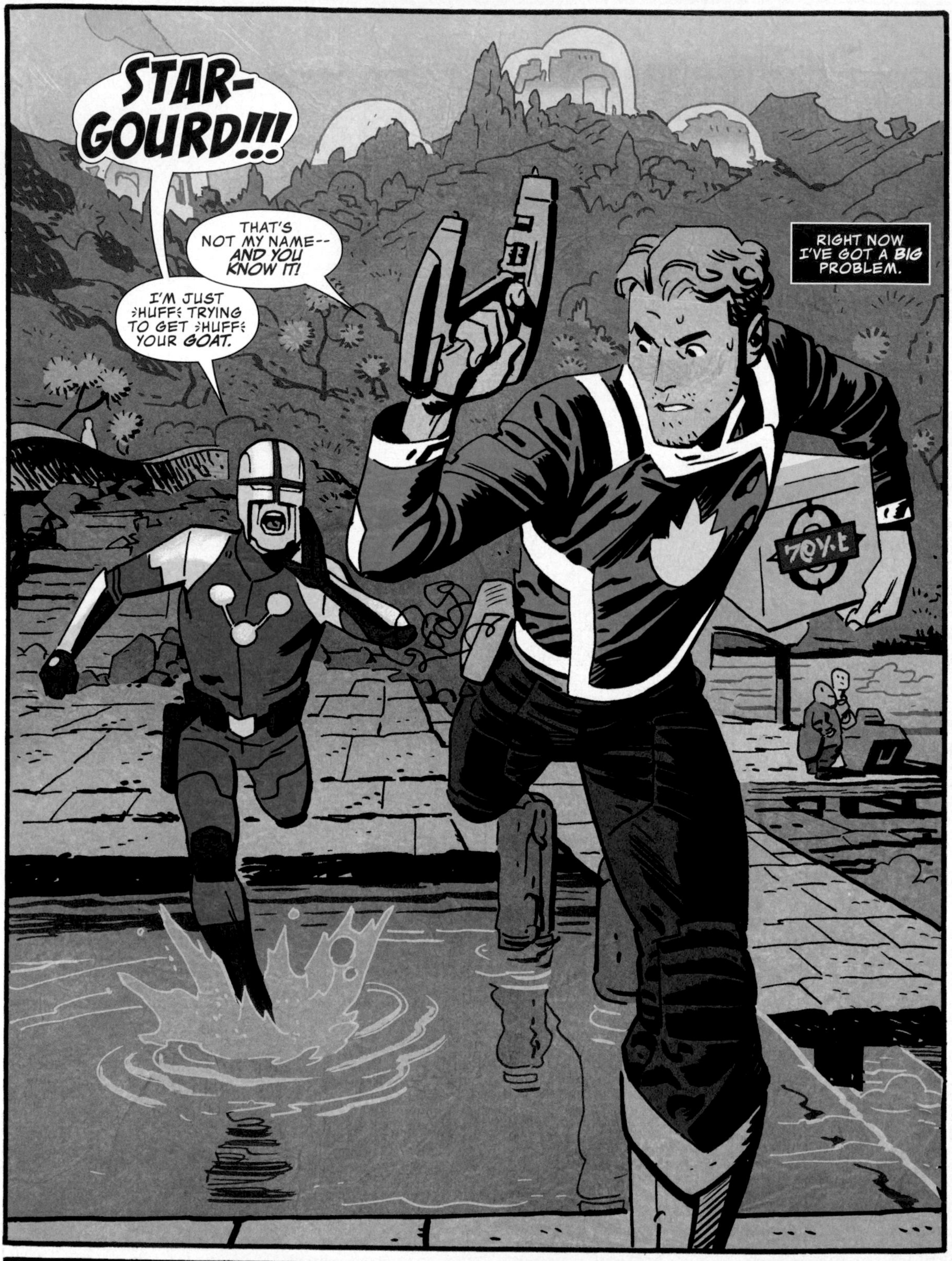
STAR-GOURD!!!
THAT'S NOT MY NAME-- AND YOU KNOW IT!
I'M JUST HUFF TRYING TO GET HUFF YOUR GOAT.
RIGHT NOW I'VE GOT A BIG PROBLEM.

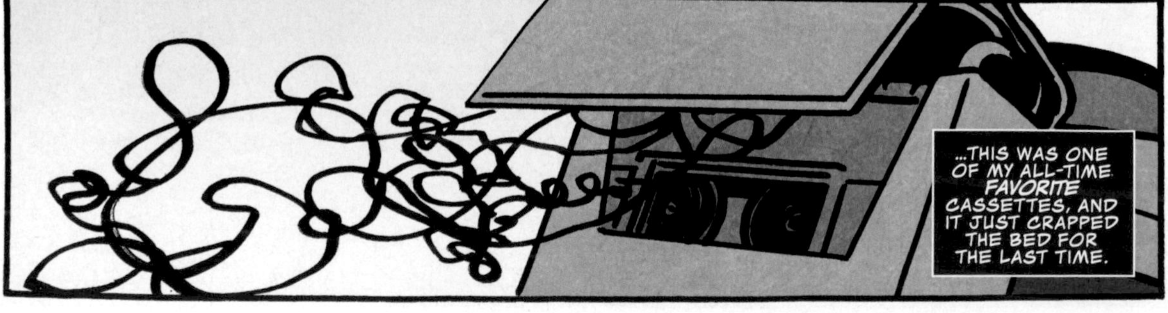
...THIS WAS ONE OF MY ALL-TIME FAVORITE CASSETTES, AND IT JUST CRAPPED THE BED FOR THE LAST TIME.

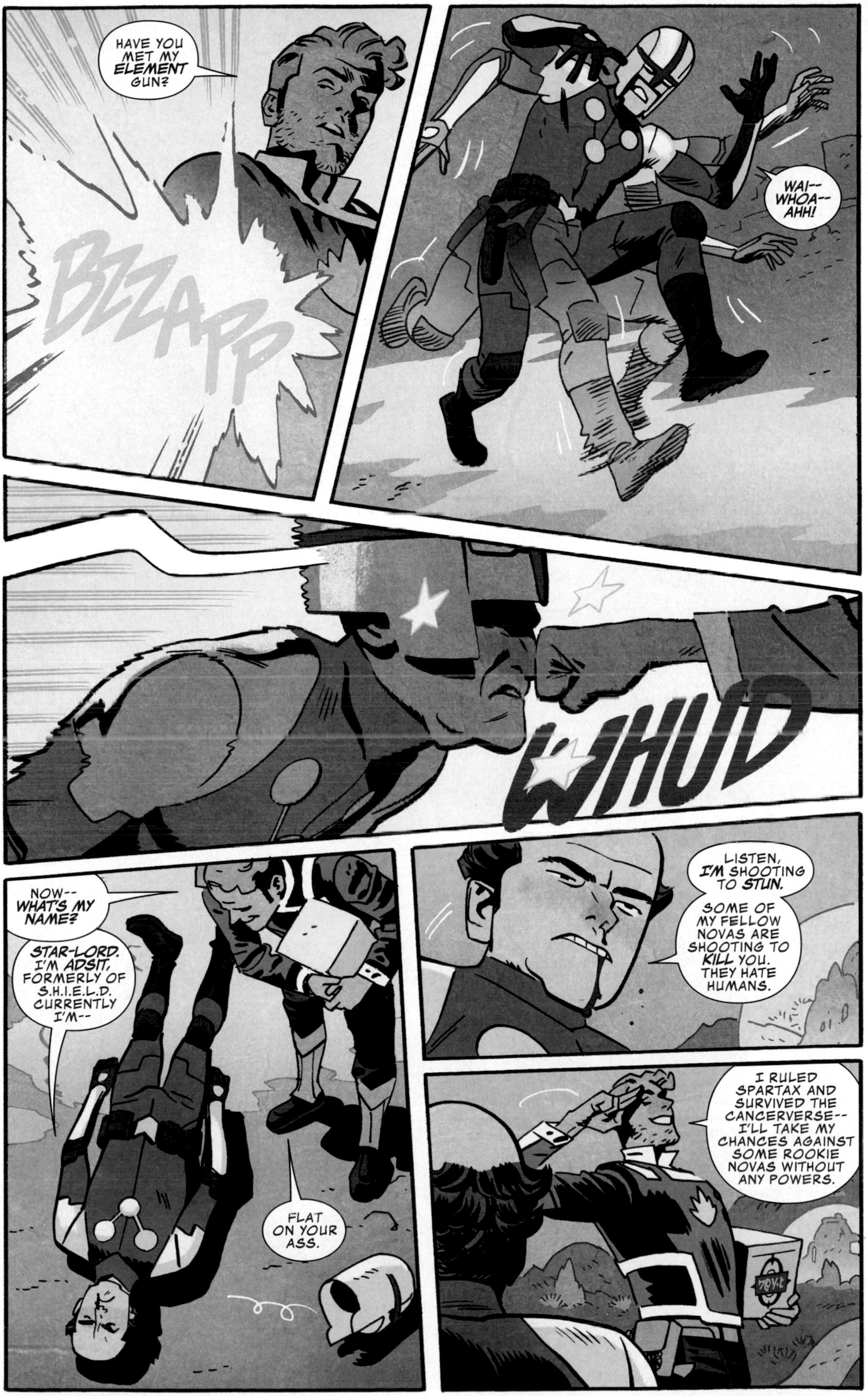
HAVE YOU MET MY ELEMENT GUN?
BZZAPP
WAI-- WHOA-- AHH!
WHUD
NOW-- WHAT'S MY NAME?
STAR-LORD. I'M ADSIT, FORMERLY OF S.H.I.E.L.D. CURRENTLY I'M--
FLAT ON YOUR ASS.
LISTEN, I'M SHOOTING TO STUN.
SOME OF MY FELLOW NOVAS ARE SHOOTING TO KILL YOU. THEY HATE HUMANS.
I RULED SPARTAX AND SURVIVED THE CANCERVERSE-- I'LL TAKE MY CHANCES AGAINST SOME ROOKIE NOVAS WITHOUT ANY POWERS.

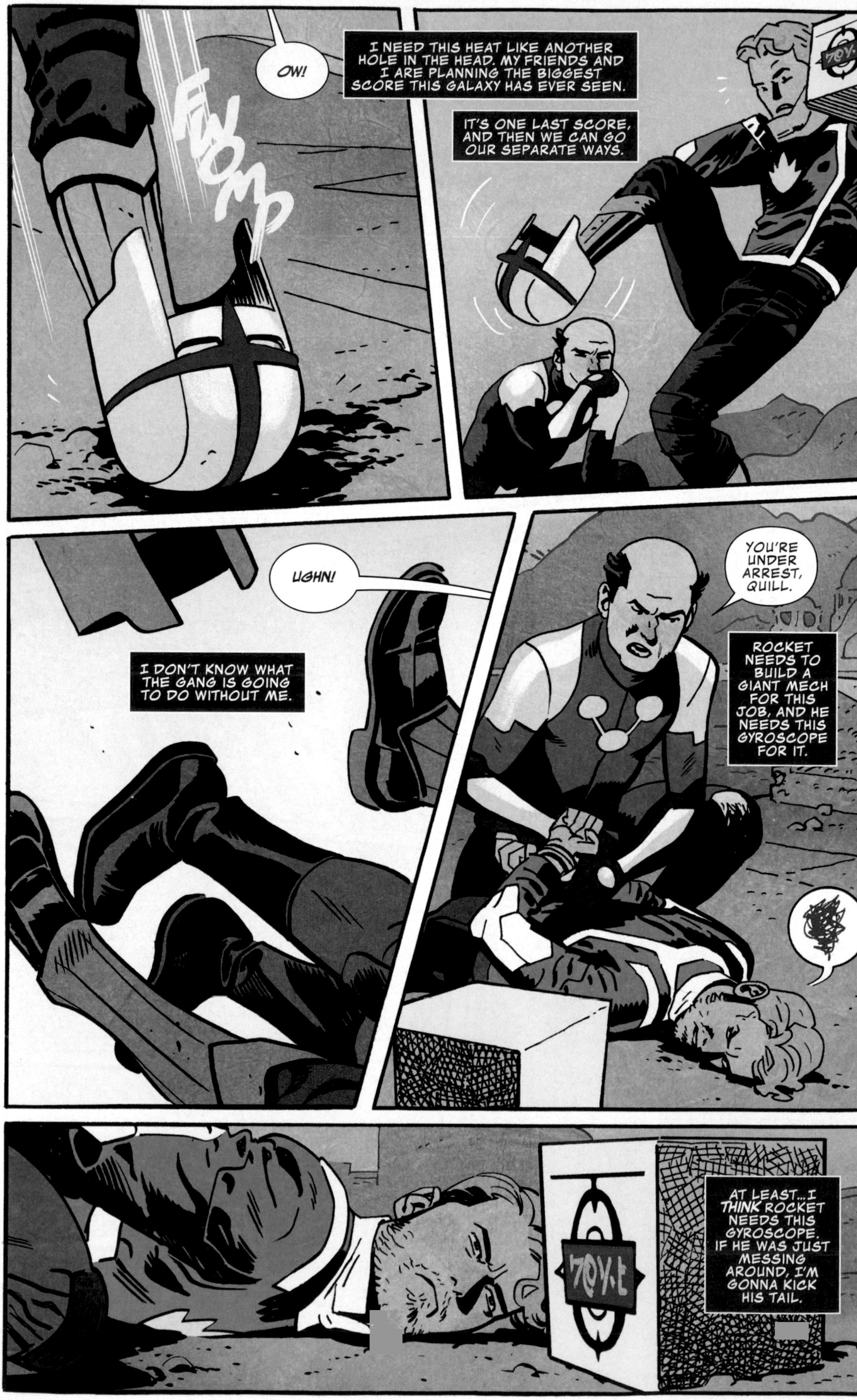
OW!
FWOMP
I NEED THIS HEAT LIKE ANOTHER HOLE IN THE HEAD. MY FRIENDS AND I ARE PLANNING THE BIGGEST SCORE THIS GALAXY HAS EVER SEEN.
IT'S ONE LAST SCORE, AND THEN WE CAN GO OUR SEPARATE WAYS.
UGHN!
I DON'T KNOW WHAT THE GANG IS GOING TO DO WITHOUT ME.
YOU'RE UNDER ARREST, QUILL.
ROCKET NEEDS TO BUILD A GIANT MECH FOR THIS JOB, AND HE NEEDS THIS GYROSCOPE FOR IT.
AT LEAST...I *THINK* ROCKET NEEDS THIS GYROSCOPE. IF HE WAS JUST MESSING AROUND, I'M GONNA KICK HIS TAIL.

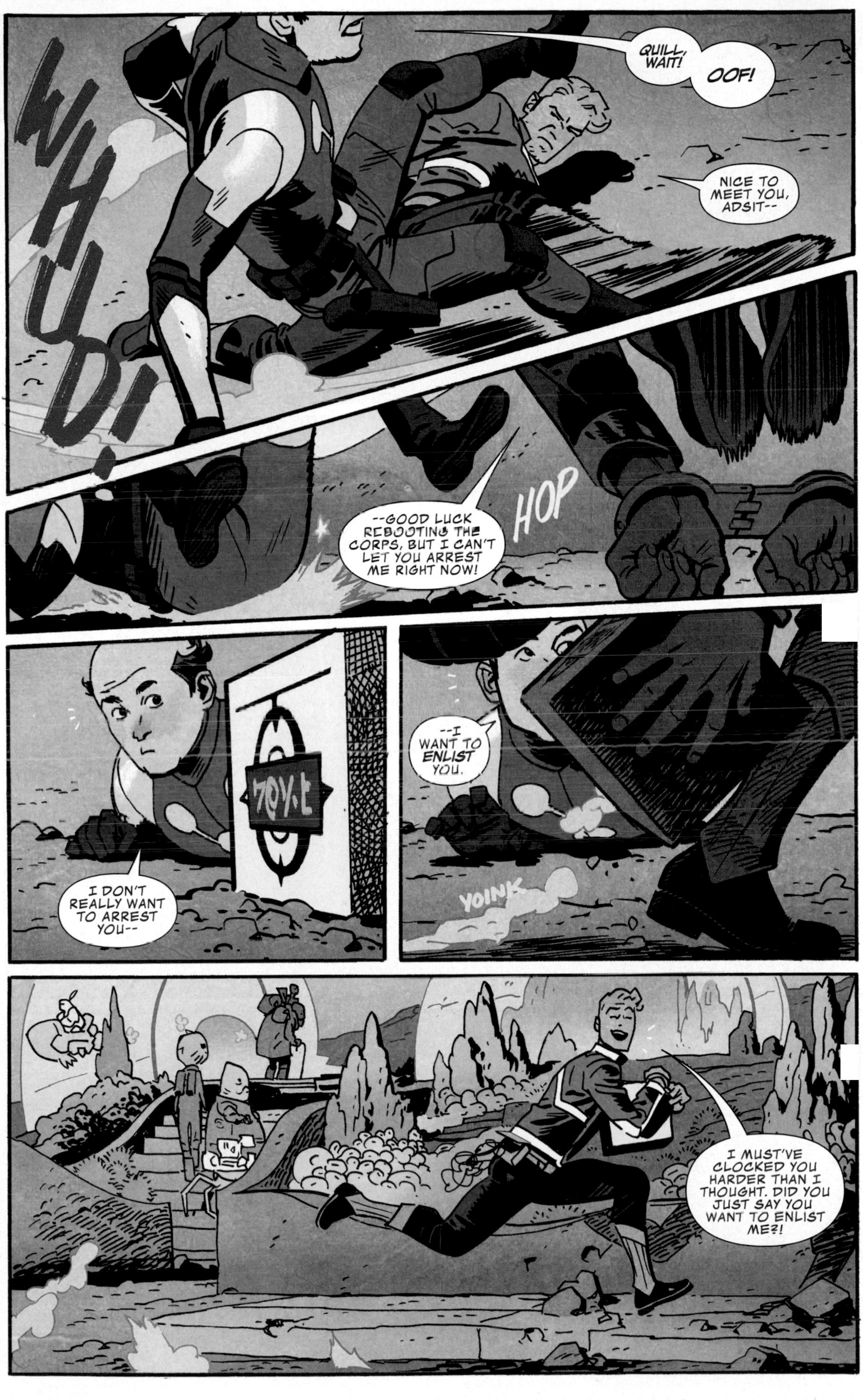
WHUD!
QUILL, WAIT!
OOF!
NICE TO MEET YOU, ADSIT--
HOP
--GOOD LUCK REBOOTING THE CORPS, BUT I CAN'T LET YOU ARREST ME RIGHT NOW!
I DON'T REALLY WANT TO ARREST YOU--
--I WANT TO ENLIST YOU.
YOINK
I MUST'VE CLOCKED YOU HARDER THAN I THOUGHT. DID YOU JUST SAY YOU WANT TO ENLIST ME?!

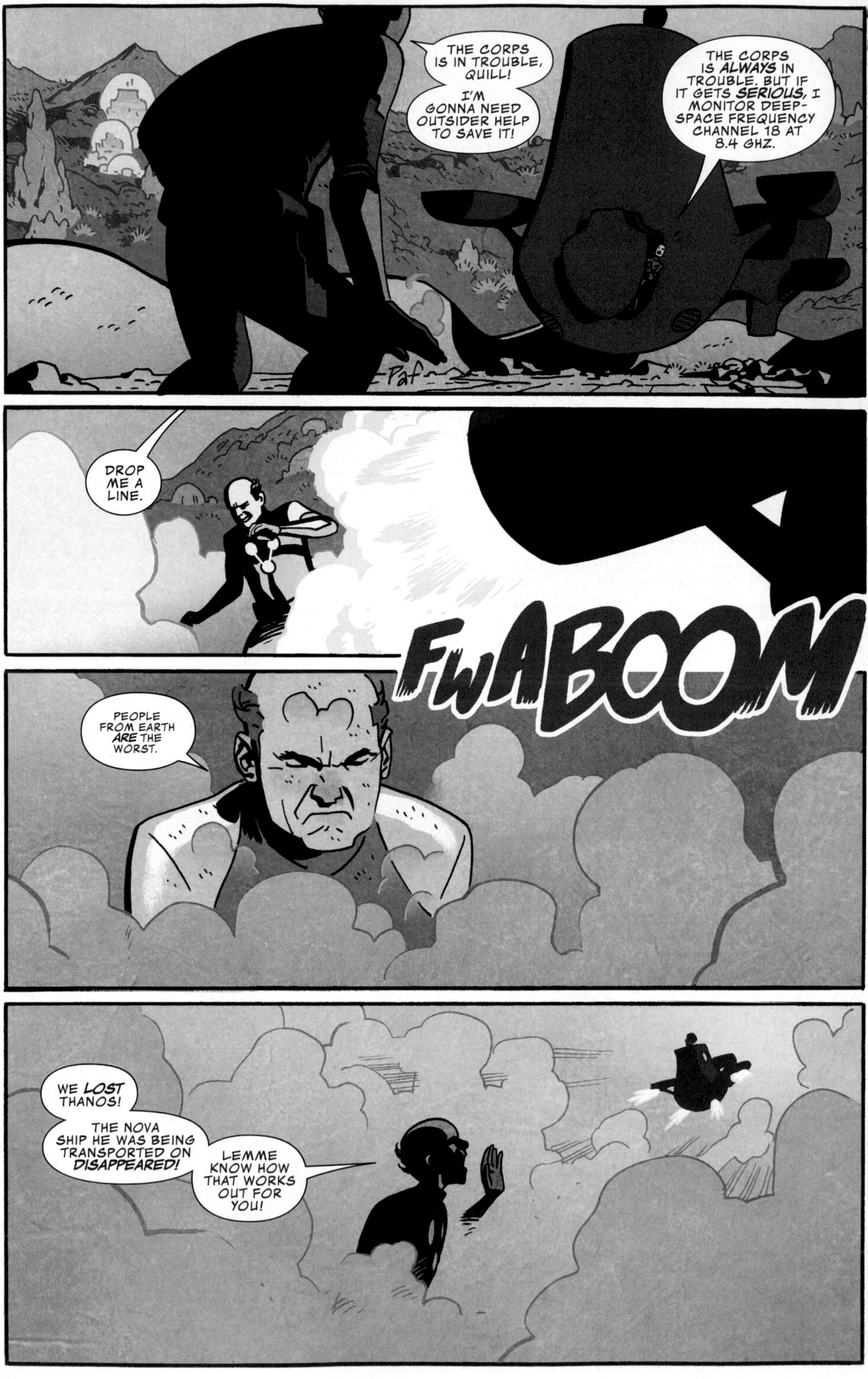

THE CORPS IS IN TROUBLE, QUILL!
I'M GONNA NEED OUTSIDER HELP TO SAVE IT!
THE CORPS IS ALWAYS IN TROUBLE. BUT IF IT GETS SERIOUS, I MONITOR DEEP-SPACE FREQUENCY CHANNEL 18 AT 8.4 GHZ.
Paf
DROP ME A LINE.
FWABOOM
PEOPLE FROM EARTH ARE THE WORST.
WE LOST THANOS!
THE NOVA SHIP HE WAS BEING TRANSPORTED ON DISAPPEARED!
LEMME KNOW HOW THAT WORKS OUT FOR YOU!

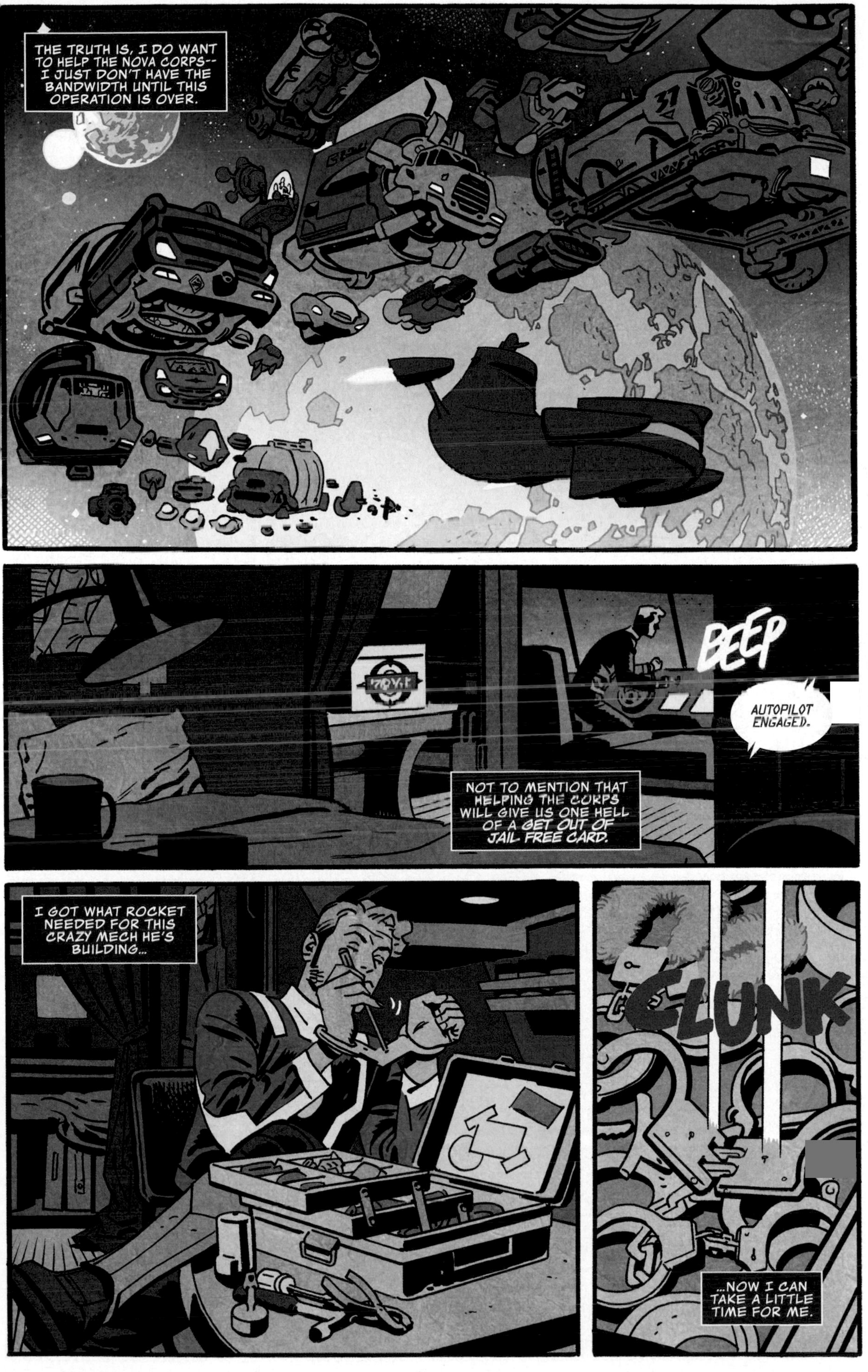
THE TRUTH IS, I DO WANT TO HELP THE NOVA CORPS-- I JUST DON'T HAVE THE BANDWIDTH UNTIL THIS OPERATION IS OVER.
BEEP
AUTOPILOT ENGAGED.
NOT TO MENTION THAT HELPING THE CORPS WILL GIVE US ONE HELL OF A GET OUT OF JAIL FREE CARD.
I GOT WHAT ROCKET NEEDED FOR THIS CRAZY MECH HE'S BUILDING...
CLUNK
...NOW I CAN TAKE A LITTLE TIME FOR ME.

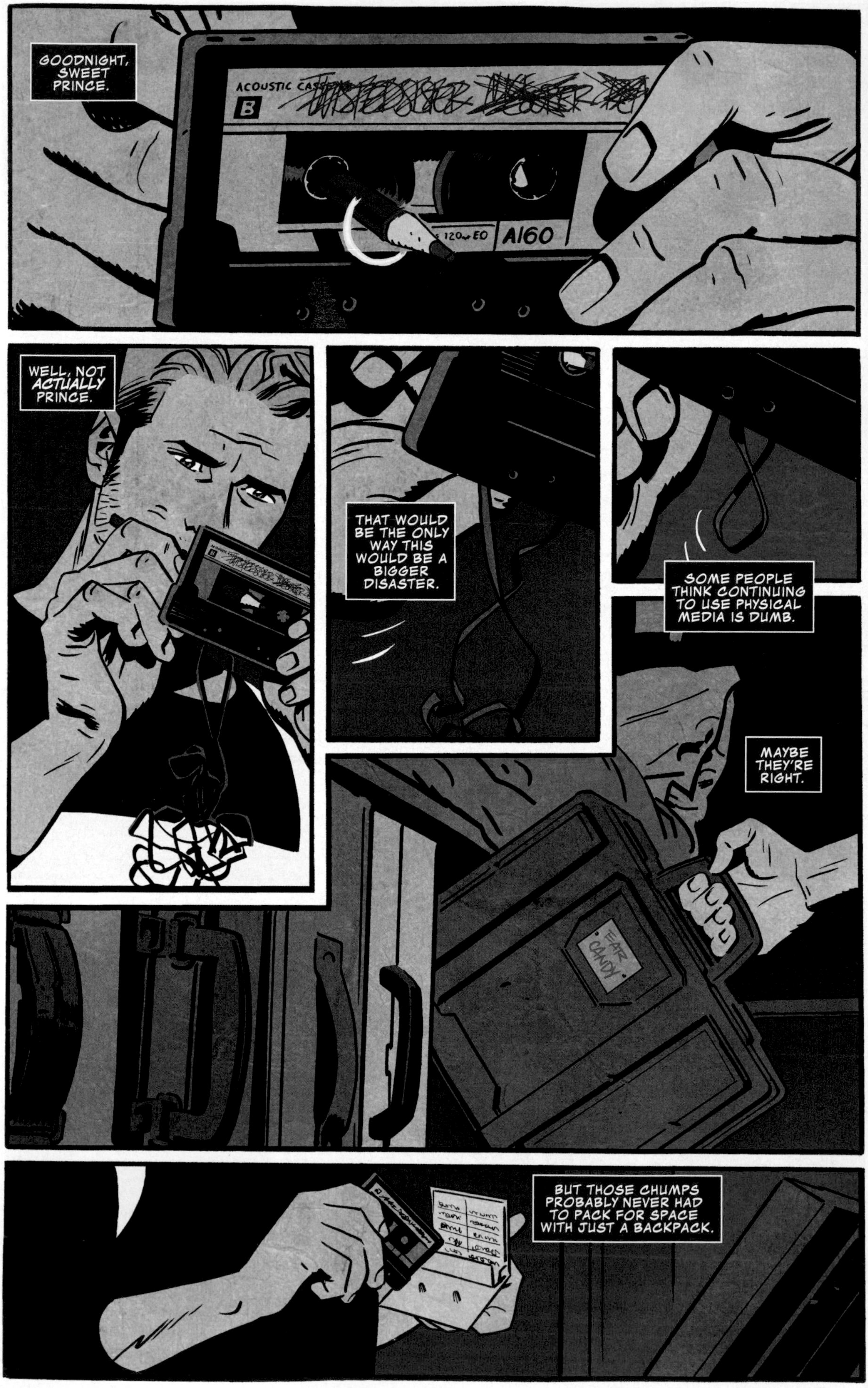
GOODNIGHT, SWEET PRINCE.
ACOUSTIC CAS
B
A160
WELL, NOT ACTUALLY PRINCE.
THAT WOULD BE THE ONLY WAY THIS WOULD BE A BIGGER DISASTER.
SOME PEOPLE THINK CONTINUING TO USE PHYSICAL MEDIA IS DUMB.
MAYBE THEY'RE RIGHT.
EAR CANDY
BUT THOSE CHUMPS PROBABLY NEVER HAD TO PACK FOR SPACE WITH JUST A BACKPACK.

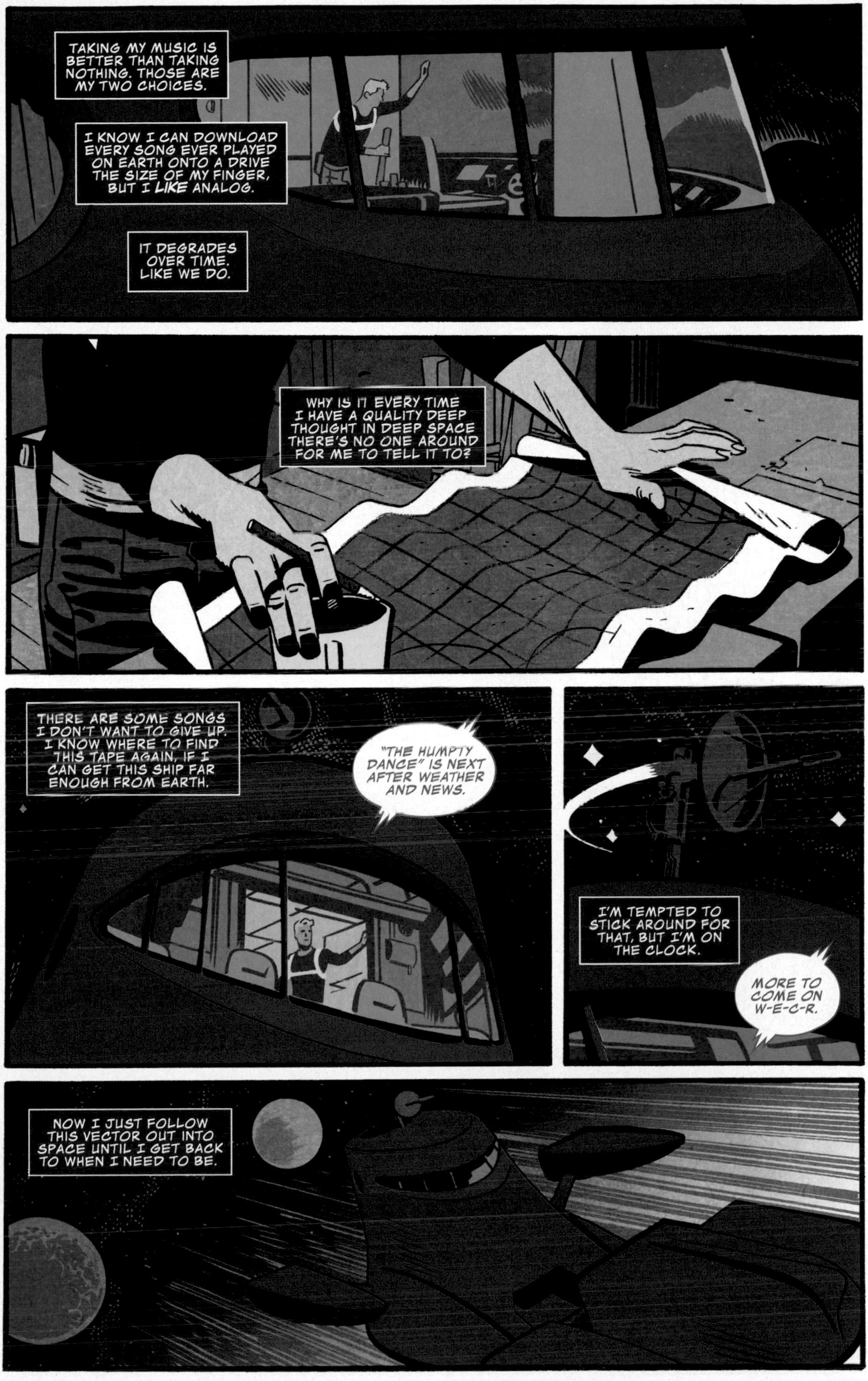
TAKING MY MUSIC IS BETTER THAN TAKING NOTHING. THOSE ARE MY TWO CHOICES.
I KNOW I CAN DOWNLOAD EVERY SONG EVER PLAYED ON EARTH ONTO A DRIVE THE SIZE OF MY FINGER, BUT I *LIKE* ANALOG.
IT DEGRADES OVER TIME. LIKE WE DO.
WHY IS IT EVERY TIME I HAVE A QUALITY DEEP THOUGHT IN DEEP SPACE THERE'S NO ONE AROUND FOR ME TO TELL IT TO?
THERE ARE SOME SONGS I DON'T WANT TO GIVE UP. I KNOW WHERE TO FIND THIS TAPE AGAIN, IF I CAN GET THIS SHIP FAR ENOUGH FROM EARTH.
"THE HUMPTY DANCE" IS NEXT AFTER WEATHER AND NEWS.
I'M TEMPTED TO STICK AROUND FOR THAT, BUT I'M ON THE CLOCK.
MORE TO COME ON W-E-C-R.
NOW I JUST FOLLOW THIS VECTOR OUT INTO SPACE UNTIL I GET BACK TO WHEN I NEED TO BE.

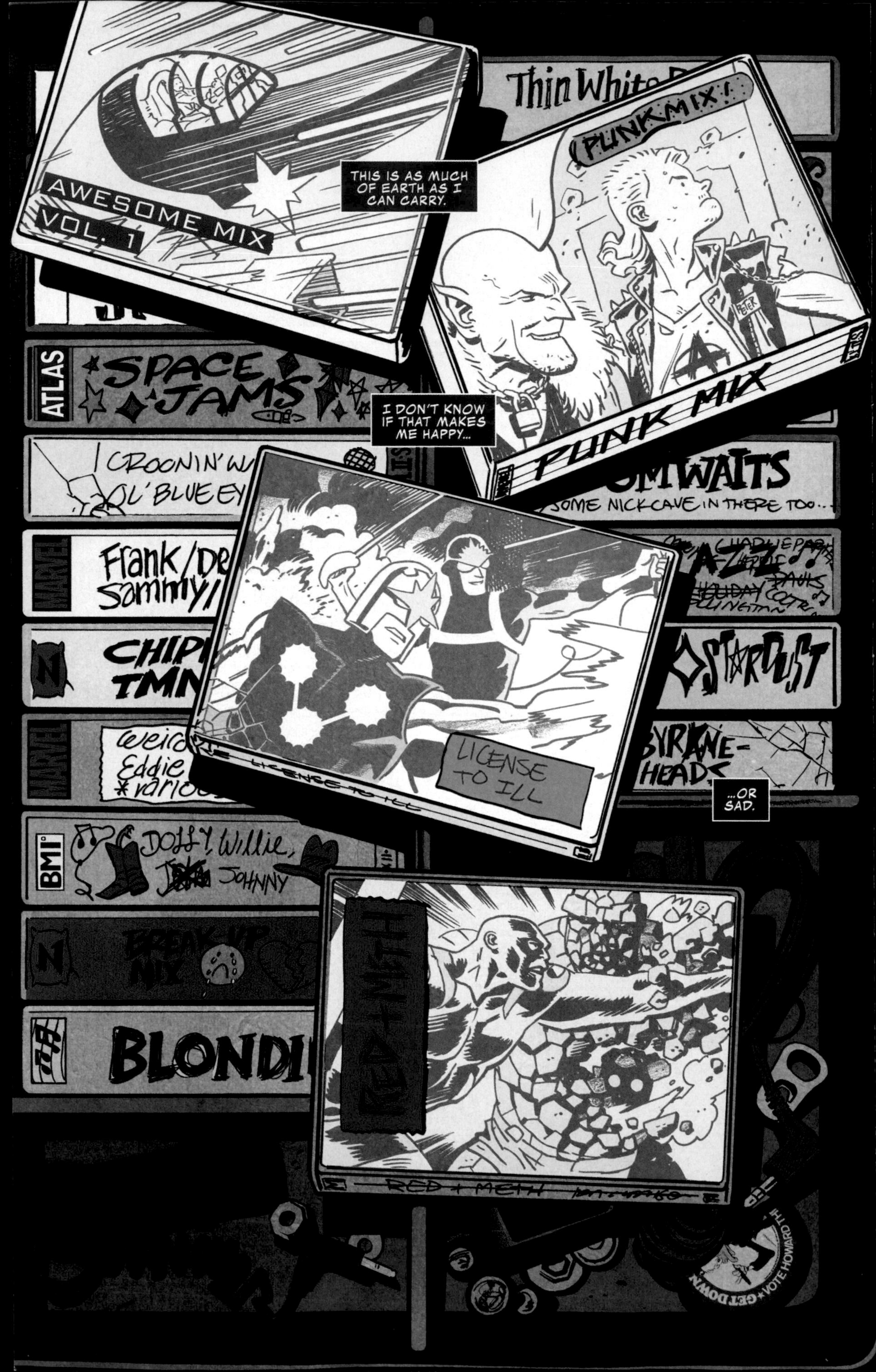
AWESOME MIX
VOL. 1
THIS IS AS MUCH OF EARTH AS I CAN CARRY.
PUNK MIX!
PUNK MIX
ATLAS
SPACE JAMS
I DON'T KNOW IF THAT MAKES ME HAPPY...
MARVEL
LICENSE TO ILL
SOME NICK CAVE IN THERE TOO...
...OR SAD.
BMI
JOHNNY
BLONDI
RED + METH
GET DOWN
VOTE HOWARD

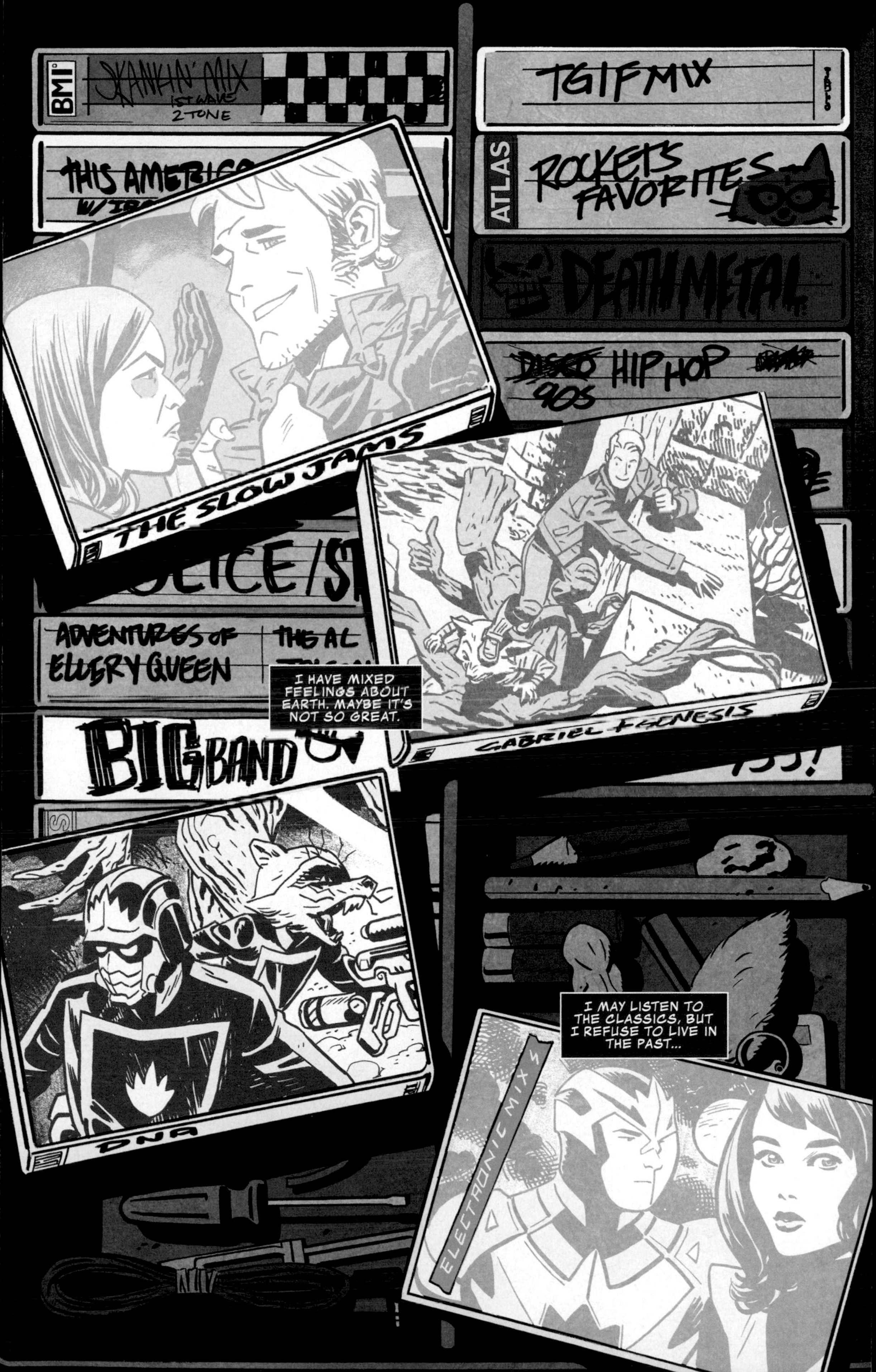

SKANKIN' MIX
1ST WAVE
2 TONE
TGIF MIX
ATLAS
ROCKET'S FAVORITES
DEATH METAL
HIP HOP
90S
THE SLOW JAMS
ADVENTURES OF ELLERY QUEEN
I HAVE MIXED FEELINGS ABOUT EARTH. MAYBE IT'S NOT SO GREAT.
BIG BAND
DNA
I MAY LISTEN TO THE CLASSICS, BUT I REFUSE TO LIVE IN THE PAST...
ELECTRONIC MIXES

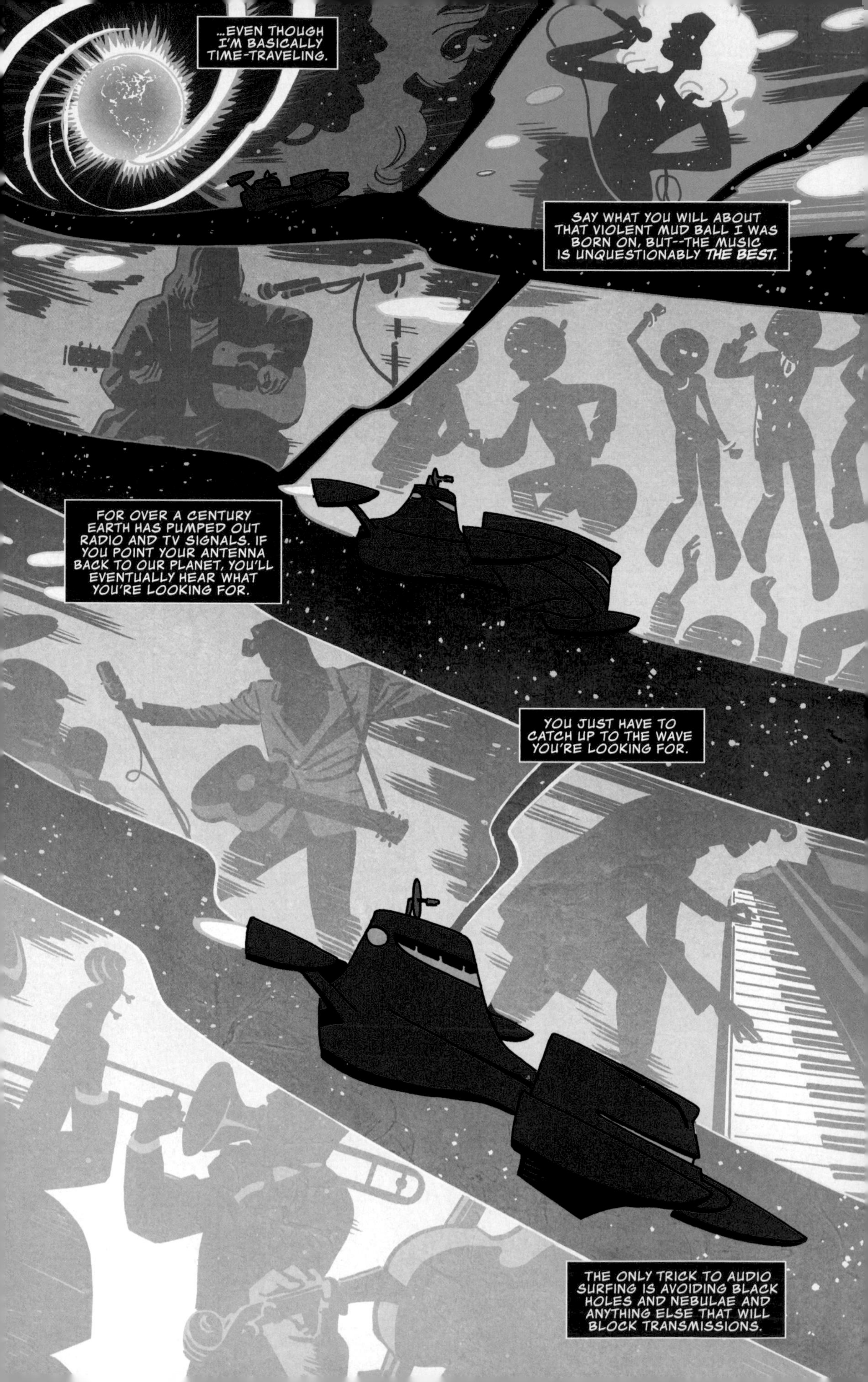
...EVEN THOUGH I'M BASICALLY TIME-TRAVELING.
SAY WHAT YOU WILL ABOUT THAT VIOLENT MUD BALL I WAS BORN ON, BUT--THE MUSIC IS UNQUESTIONABLY *THE BEST.*
FOR OVER A CENTURY EARTH HAS PUMPED OUT RADIO AND TV SIGNALS. IF YOU POINT YOUR ANTENNA BACK TO OUR PLANET, YOU'LL EVENTUALLY HEAR WHAT YOU'RE LOOKING FOR.
YOU JUST HAVE TO CATCH UP TO THE WAVE YOU'RE LOOKING FOR.
THE ONLY TRICK TO AUDIO SURFING IS AVOIDING BLACK HOLES AND NEBULAE AND ANYTHING ELSE THAT WILL BLOCK TRANSMISSIONS.

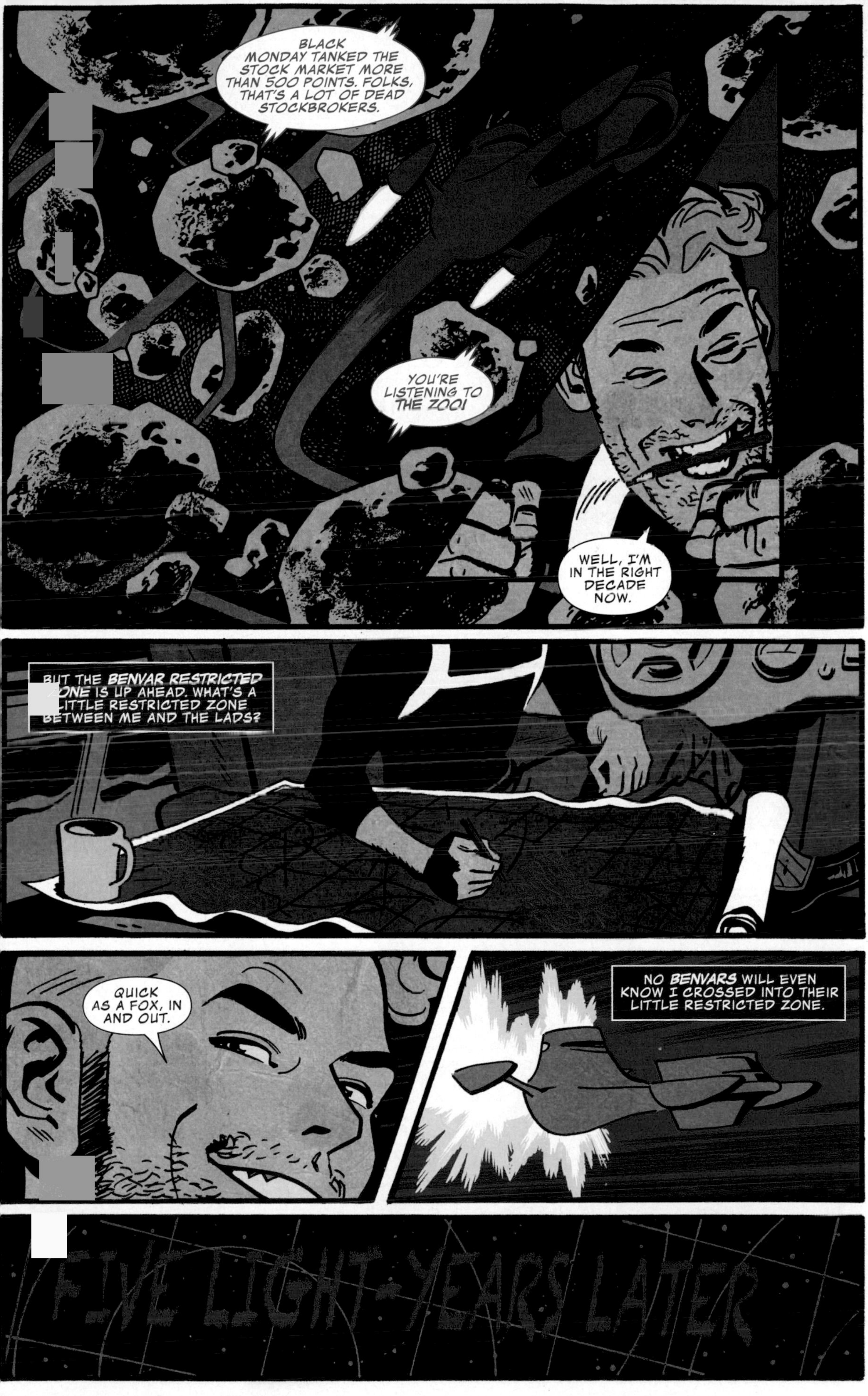
BLACK MONDAY TANKED THE STOCK MARKET MORE THAN 500 POINTS. FOLKS, THAT'S A LOT OF DEAD STOCKBROKERS.
YOU'RE LISTENING TO THE ZOO!
WELL, I'M IN THE RIGHT DECADE NOW.
BUT THE BENVAR RESTRICTED ZONE IS UP AHEAD. WHAT'S A LITTLE RESTRICTED ZONE BETWEEN ME AND THE LADS?
QUICK AS A FOX, IN AND OUT.
NO BENVARS WILL EVEN KNOW I CROSSED INTO THEIR LITTLE RESTRICTED ZONE.
FIVE LIGHT-YEARS LATER

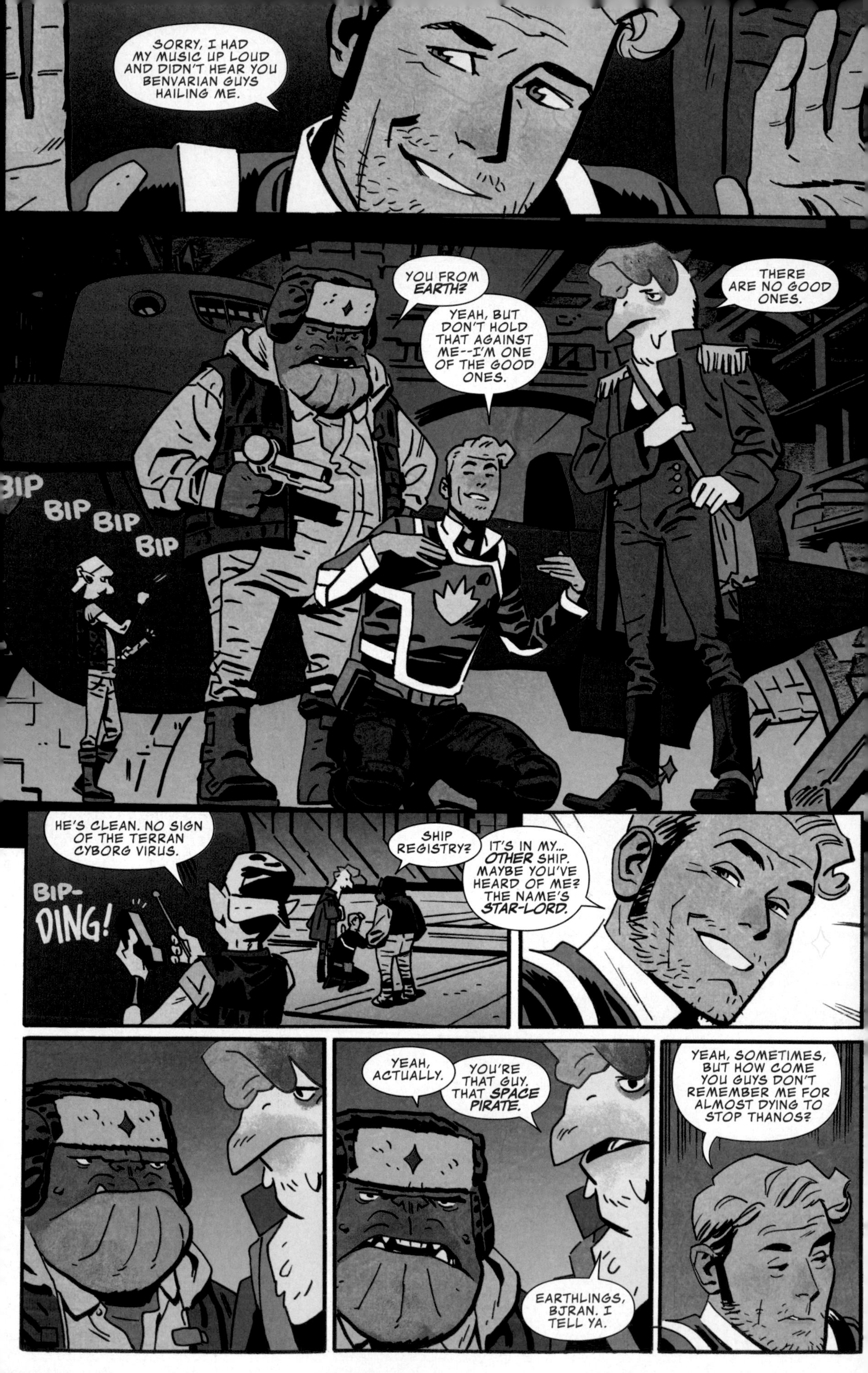
SORRY, I HAD MY MUSIC UP LOUD AND DIDN'T HEAR YOU BENVARIAN GUYS HAILING ME.
YOU FROM EARTH?
YEAH, BUT DON'T HOLD THAT AGAINST ME--I'M ONE OF THE GOOD ONES.
THERE ARE NO GOOD ONES.
BIP BIP BIP BIP
HE'S CLEAN. NO SIGN OF THE TERRAN CYBORG VIRUS.
BIP-DING!
SHIP REGISTRY?
IT'S IN MY... OTHER SHIP. MAYBE YOU'VE HEARD OF ME? THE NAME'S STAR-LORD.
YEAH, ACTUALLY.
YOU'RE THAT GUY. THAT SPACE PIRATE.
EARTHLINGS, BJRAN. I TELL YA.
YEAH, SOMETIMES, BUT HOW COME YOU GUYS DON'T REMEMBER ME FOR ALMOST DYING TO STOP THANOS?

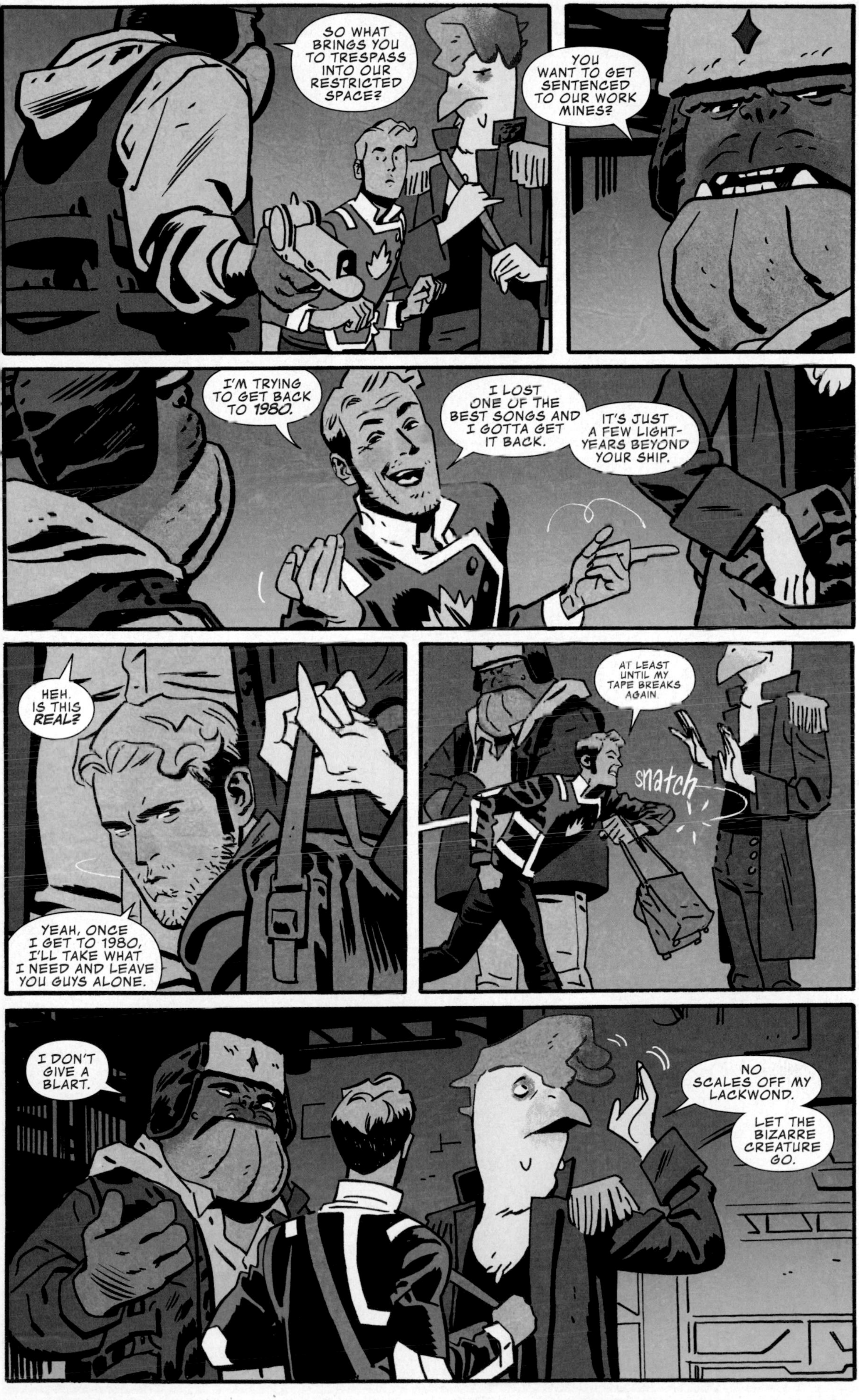
SO WHAT BRINGS YOU TO TRESPASS INTO OUR RESTRICTED SPACE?
YOU WANT TO GET SENTENCED TO OUR WORK MINES?
I'M TRYING TO GET BACK TO 1980.
I LOST ONE OF THE BEST SONGS AND I GOTTA GET IT BACK.
IT'S JUST A FEW LIGHT-YEARS BEYOND YOUR SHIP.
HEH. IS THIS REAL?
YEAH, ONCE I GET TO 1980, I'LL TAKE WHAT I NEED AND LEAVE YOU GUYS ALONE.
AT LEAST UNTIL MY TAPE BREAKS AGAIN.
snatch
I DON'T GIVE A BLART.
NO SCALES OFF MY LACKWOND.
LET THE BIZARRE CREATURE GO.

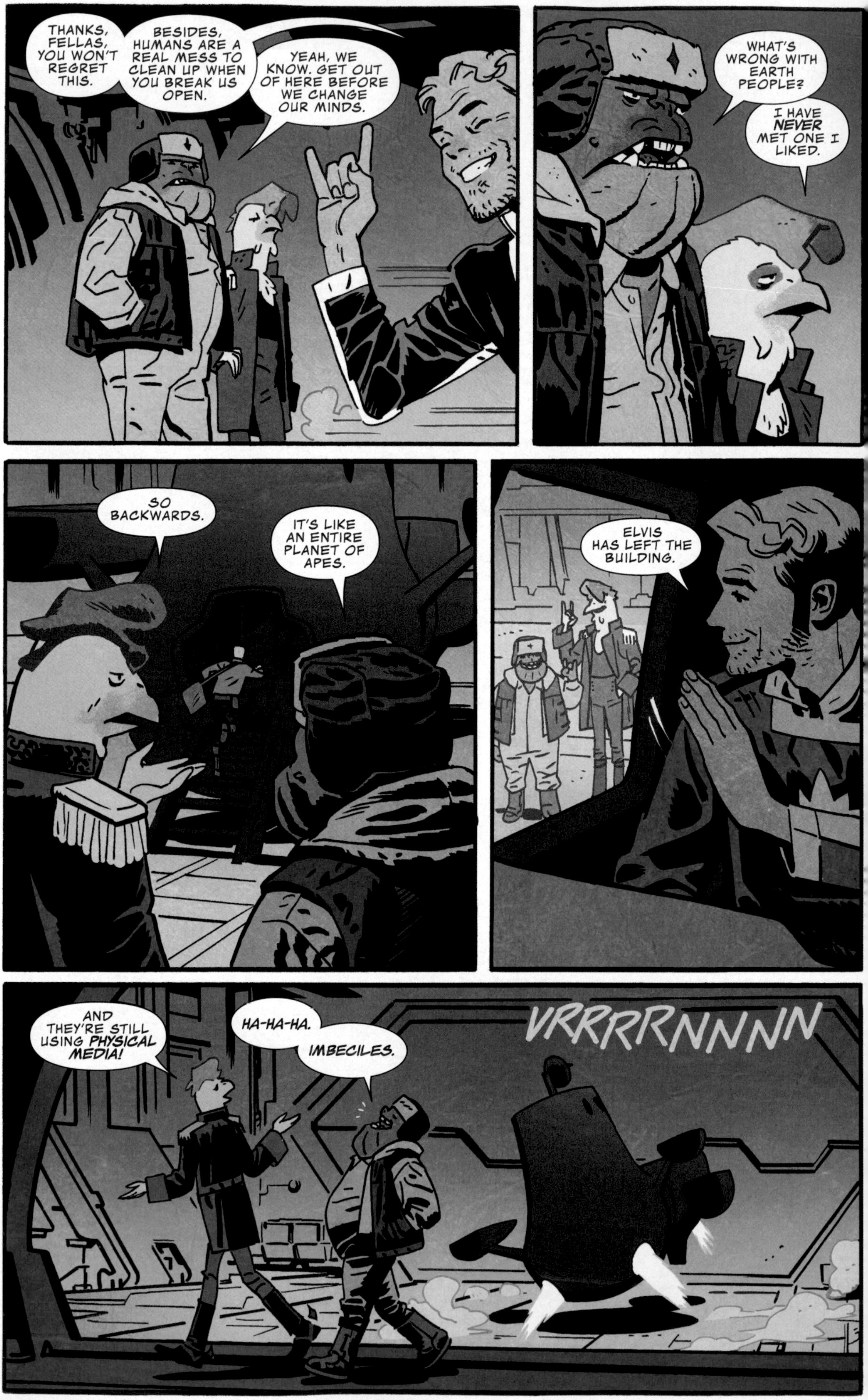
THANKS, FELLAS, YOU WON'T REGRET THIS.
BESIDES, HUMANS ARE A REAL MESS TO CLEAN UP WHEN YOU BREAK US OPEN.
YEAH, WE KNOW. GET OUT OF HERE BEFORE WE CHANGE OUR MINDS.
WHAT'S WRONG WITH EARTH PEOPLE?
I HAVE NEVER MET ONE I LIKED.
SO BACKWARDS.
IT'S LIKE AN ENTIRE PLANET OF APES.
ELVIS HAS LEFT THE BUILDING.
AND THEY'RE STILL USING PHYSICAL MEDIA!
HA-HA-HA.
IMBECILES.
VRRRRNNNNN

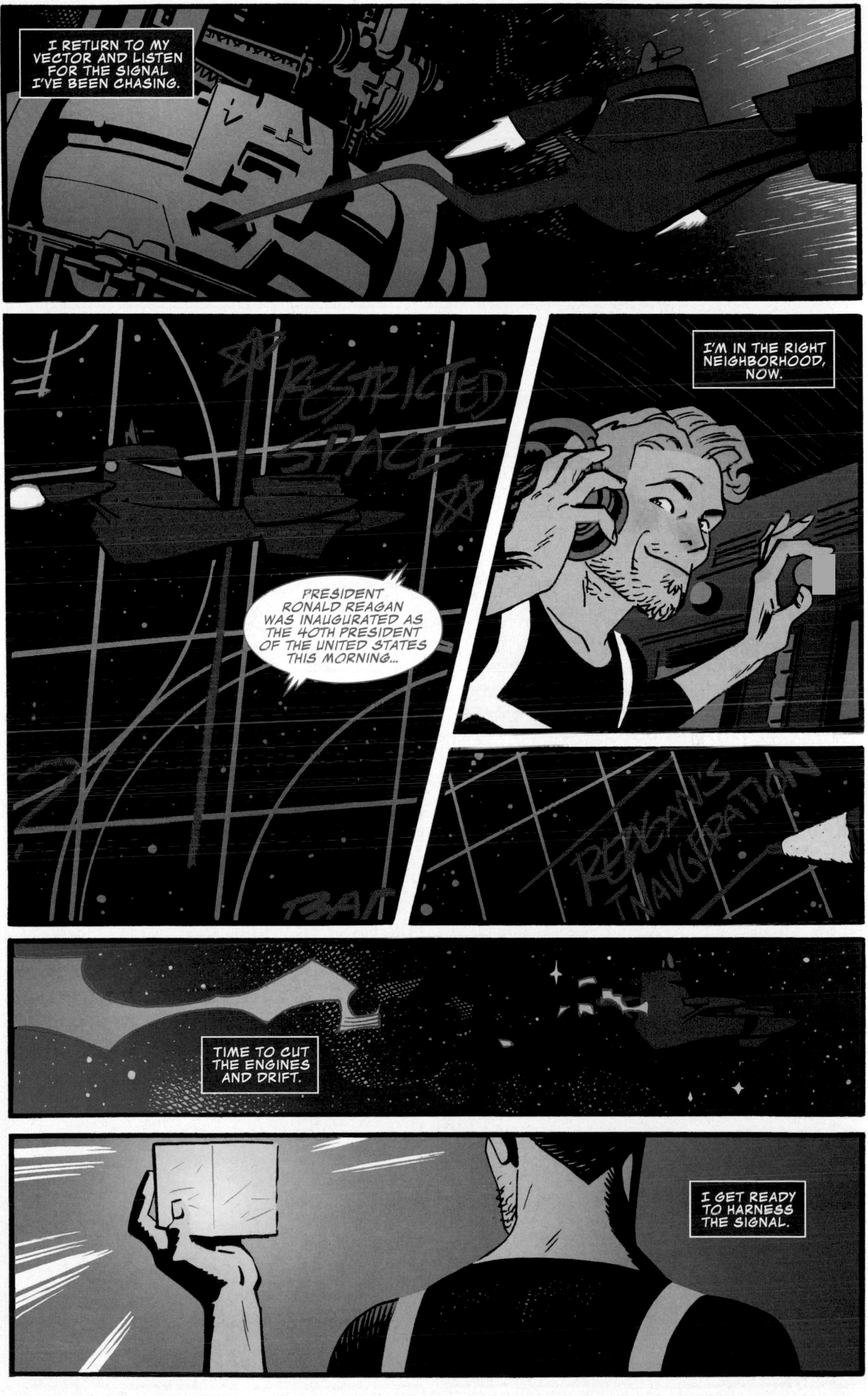
I RETURN TO MY VECTOR AND LISTEN FOR THE SIGNAL I'VE BEEN CHASING.
RESTRICTED SPACE
PRESIDENT RONALD REAGAN WAS INAUGURATED AS THE 40TH PRESIDENT OF THE UNITED STATES THIS MORNING...
I'M IN THE RIGHT NEIGHBORHOOD, NOW.
REAGAN'S INAUGURATION
TIME TO CUT THE ENGINES AND DRIFT.
I GET READY TO HARNESS THE SIGNAL.

JUST A COUPLE OF LIGHT-YEARS OUT.

GOTTA BE READY.

ATLAS
AUDIO CASSETTE
NORMAL BIAS
UR
SUPER SIZE

KCHAKT

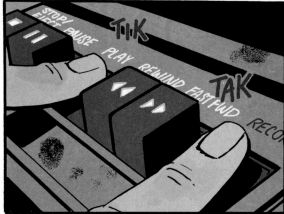

STOP/EJECT
PAUSE
PLAY REWIND FASTFWD RECOR

TIIK
TAK

TZZT
ATLAS
LUNA

EVERYONE AT W-E-C-R IS STILL REELING FROM THE DEVASTATING NEWS OUT OF NEW YORK THIS MORNING...

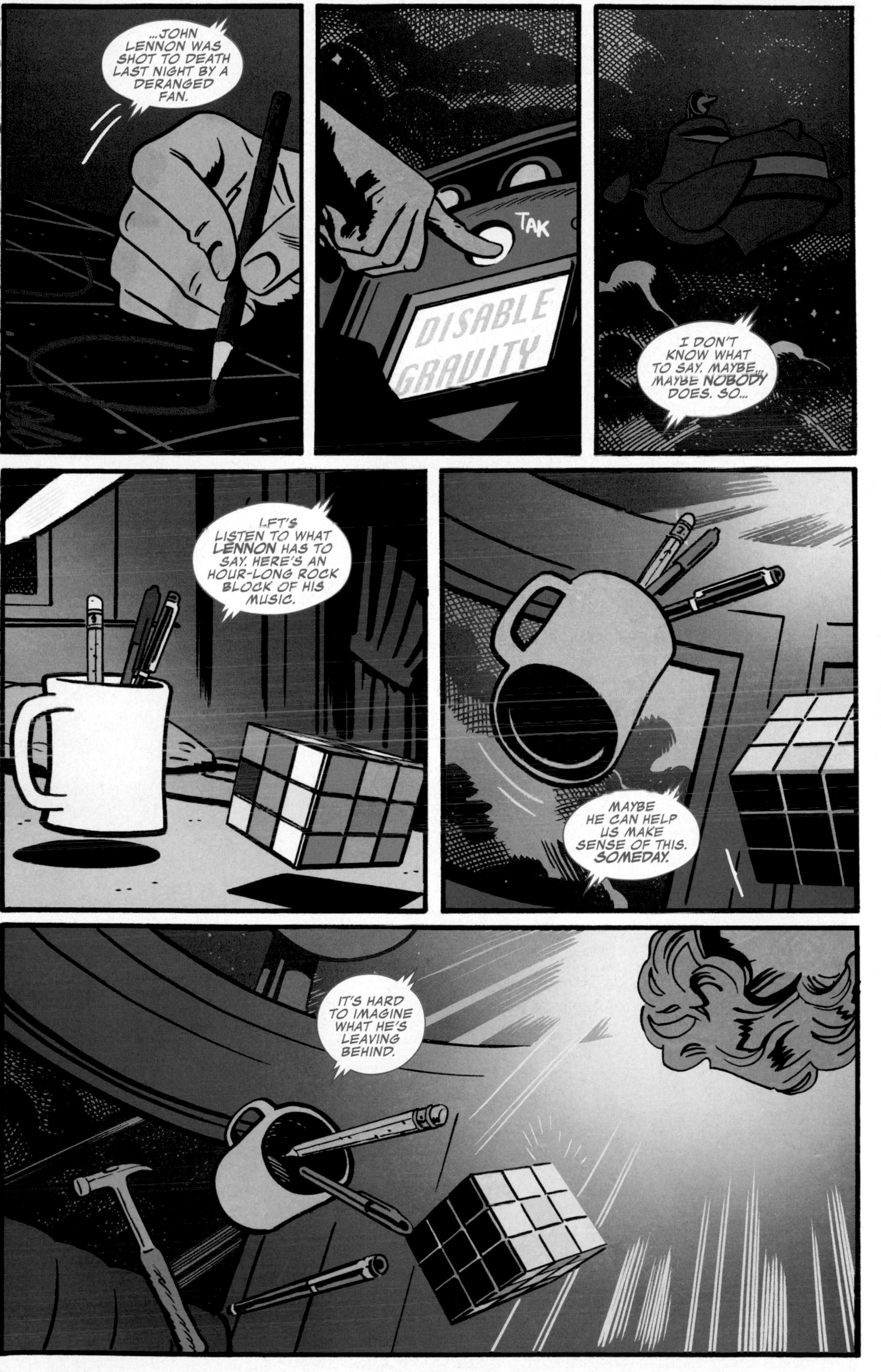
...JOHN LENNON WAS SHOT TO DEATH LAST NIGHT BY A DERANGED FAN.
TAK
DISABLE GRAVITY
I DON'T KNOW WHAT TO SAY. MAYBE... MAYBE NOBODY DOES. SO...
LET'S LISTEN TO WHAT LENNON HAS TO SAY. HERE'S AN HOUR-LONG ROCK BLOCK OF HIS MUSIC.
MAYBE HE CAN HELP US MAKE SENSE OF THIS. SOMEDAY.
IT'S HARD TO IMAGINE WHAT HE'S LEAVING BEHIND.

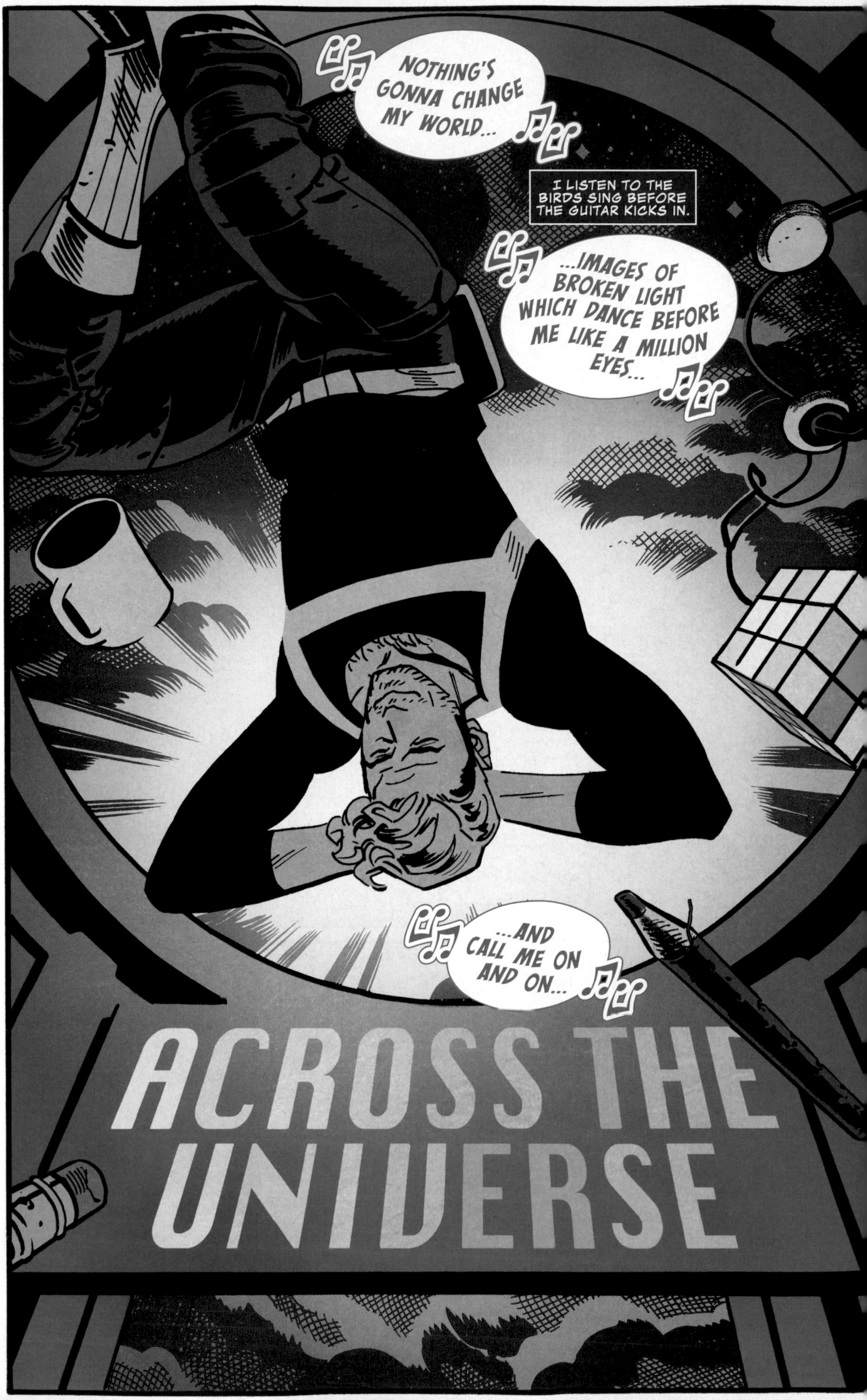
NOTHING'S GONNA CHANGE MY WORLD...
I LISTEN TO THE BIRDS SING BEFORE THE GUITAR KICKS IN.
...IMAGES OF BROKEN LIGHT WHICH DANCE BEFORE ME LIKE A MILLION EYES...
...AND CALL ME ON AND ON...
ACROSS THE UNIVERSE

7

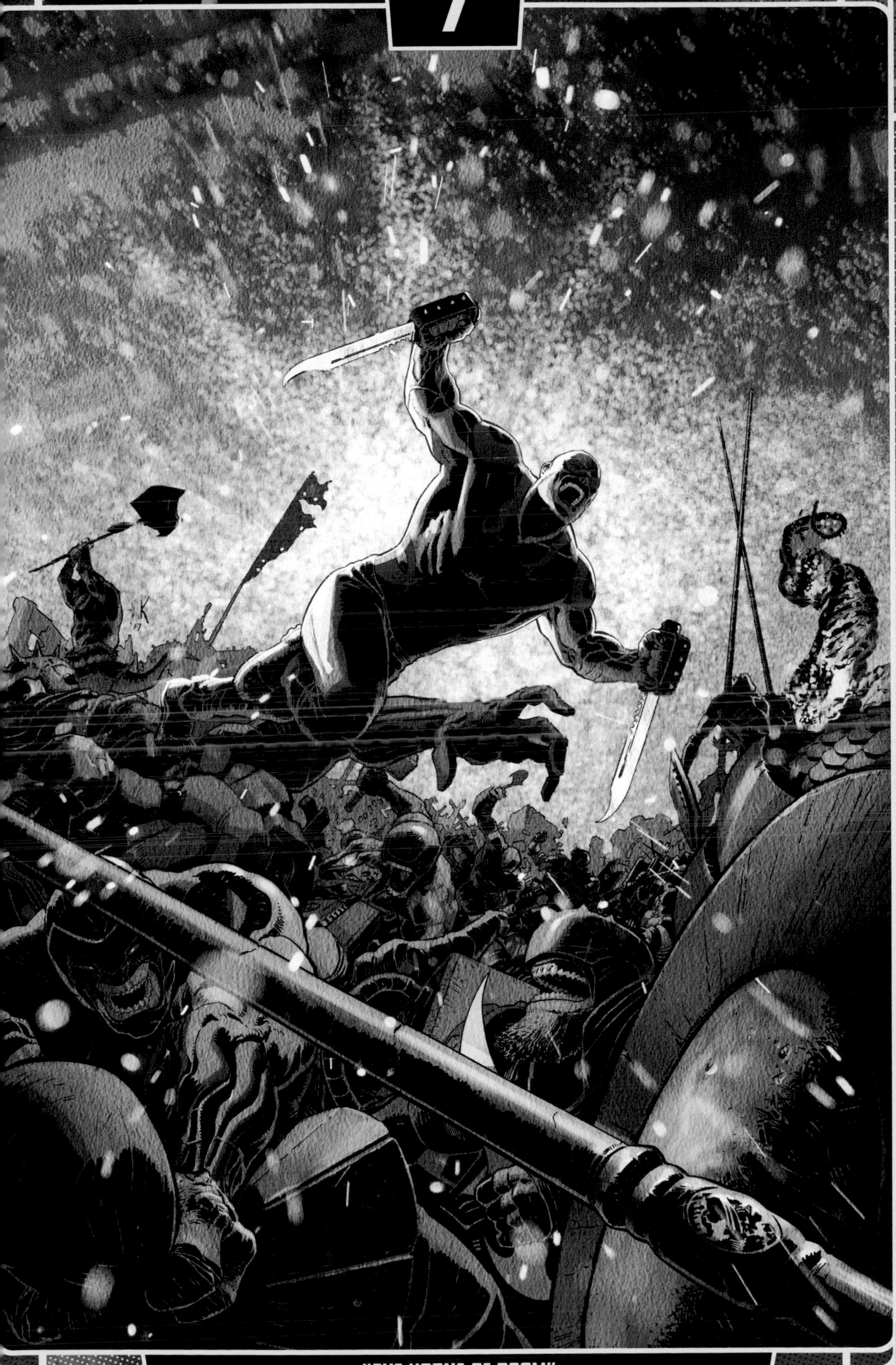

"THE HORNS OF DOOM"

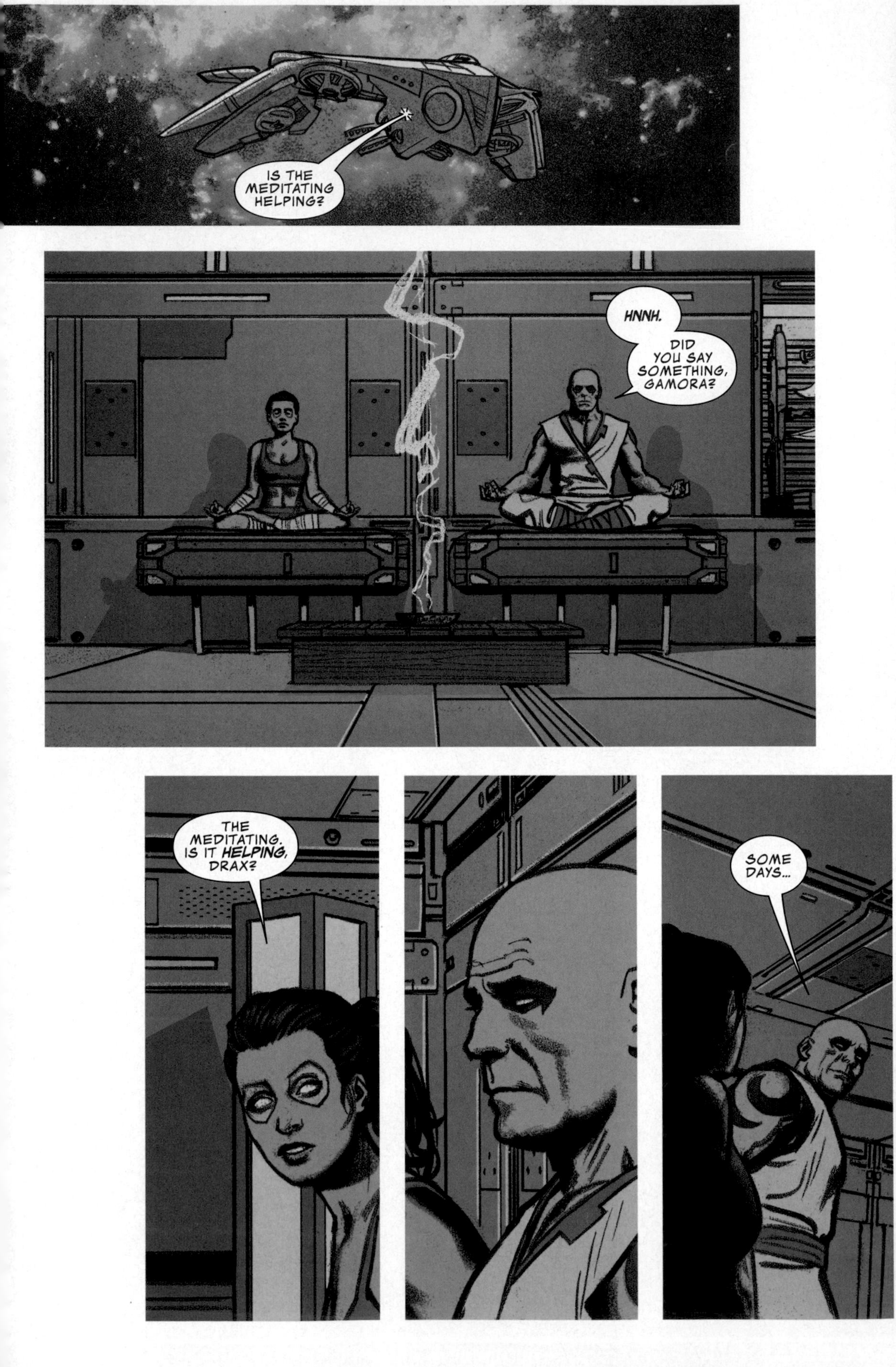
IS THE MEDITATING HELPING?
HNNH.
DID YOU SAY SOMETHING, GAMORA?
THE MEDITATING. IS IT HELPING, DRAX?
SOME DAYS...

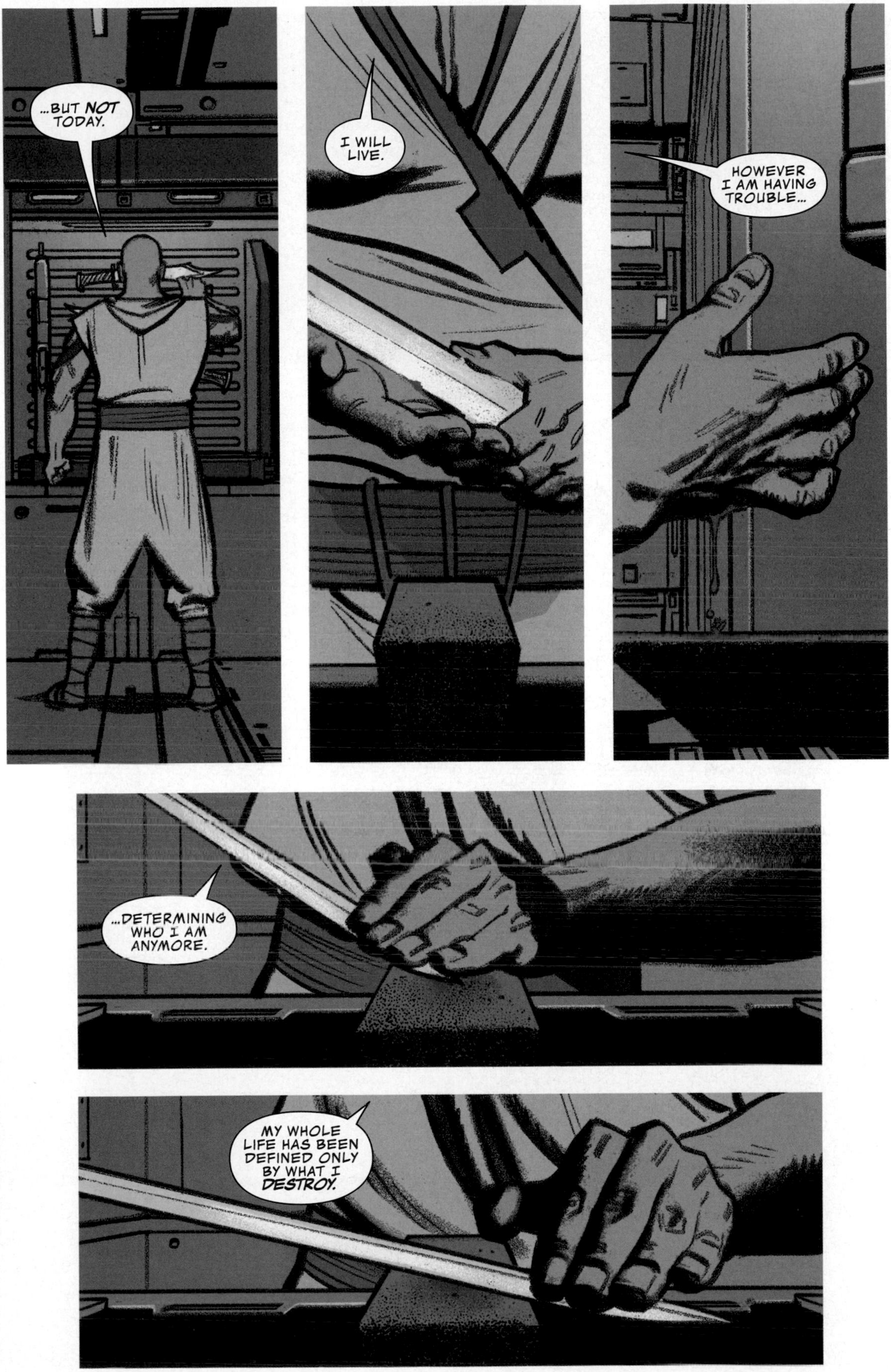
...BUT NOT TODAY.
I WILL LIVE.
HOWEVER I AM HAVING TROUBLE...
...DETERMINING WHO I AM ANYMORE.
MY WHOLE LIFE HAS BEEN DEFINED ONLY BY WHAT I DESTROY.

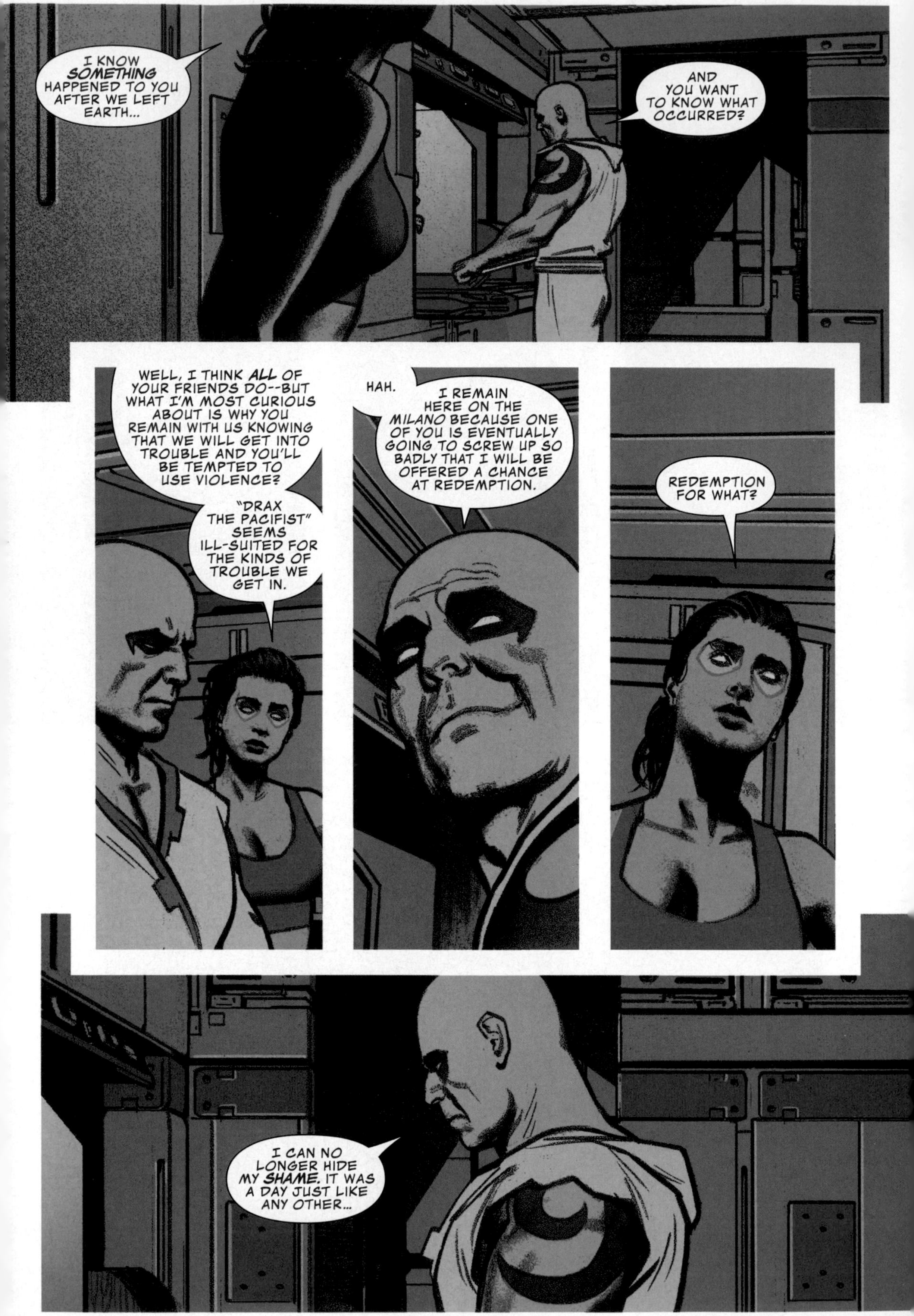
I KNOW **SOMETHING** HAPPENED TO YOU AFTER WE LEFT EARTH...
AND YOU WANT TO KNOW WHAT OCCURRED?
WELL, I THINK **ALL** OF YOUR FRIENDS DO--BUT WHAT I'M *MOST* CURIOUS ABOUT IS WHY YOU REMAIN WITH US KNOWING THAT WE WILL GET INTO TROUBLE AND YOU'LL BE TEMPTED TO USE VIOLENCE?
"DRAX THE PACIFIST" SEEMS ILL-SUITED FOR THE KINDS OF TROUBLE WE GET IN.
HAH.
I REMAIN HERE ON THE *MILANO* BECAUSE ONE OF YOU IS EVENTUALLY GOING TO SCREW UP SO BADLY THAT I WILL BE OFFERED A CHANCE AT REDEMPTION.
REDEMPTION FOR WHAT?
I CAN NO LONGER HIDE MY **SHAME**. IT WAS A DAY JUST LIKE ANY OTHER...

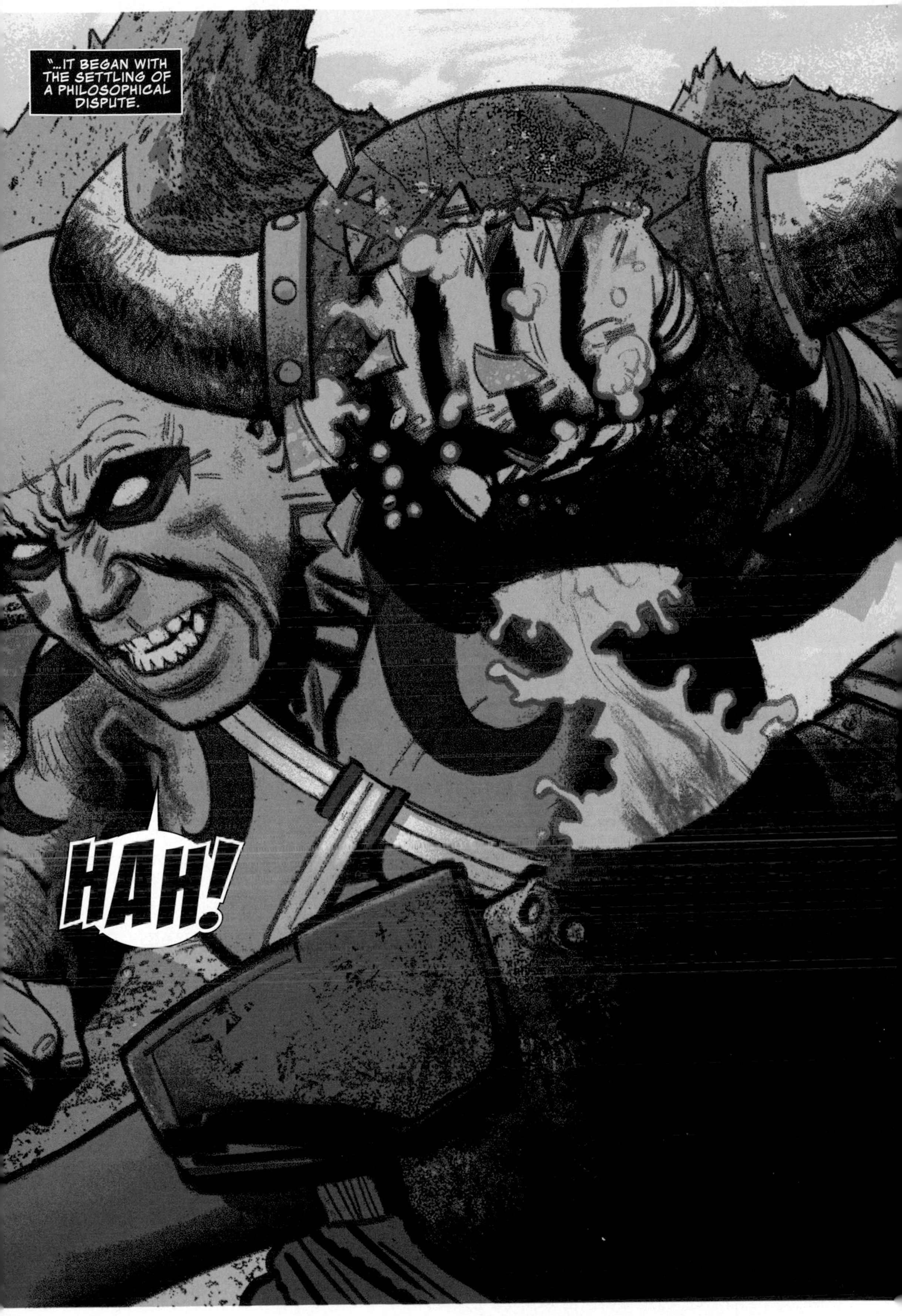
"...IT BEGAN WITH THE SETTLING OF A PHILOSOPHICAL DISPUTE.
HAH!

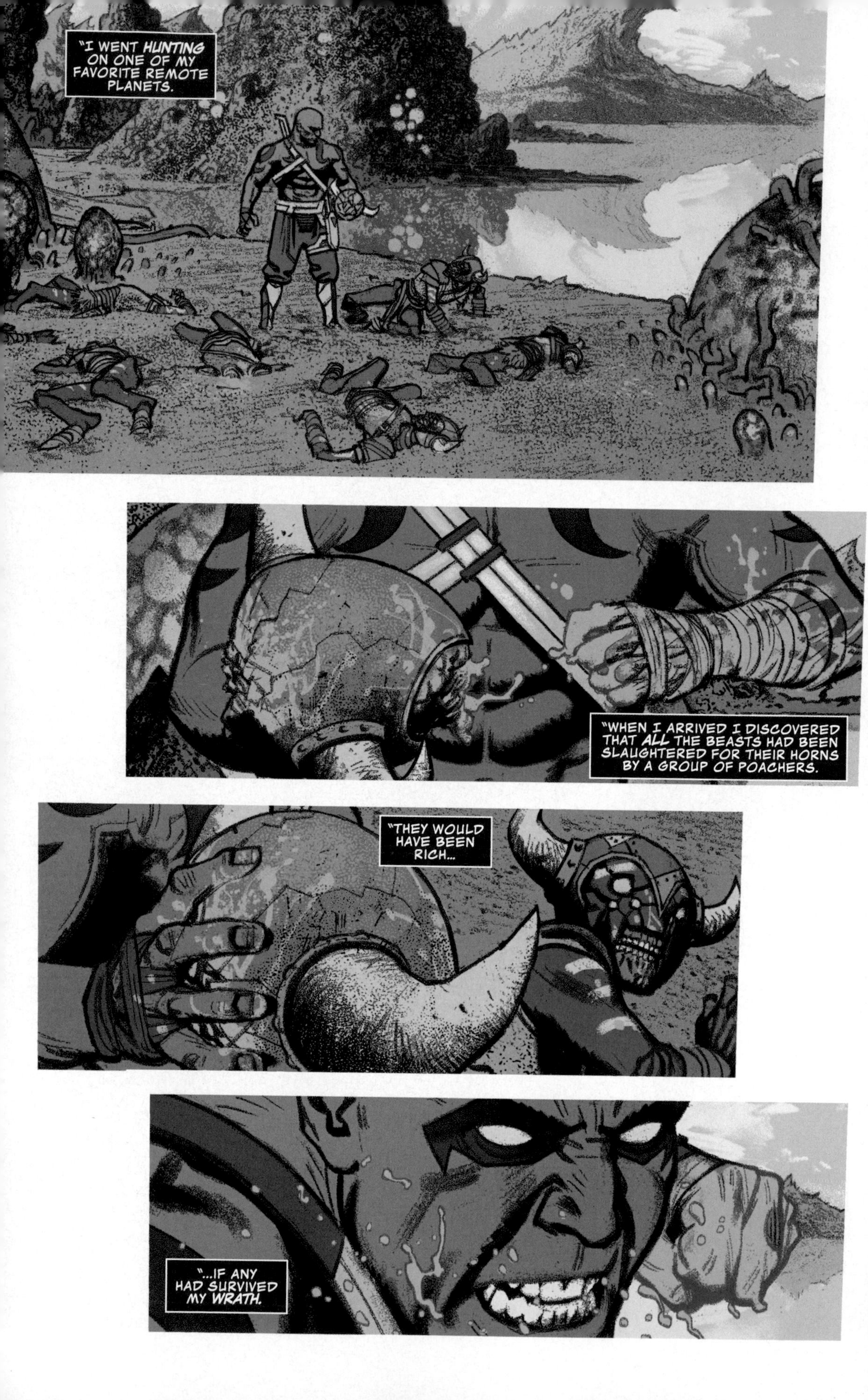
"I WENT HUNTING ON ONE OF MY FAVORITE REMOTE PLANETS.
"WHEN I ARRIVED I DISCOVERED THAT ALL THE BEASTS HAD BEEN SLAUGHTERED FOR THEIR HORNS BY A GROUP OF POACHERS.
"THEY WOULD HAVE BEEN RICH...
"...IF ANY HAD SURVIVED MY WRATH.

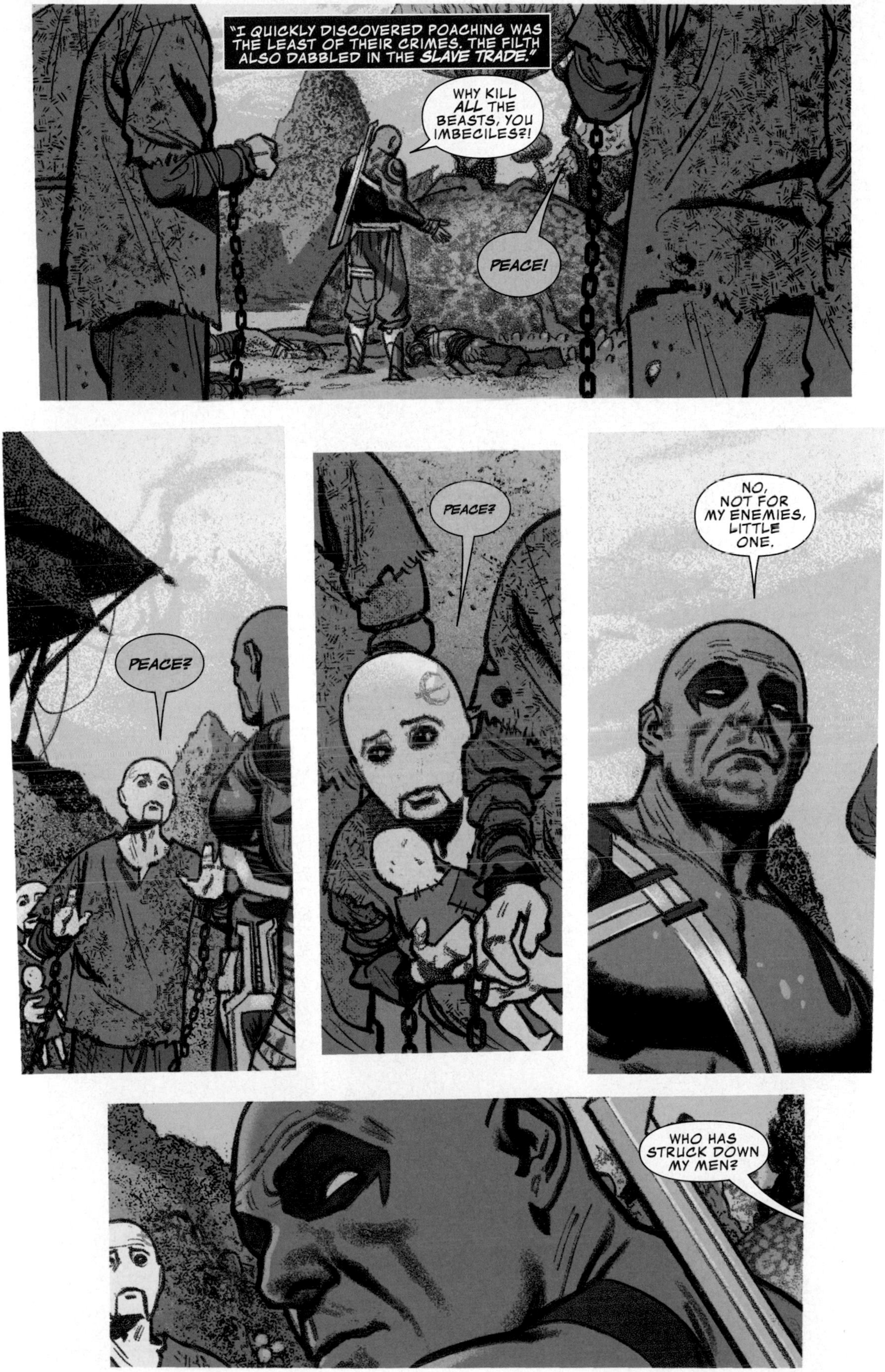
"I QUICKLY DISCOVERED POACHING WAS THE LEAST OF THEIR CRIMES. THE FILTH ALSO DABBLED IN THE SLAVE TRADE."
WHY KILL ALL THE BEASTS, YOU IMBECILES?!
PEACE!
PEACE?
PEACE?
NO, NOT FOR MY ENEMIES, LITTLE ONE.
WHO HAS STRUCK DOWN MY MEN?

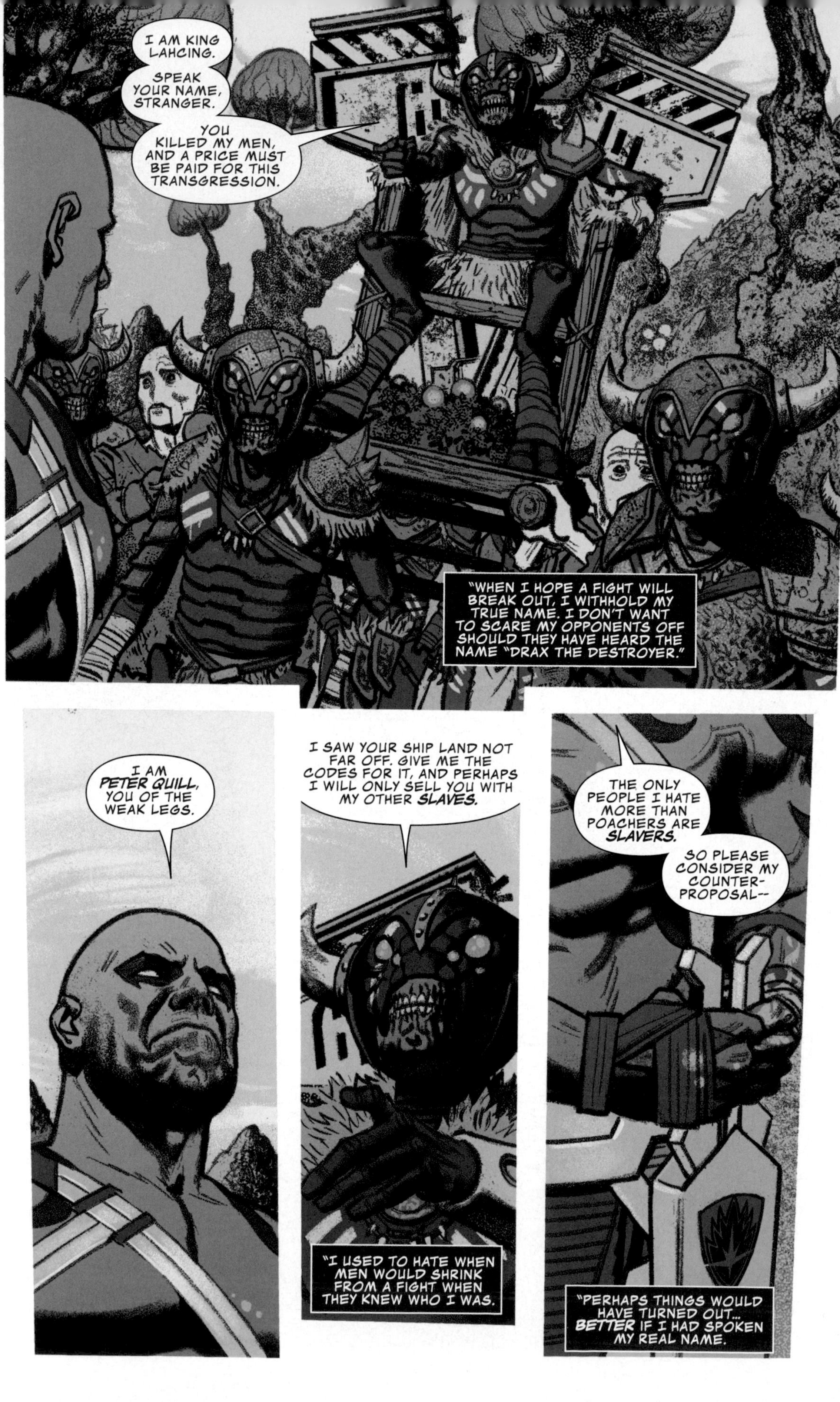
I AM KING LAHCING.
SPEAK YOUR NAME, STRANGER.
YOU KILLED MY MEN, AND A PRICE MUST BE PAID FOR THIS TRANSGRESSION.
"WHEN I HOPE A FIGHT WILL BREAK OUT, I WITHHOLD MY TRUE NAME. I DON'T WANT TO SCARE MY OPPONENTS OFF SHOULD THEY HAVE HEARD THE NAME "DRAX THE DESTROYER."
I AM PETER QUILL, YOU OF THE WEAK LEGS.
I SAW YOUR SHIP LAND NOT FAR OFF. GIVE ME THE CODES FOR IT, AND PERHAPS I WILL ONLY SELL YOU WITH MY OTHER SLAVES.
"I USED TO HATE WHEN MEN WOULD SHRINK FROM A FIGHT WHEN THEY KNEW WHO I WAS.
THE ONLY PEOPLE I HATE MORE THAN POACHERS ARE SLAVERS.
SO PLEASE CONSIDER MY COUNTER-PROPOSAL--
"PERHAPS THINGS WOULD HAVE TURNED OUT... BETTER IF I HAD SPOKEN MY REAL NAME.

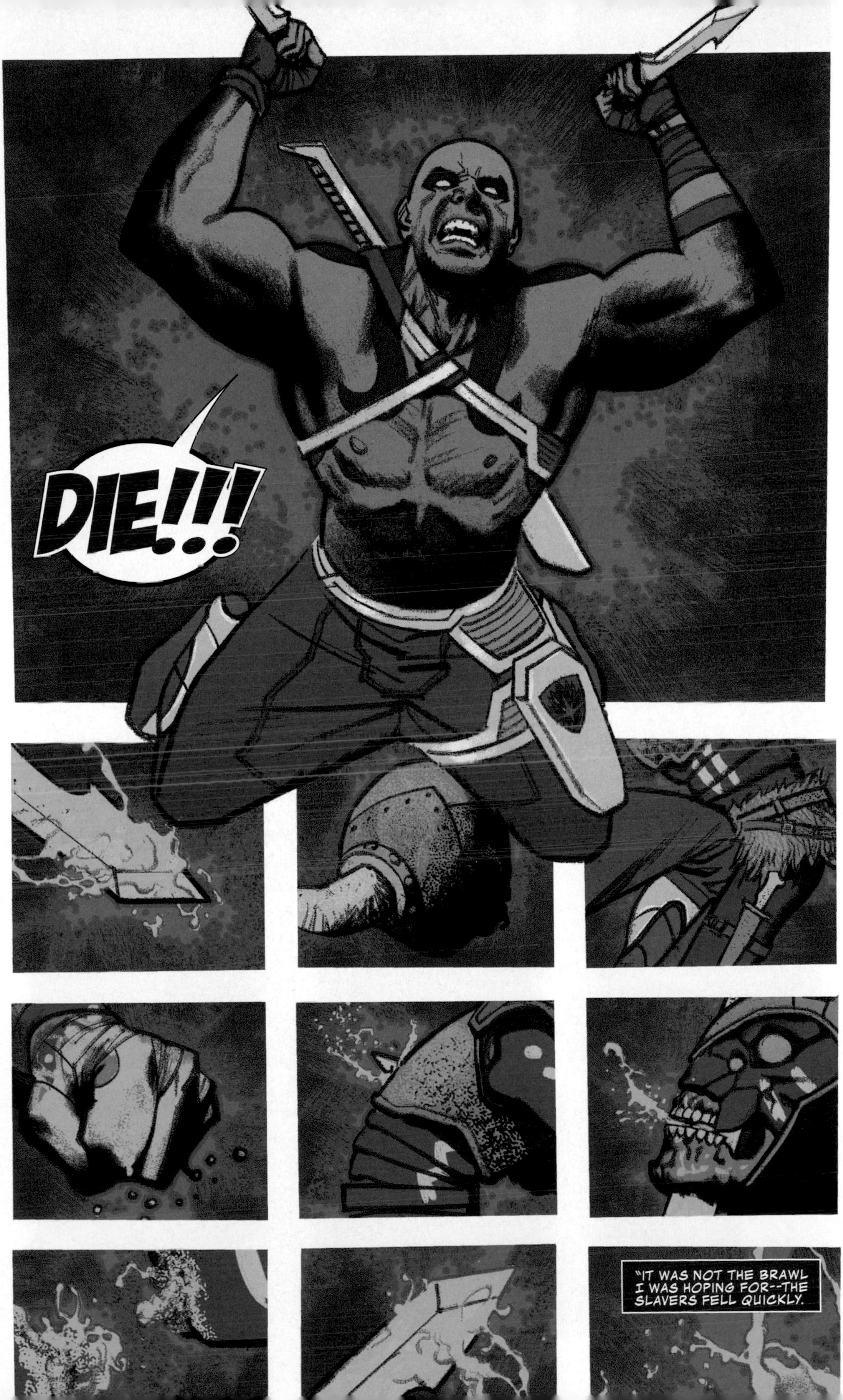
DIE!!!
"IT WAS NOT THE BRAWL I WAS HOPING FOR--THE SLAVERS FELL QUICKLY.

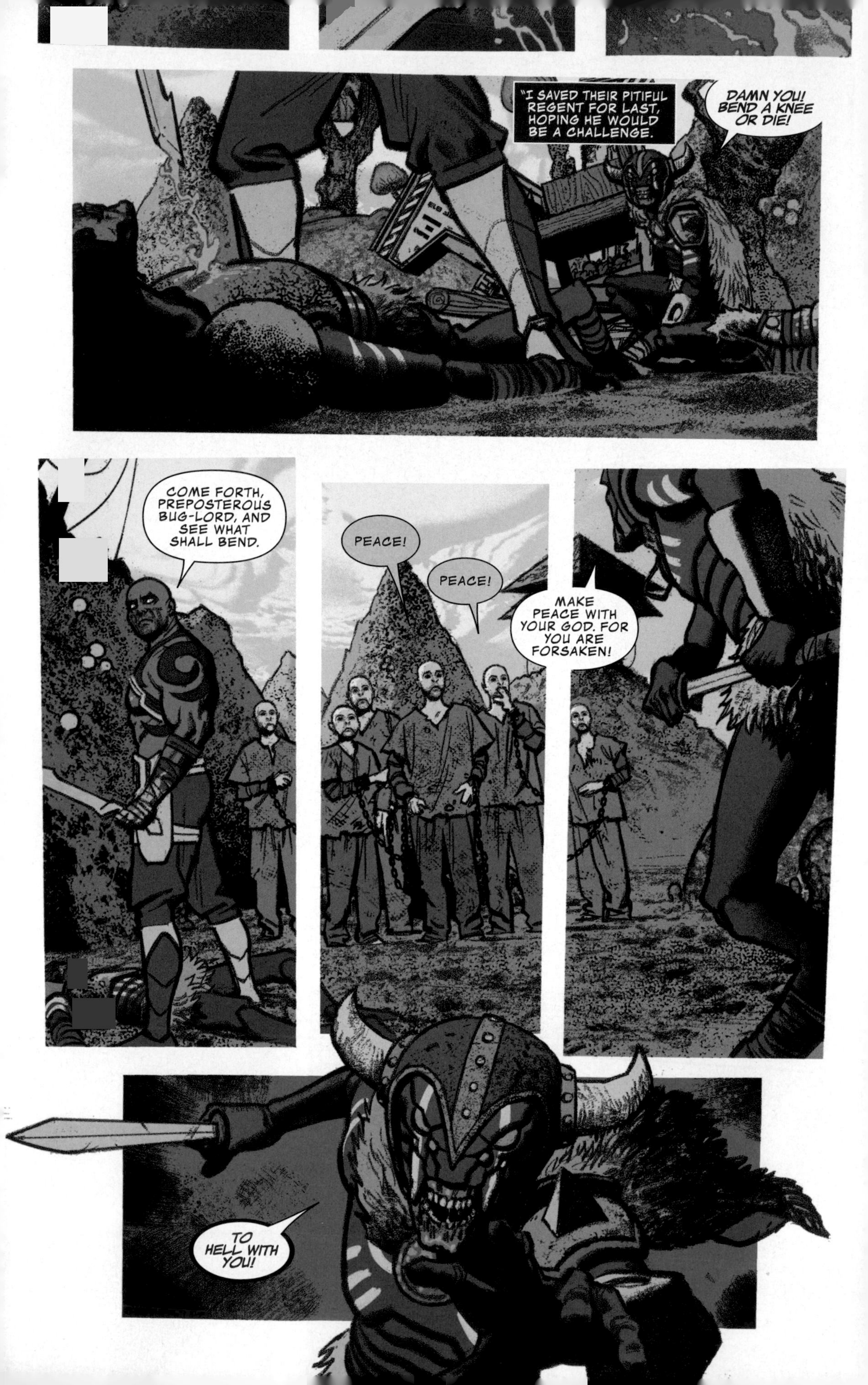
"I SAVED THEIR PITIFUL REGENT FOR LAST, HOPING HE WOULD BE A CHALLENGE.
DAMN YOU! BEND A KNEE OR DIE!
COME FORTH, PREPOSTEROUS BUG-LORD, AND SEE WHAT SHALL BEND.
PEACE!
PEACE!
MAKE PEACE WITH YOUR GOD. FOR YOU ARE FORSAKEN!
TO HELL WITH YOU!

SLASH·K·K

"I HAD COME TO HUNT.

"TO KILL WITH HONOR.

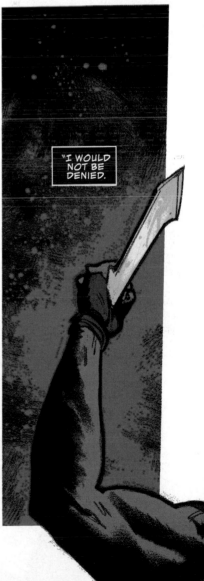

"I WOULD NOT BE DENIED.

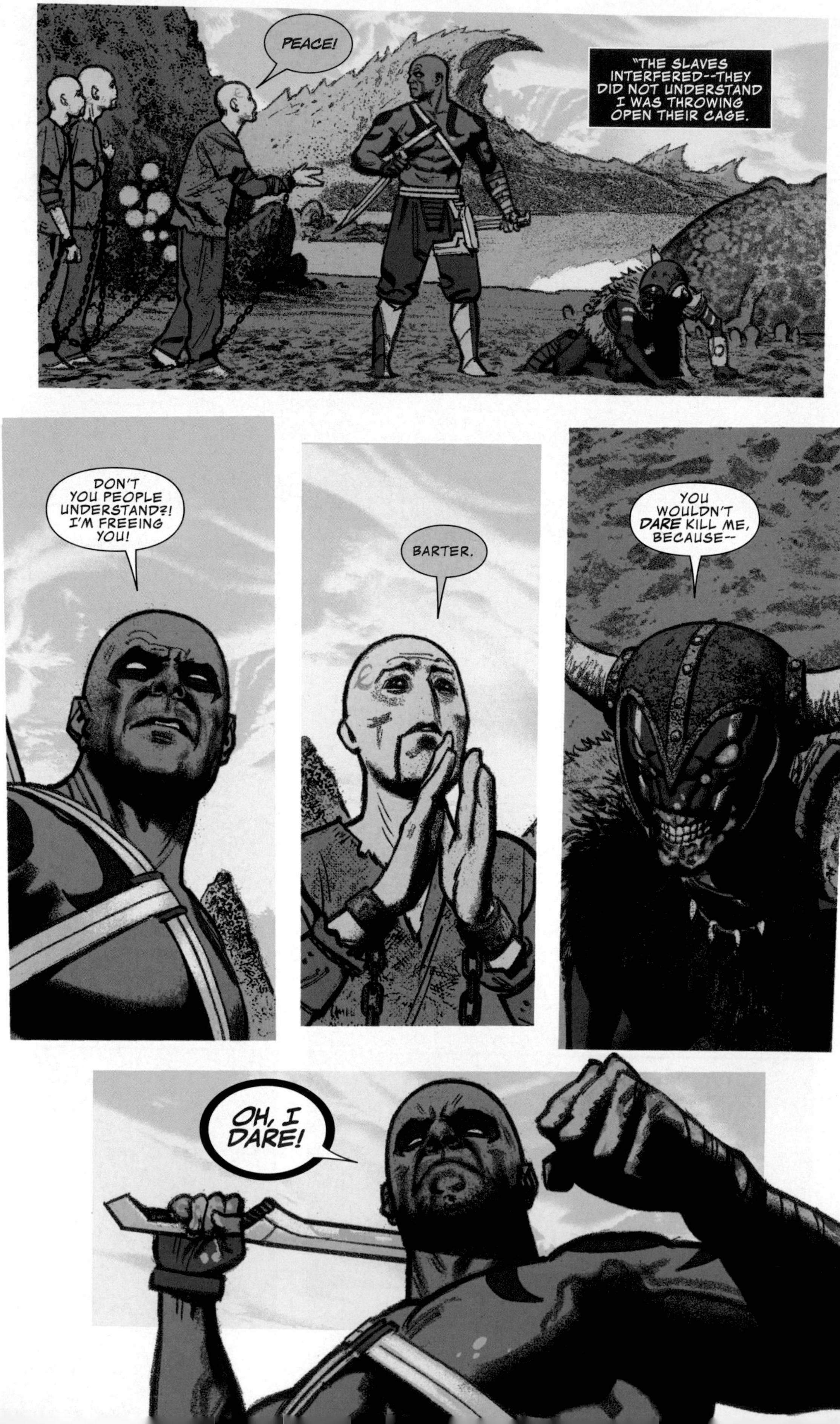
PEACE!
"THE SLAVES INTERFERED--THEY DID NOT UNDERSTAND I WAS THROWING OPEN THEIR CAGE.
DON'T YOU PEOPLE UNDERSTAND?! I'M FREEING YOU!
BARTER.
YOU WOULDN'T DARE KILL ME, BECAUSE--
OH, I DARE!

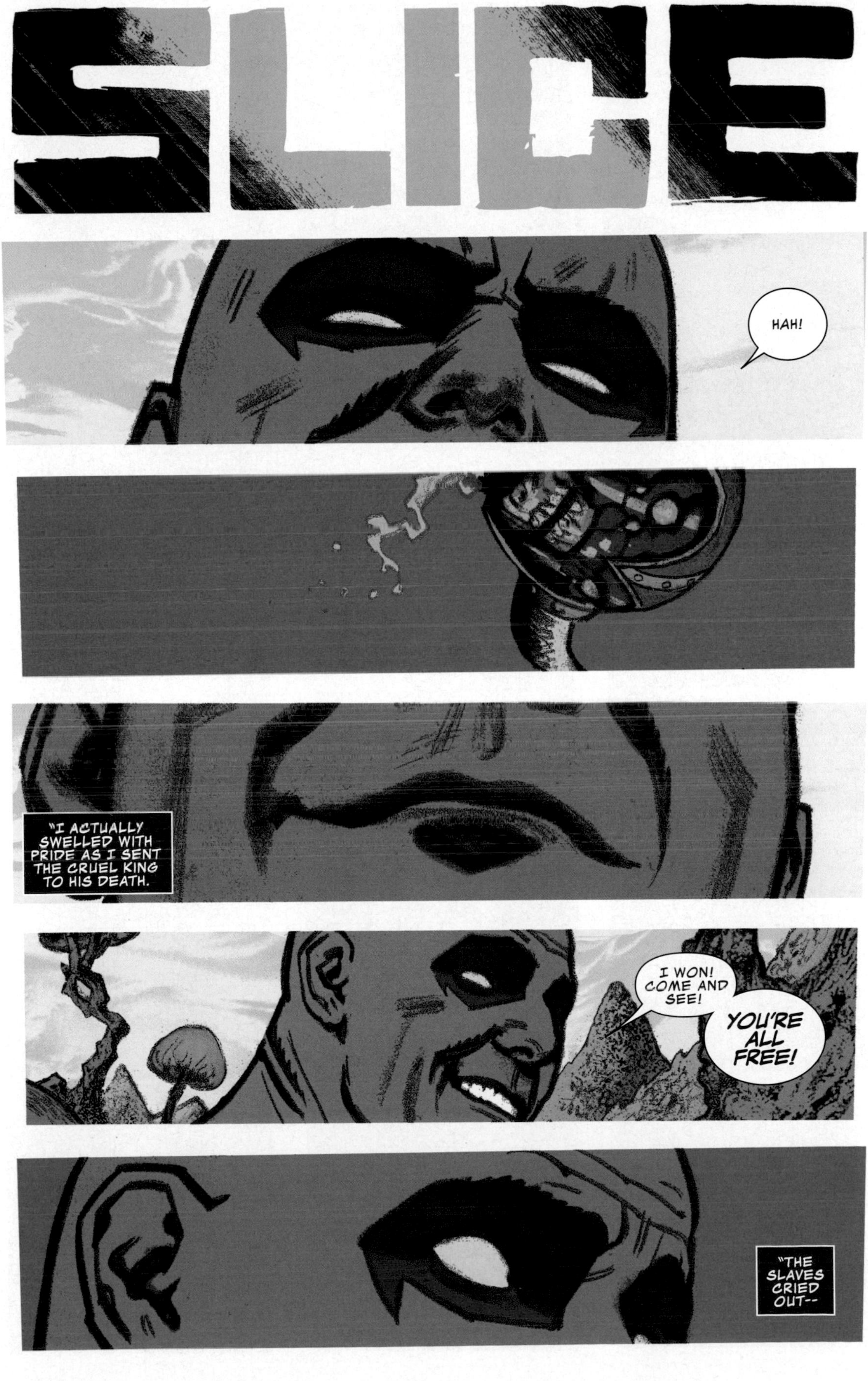
SLICE
HAH!
"I ACTUALLY SWELLED WITH PRIDE AS I SENT THE CRUEL KING TO HIS DEATH.
I WON! COME AND SEE!
YOU'RE ALL FREE!
"THE SLAVES CRIED OUT--

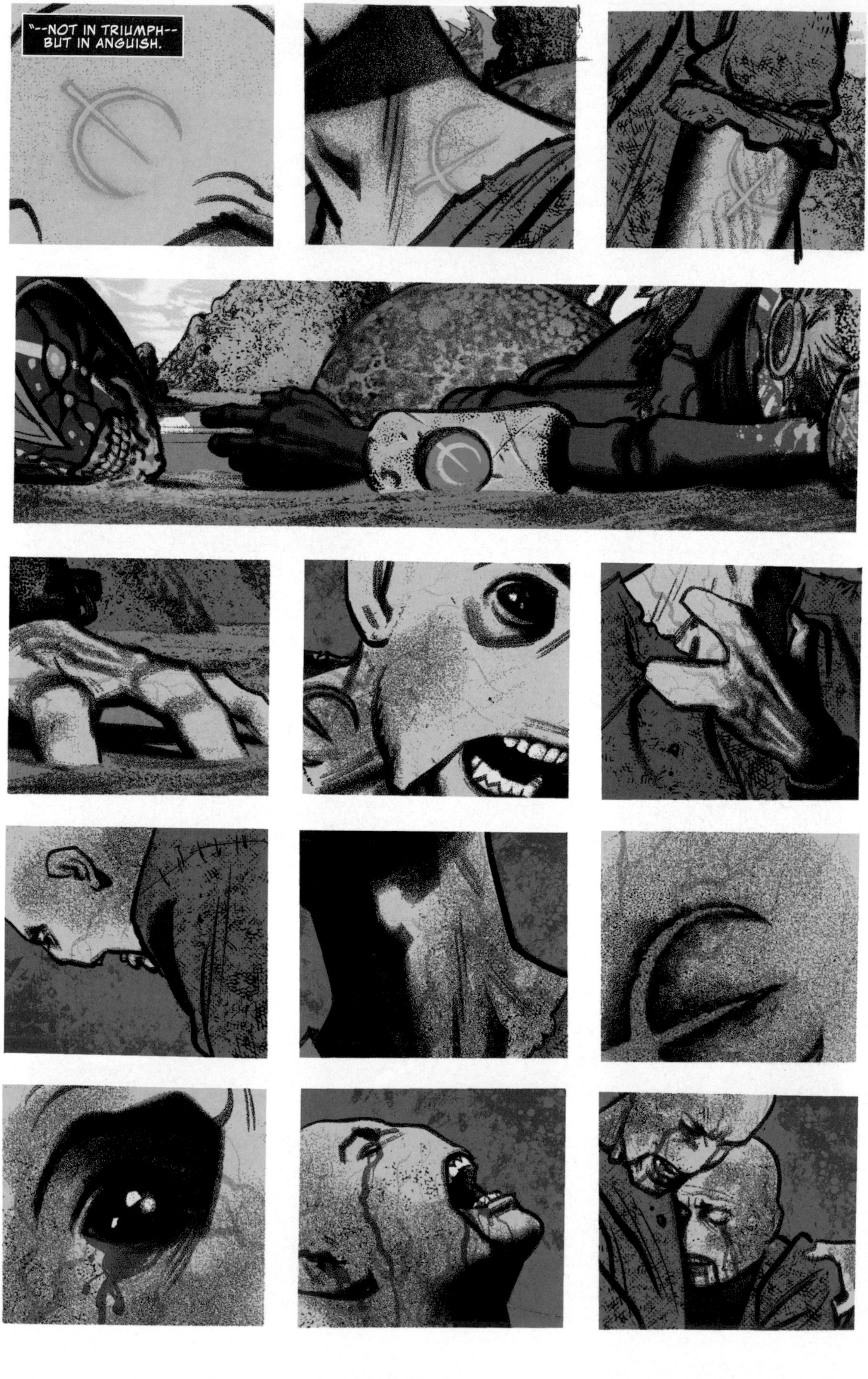
"--NOT IN TRIUMPH--
BUT IN ANGUISH.

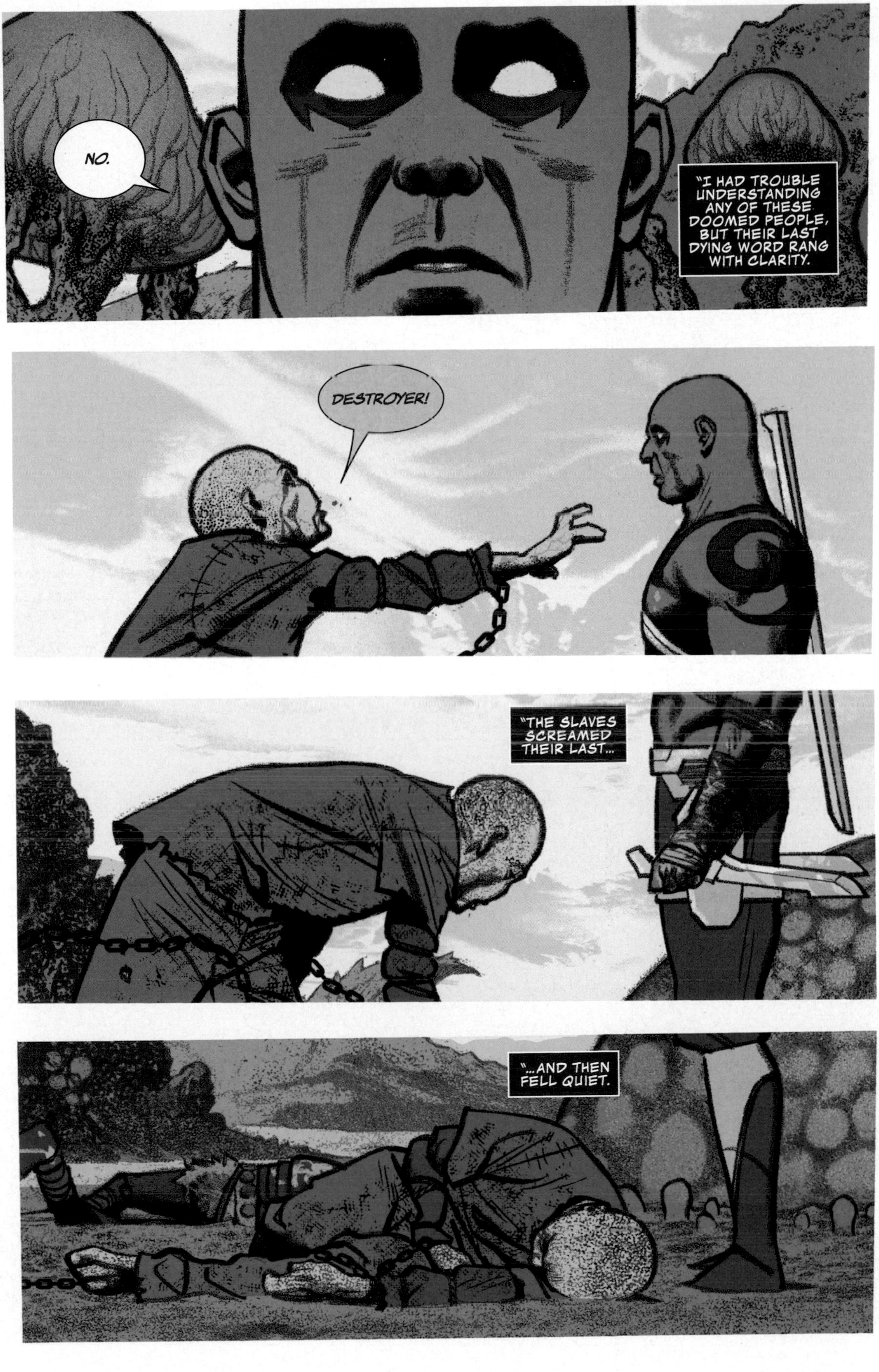
NO.
"I HAD TROUBLE UNDERSTANDING ANY OF THESE DOOMED PEOPLE, BUT THEIR LAST DYING WORD RANG WITH CLARITY.
DESTROYER!
"THE SLAVES SCREAMED THEIR LAST...
"...AND THEN FELL QUIET.

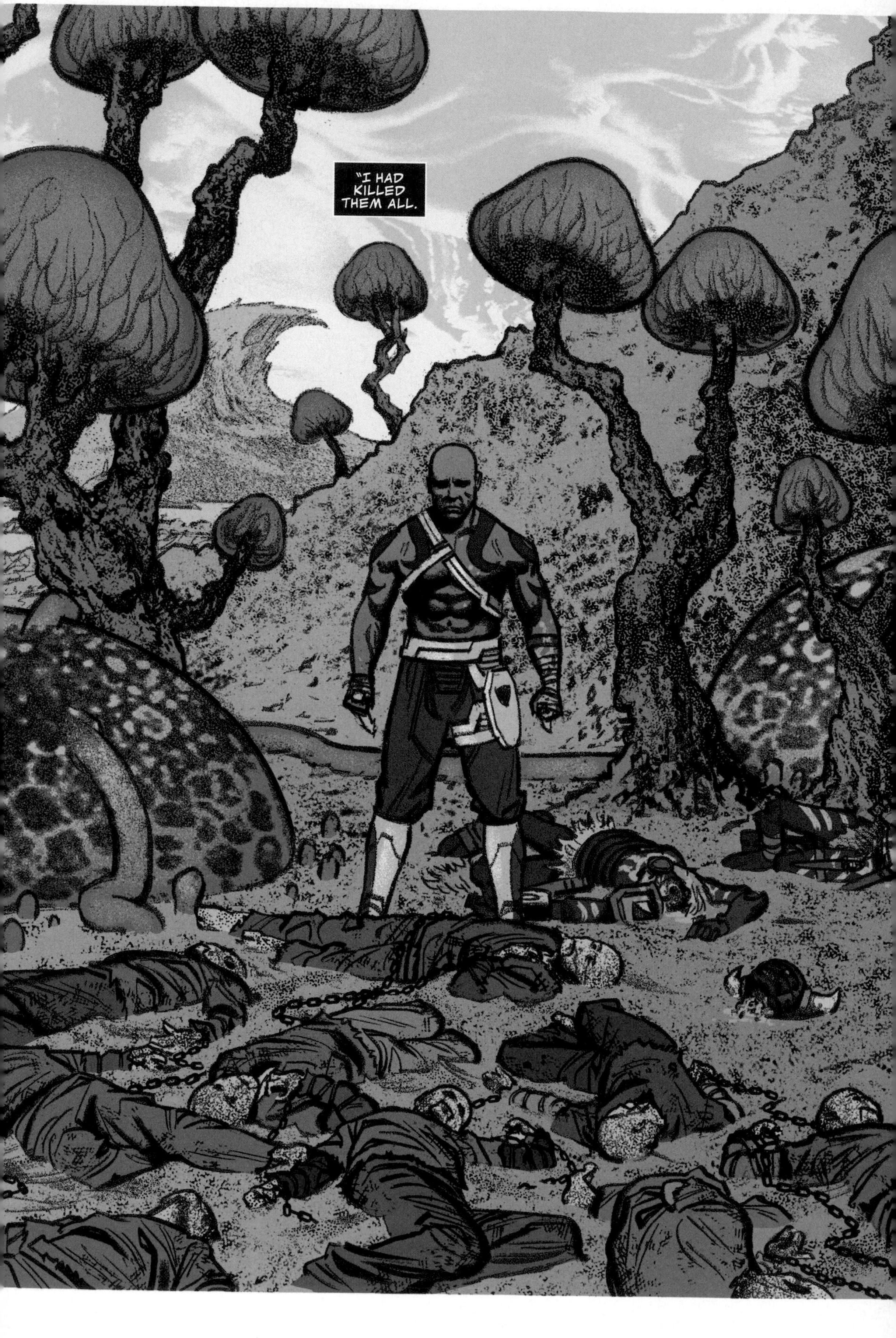
"I HAD KILLED THEM ALL.

"AND WITH THEM--MY *SPIRIT* FOR BATTLE.

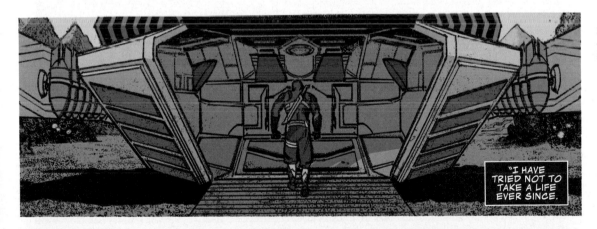

"THE SLAVE KING HAD BOUND HIS LIFE TO THE SLAVES WITH THE POISON IN THEIR BRANDS.

"I MISTOOK THEIR DESIRE FOR PEACE AS A *WEAKNESS.*

"I HAVE TRIED NOT TO TAKE A LIFE EVER SINCE.

"DO NOT WASTE YOUR BREATH, *GAMORA...*"

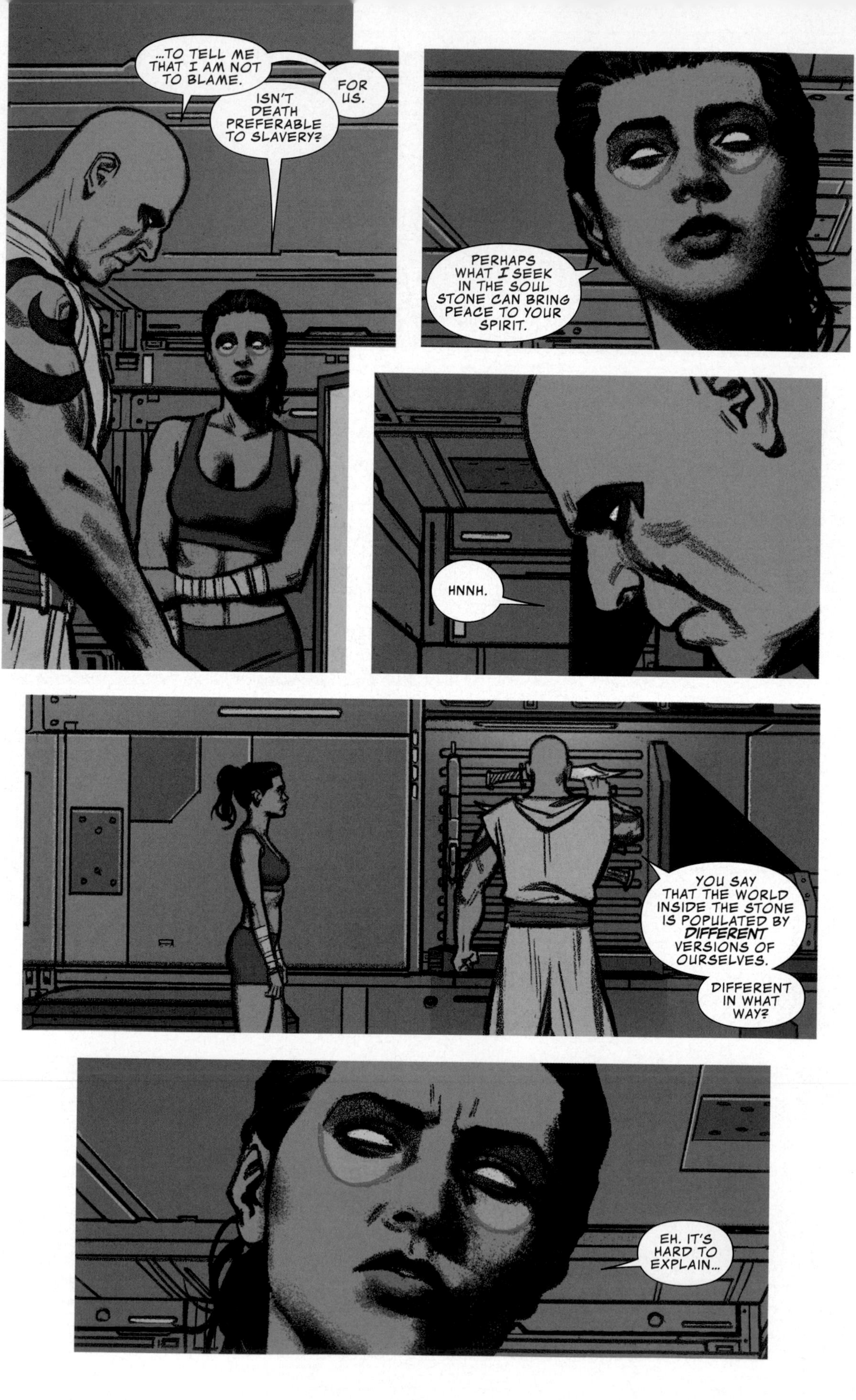
...TO TELL ME THAT I AM NOT TO BLAME.
FOR US.
ISN'T DEATH PREFERABLE TO SLAVERY?
PERHAPS WHAT *I* SEEK IN THE SOUL STONE CAN BRING PEACE TO YOUR SPIRIT.
HNNH.
YOU SAY THAT THE WORLD INSIDE THE STONE IS POPULATED BY *DIFFERENT* VERSIONS OF OURSELVES.
DIFFERENT IN WHAT WAY?
EH. IT'S HARD TO EXPLAIN...

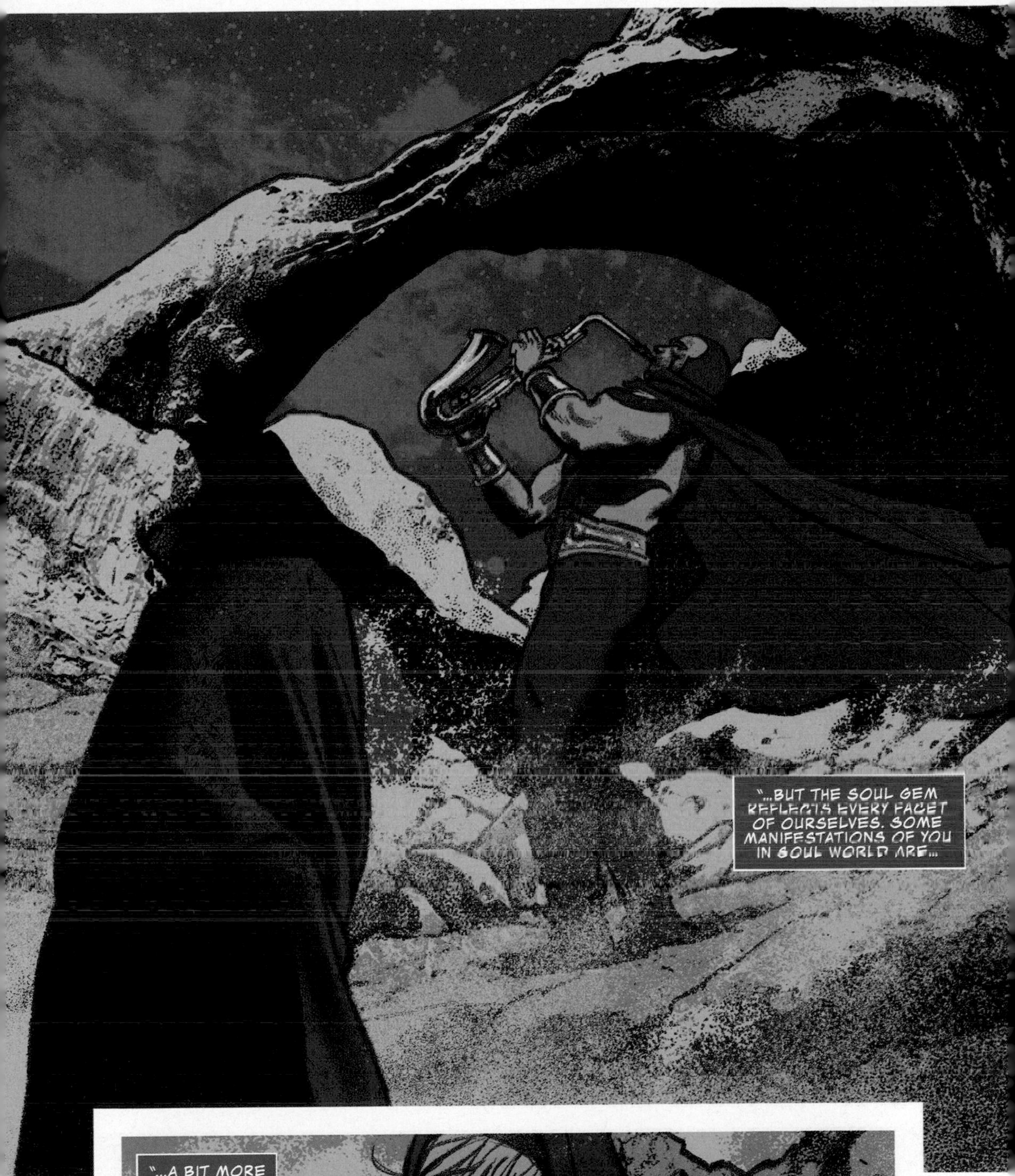
"...BUT THE SOUL GEM REFLECTS EVERY FACET OF OURSELVES. SOME MANIFESTATIONS OF YOU IN SOUL WORLD ARE...

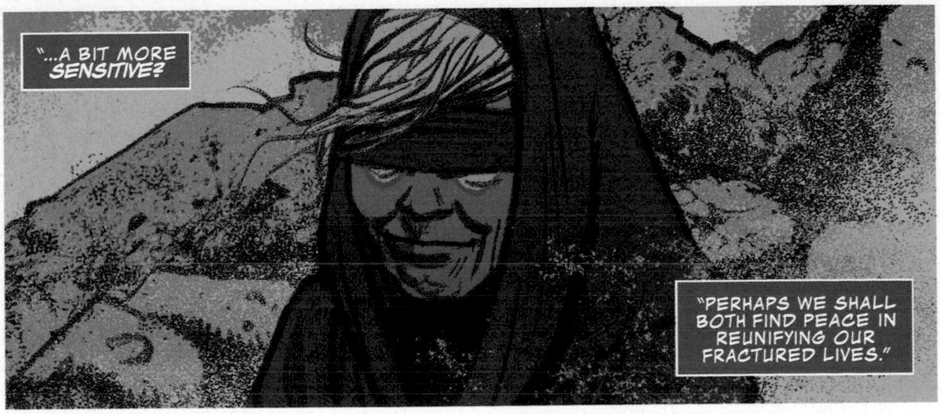
"...A BIT MORE *SENSITIVE?*
"PERHAPS WE SHALL BOTH FIND PEACE IN REUNIFYING OUR FRACTURED LIVES."

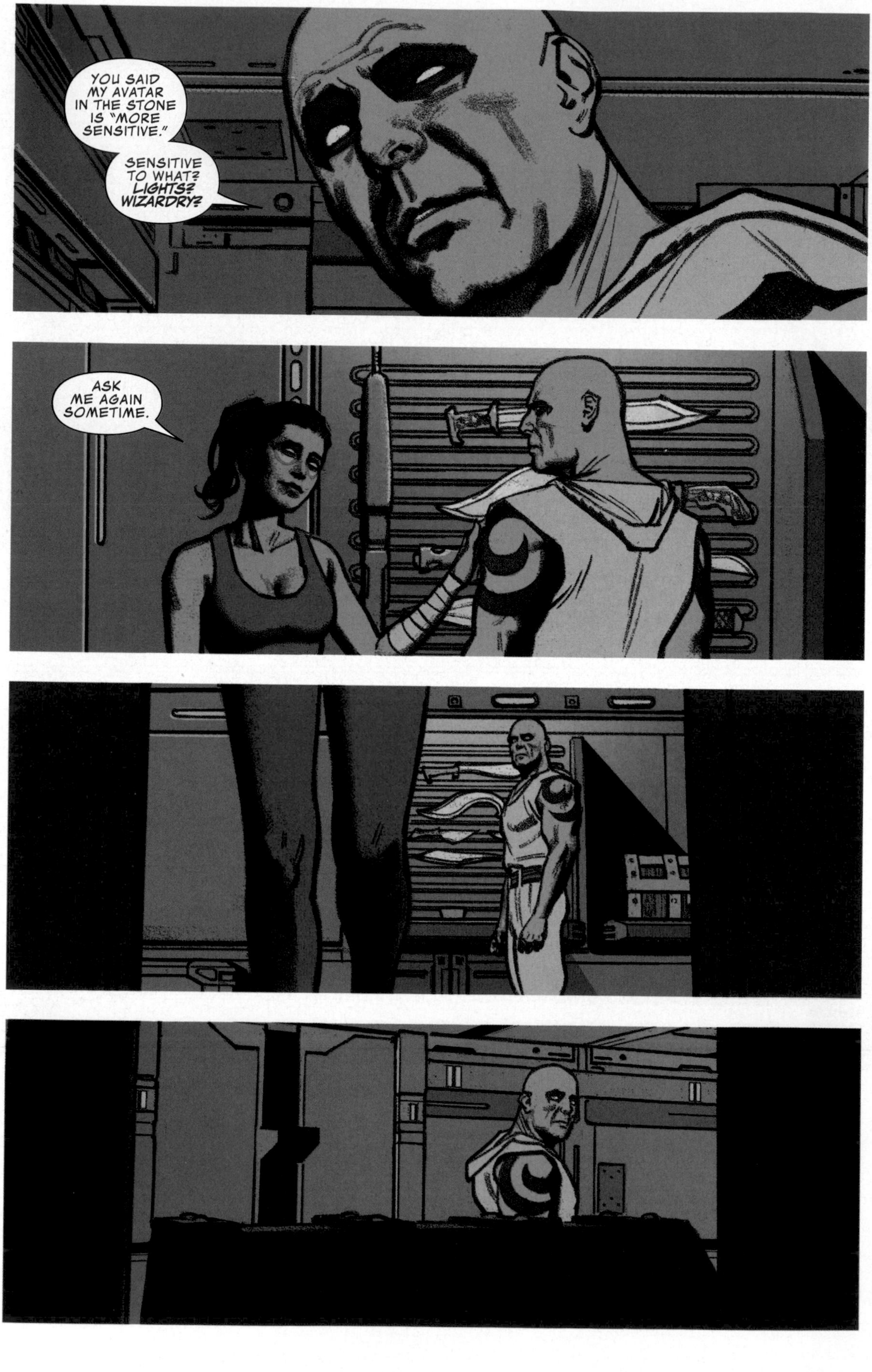
YOU SAID MY AVATAR IN THE STONE IS "MORE SENSITIVE."
SENSITIVE TO WHAT? *LIGHTS?* *WIZARDRY?*
ASK ME AGAIN SOMETIME.

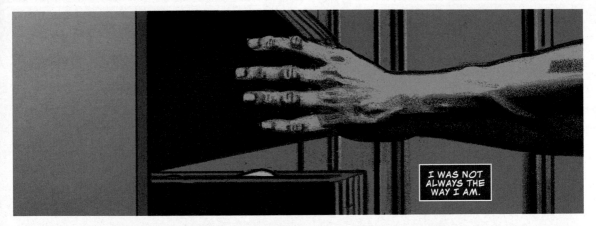

I WAS NOT ALWAYS THE WAY I AM.

A PART OF ME FEELS LOCKED AWAY, TOO.

I KNOW HOW TO FIX IT.

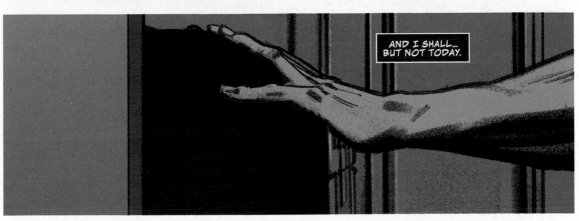

AND I SHALL... BUT NOT TODAY.

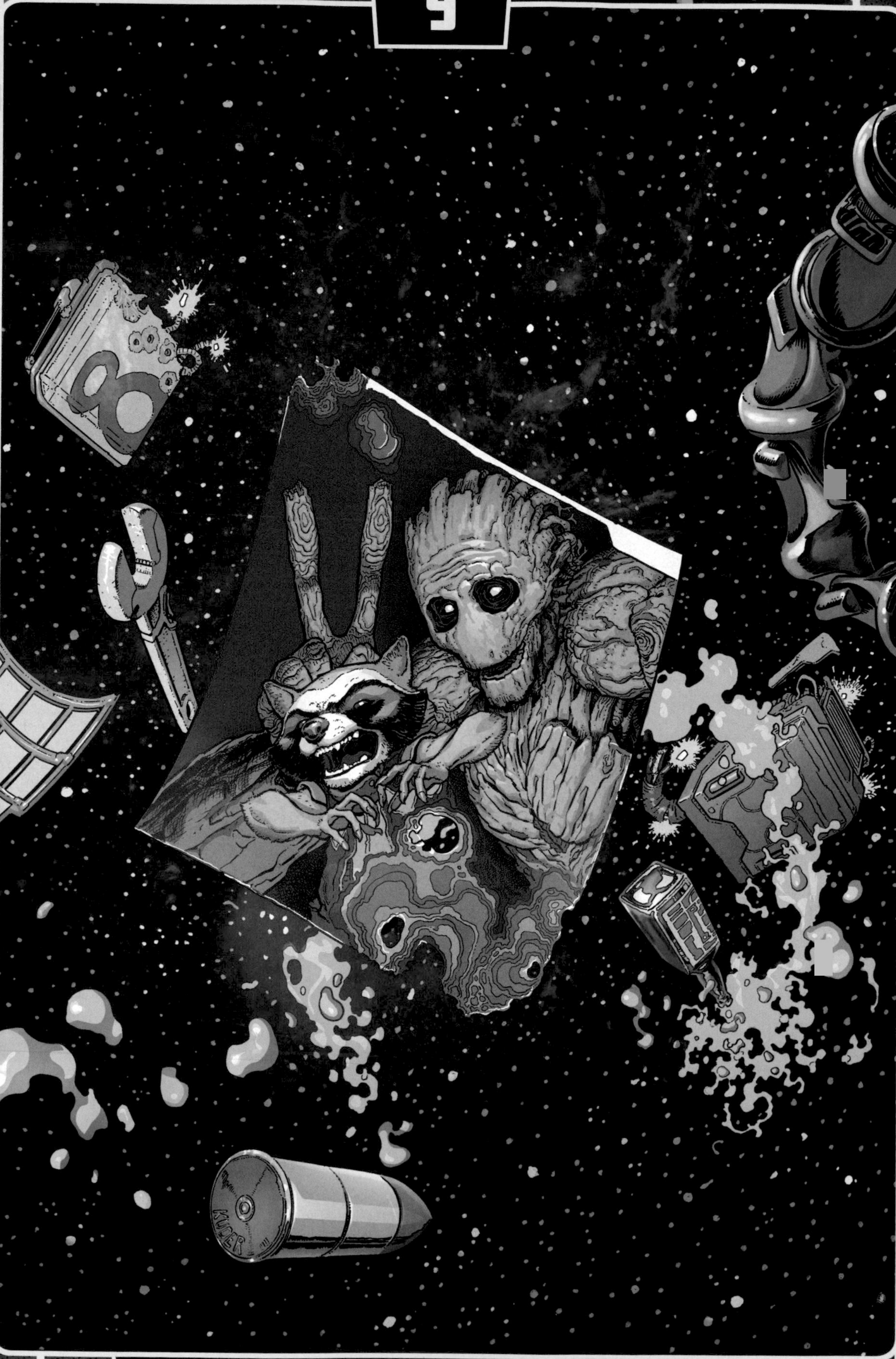

"SHATTERED"

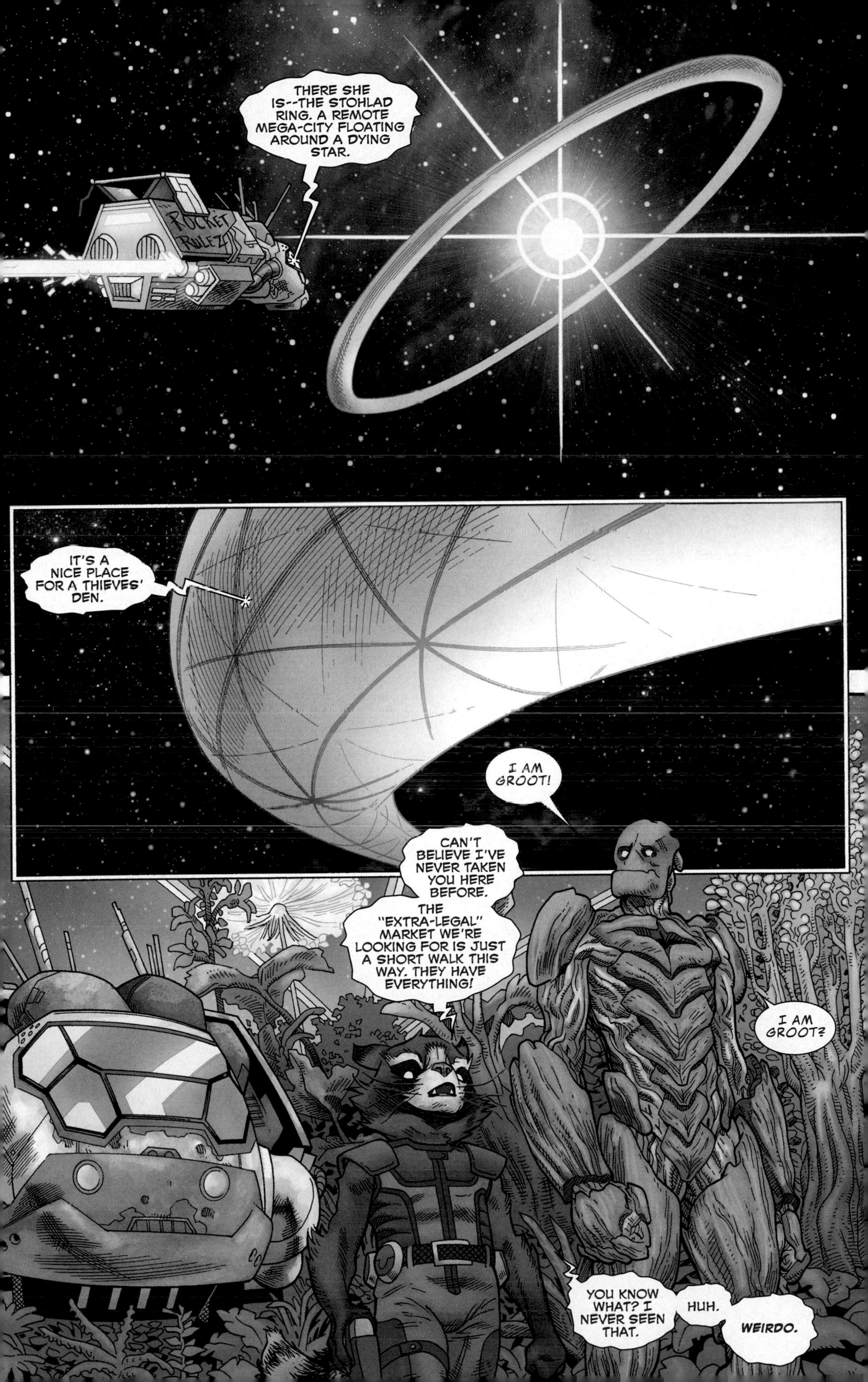
THERE SHE IS--THE STOHLAD RING. A REMOTE MEGA-CITY FLOATING AROUND A DYING STAR.
ROCKET RULEZ
IT'S A NICE PLACE FOR A THIEVES' DEN.
I AM GROOT!
CAN'T BELIEVE I'VE NEVER TAKEN YOU HERE BEFORE.
THE "EXTRA-LEGAL" MARKET WE'RE LOOKING FOR IS JUST A SHORT WALK THIS WAY. THEY HAVE EVERYTHING!
I AM GROOT?
YOU KNOW WHAT? I NEVER SEEN THAT.
HUH.
WEIRDO.

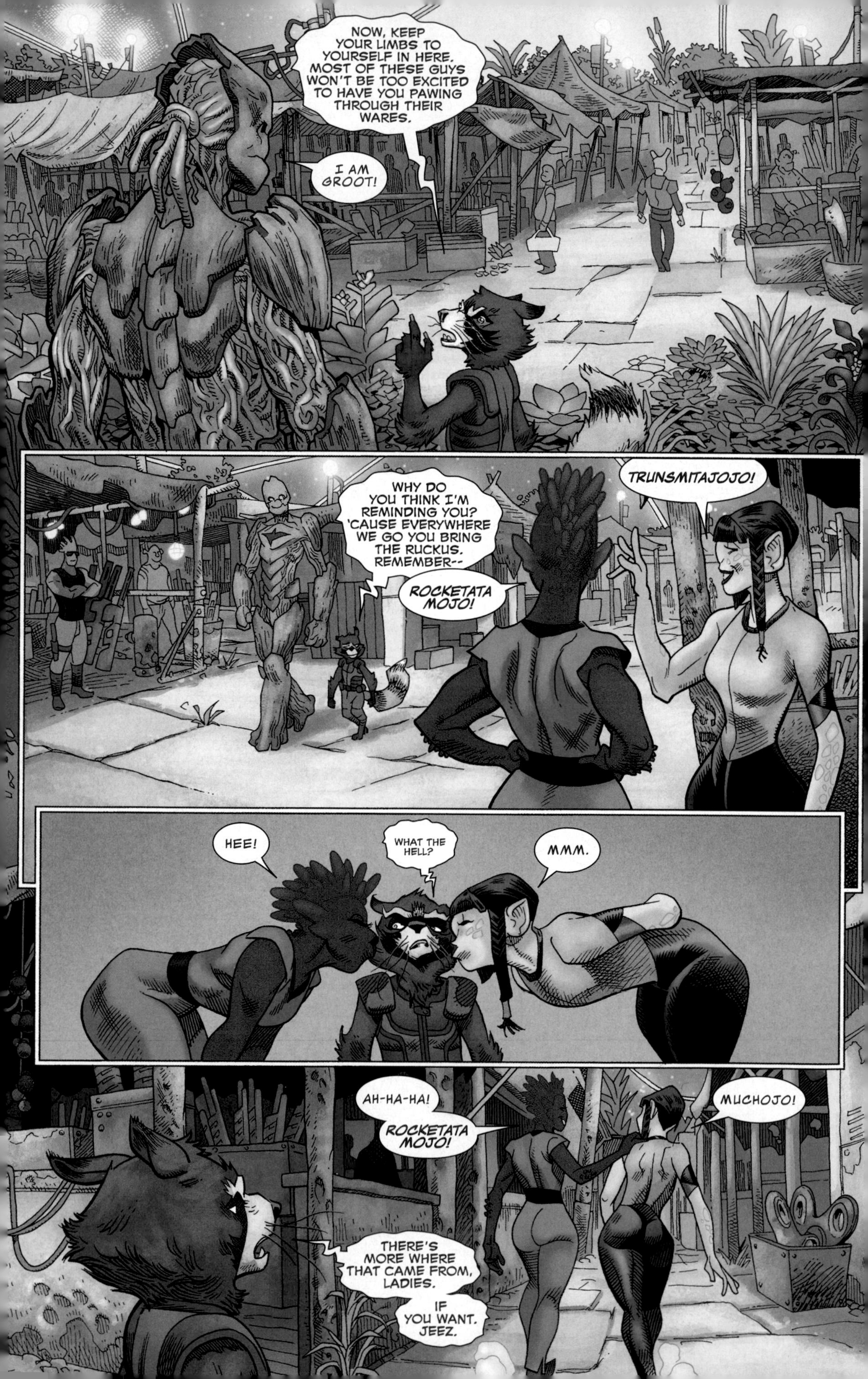
NOW, KEEP YOUR LIMBS TO YOURSELF IN HERE. MOST OF THESE GUYS WON'T BE TOO EXCITED TO HAVE YOU PAWING THROUGH THEIR WARES.
I AM GROOT!
WHY DO YOU THINK I'M REMINDING YOU? 'CAUSE EVERYWHERE WE GO YOU BRING THE RUCKUS. REMEMBER--
TRUNSMITAJOJO!
ROCKETATA MOJO!
HEE!
WHAT THE HELL?
MMM.
AH-HA-HA!
ROCKETATA MOJO!
MUCHOJO!
THERE'S MORE WHERE THAT CAME FROM, LADIES.
IF YOU WANT. JEEZ.

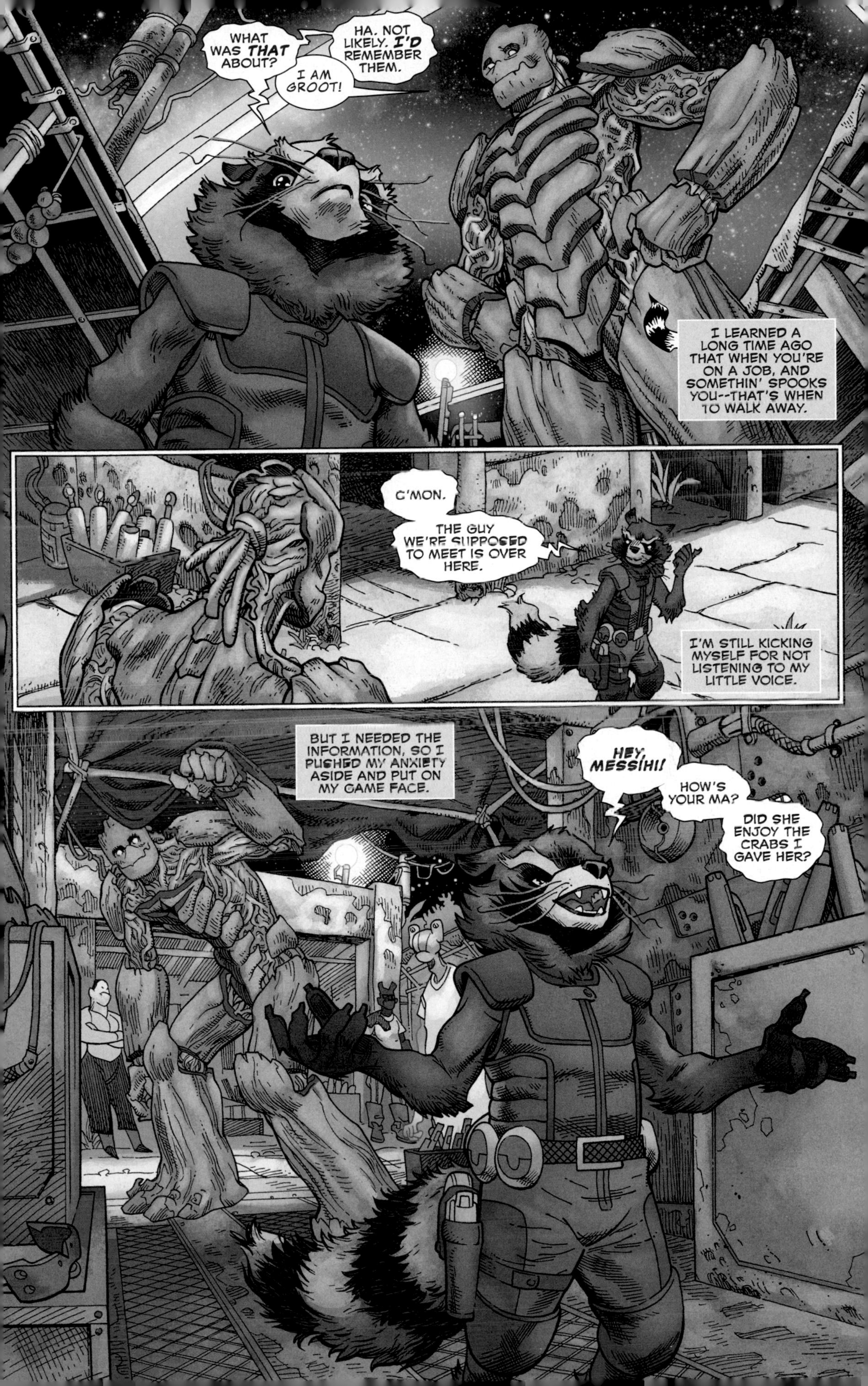
WHAT WAS THAT ABOUT?
HA. NOT LIKELY. I'D REMEMBER THEM.
I AM GROOT!
I LEARNED A LONG TIME AGO THAT WHEN YOU'RE ON A JOB, AND SOMETHIN' SPOOKS YOU--THAT'S WHEN TO WALK AWAY.
C'MON.
THE GUY WE'RE SUPPOSED TO MEET IS OVER HERE.
I'M STILL KICKING MYSELF FOR NOT LISTENING TO MY LITTLE VOICE.
BUT I NEEDED THE INFORMATION, SO I PUSHED MY ANXIETY ASIDE AND PUT ON MY GAME FACE.
HEY, MESSIHI!
HOW'S YOUR MA?
DID SHE ENJOY THE CRABS I GAVE HER?

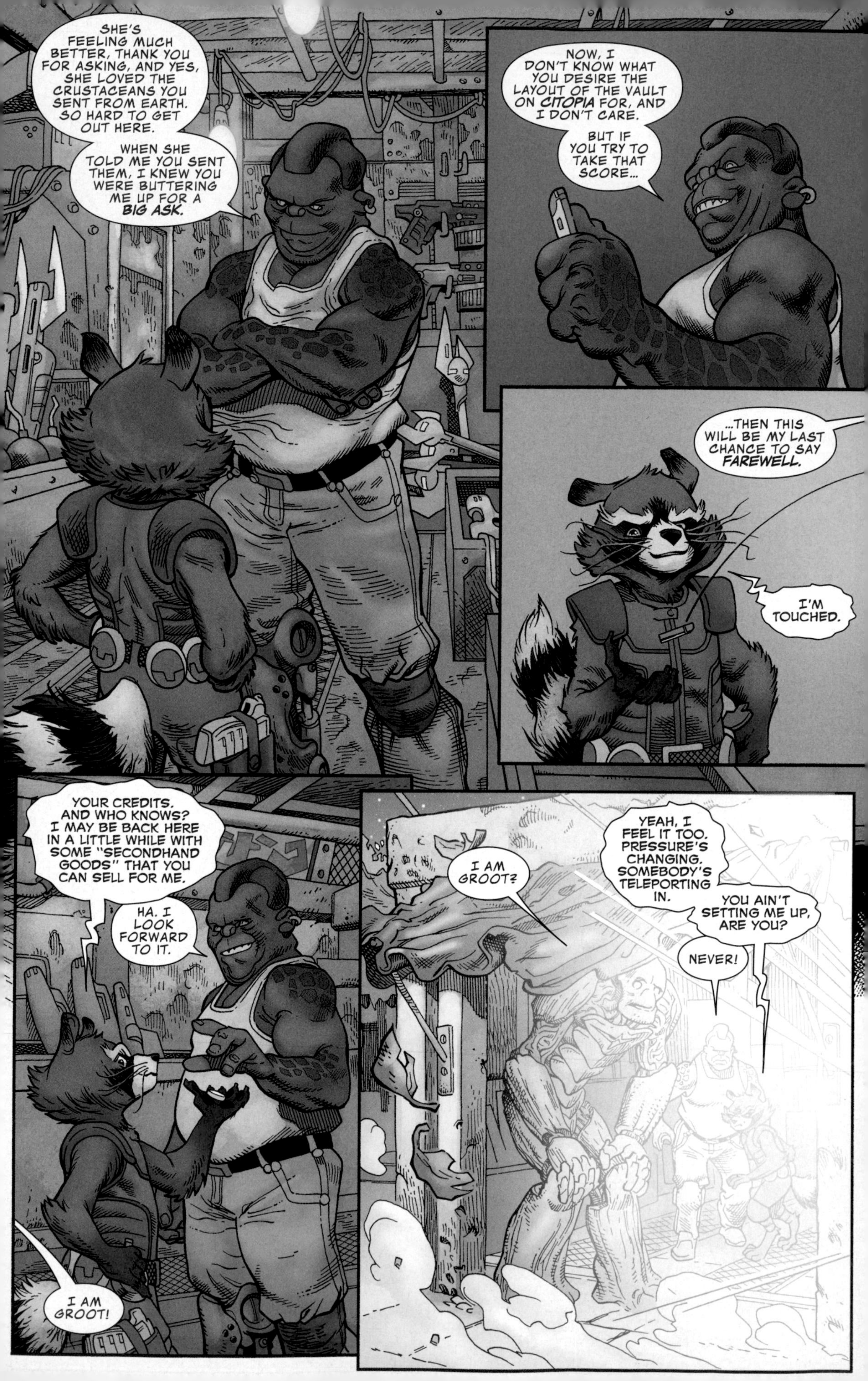
SHE'S FEELING MUCH BETTER, THANK YOU FOR ASKING, AND YES, SHE LOVED THE CRUSTACEANS YOU SENT FROM EARTH. SO HARD TO GET OUT HERE.
WHEN SHE TOLD ME YOU SENT THEM, I KNEW YOU WERE BUTTERING ME UP FOR A **BIG ASK.**
NOW, I DON'T KNOW WHAT YOU DESIRE THE LAYOUT OF THE VAULT ON *CITOPIA* FOR, AND I DON'T CARE.
BUT IF YOU TRY TO TAKE THAT SCORE...
...THEN THIS WILL BE MY LAST CHANCE TO SAY *FAREWELL.*
I'M TOUCHED.
YOUR CREDITS. AND WHO KNOWS? I MAY BE BACK HERE IN A LITTLE WHILE WITH SOME "SECONDHAND GOODS" THAT YOU CAN SELL FOR ME.
HA. I LOOK FORWARD TO IT.
I AM GROOT!
I AM GROOT?
YEAH, I FEEL IT TOO. PRESSURE'S CHANGING. SOMEBODY'S TELEPORTING IN.
YOU AIN'T SETTING ME UP, ARE YOU?
NEVER!

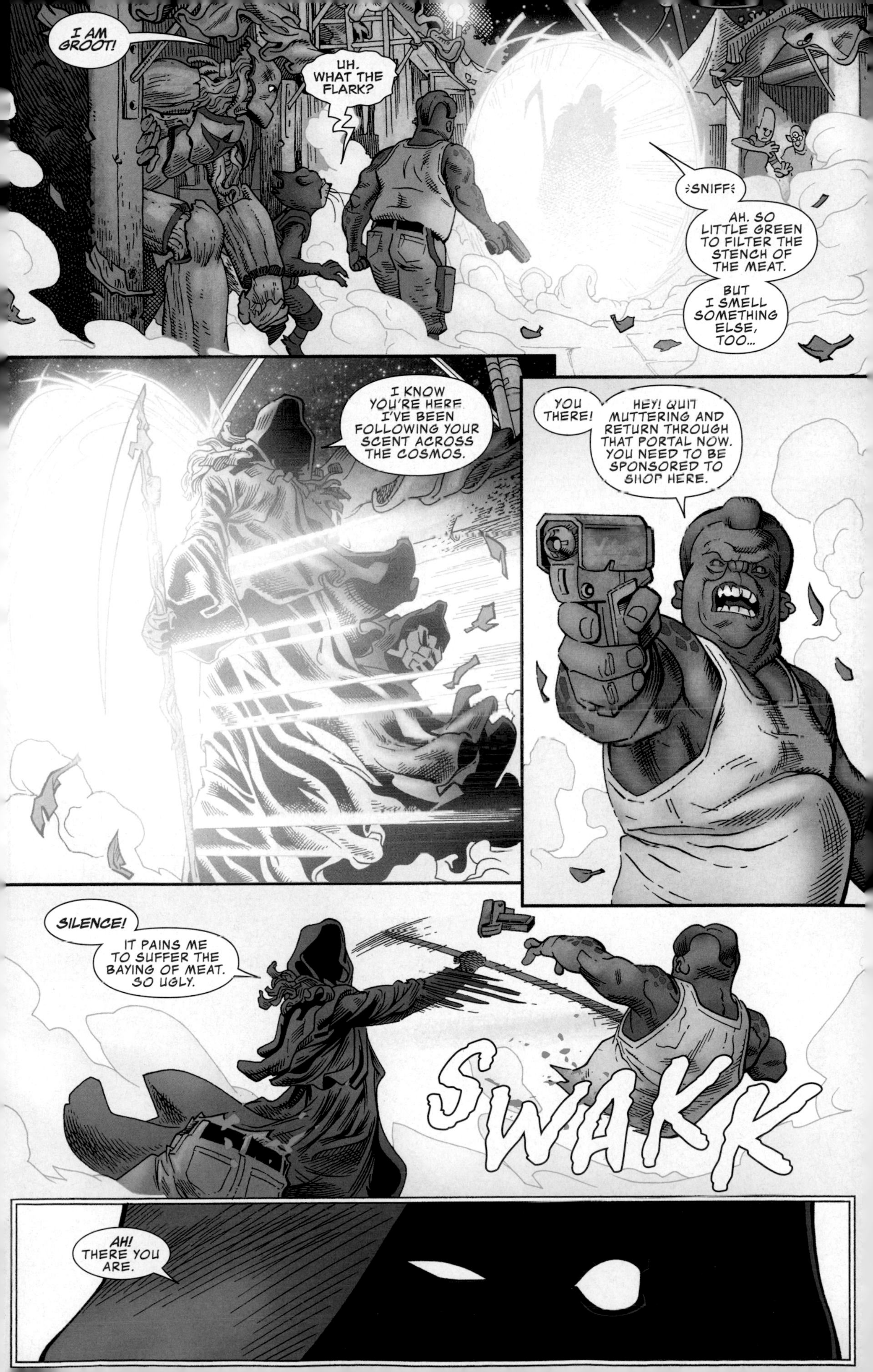
I AM GROOT!
UH. WHAT THE FLARK?
⊰SNIFF⊱
AH. SO LITTLE GREEN TO FILTER THE STENCH OF THE MEAT.
BUT I SMELL SOMETHING ELSE, TOO...
I KNOW YOU'RE HERE. I'VE BEEN FOLLOWING YOUR SCENT ACROSS THE COSMOS.
YOU THERE!
HEY! QUIT MUTTERING AND RETURN THROUGH THAT PORTAL NOW. YOU NEED TO BE SPONSORED TO SHOP HERE.
SILENCE!
IT PAINS ME TO SUFFER THE BAYING OF MEAT. SO UGLY.
SWAKK
AH! THERE YOU ARE.

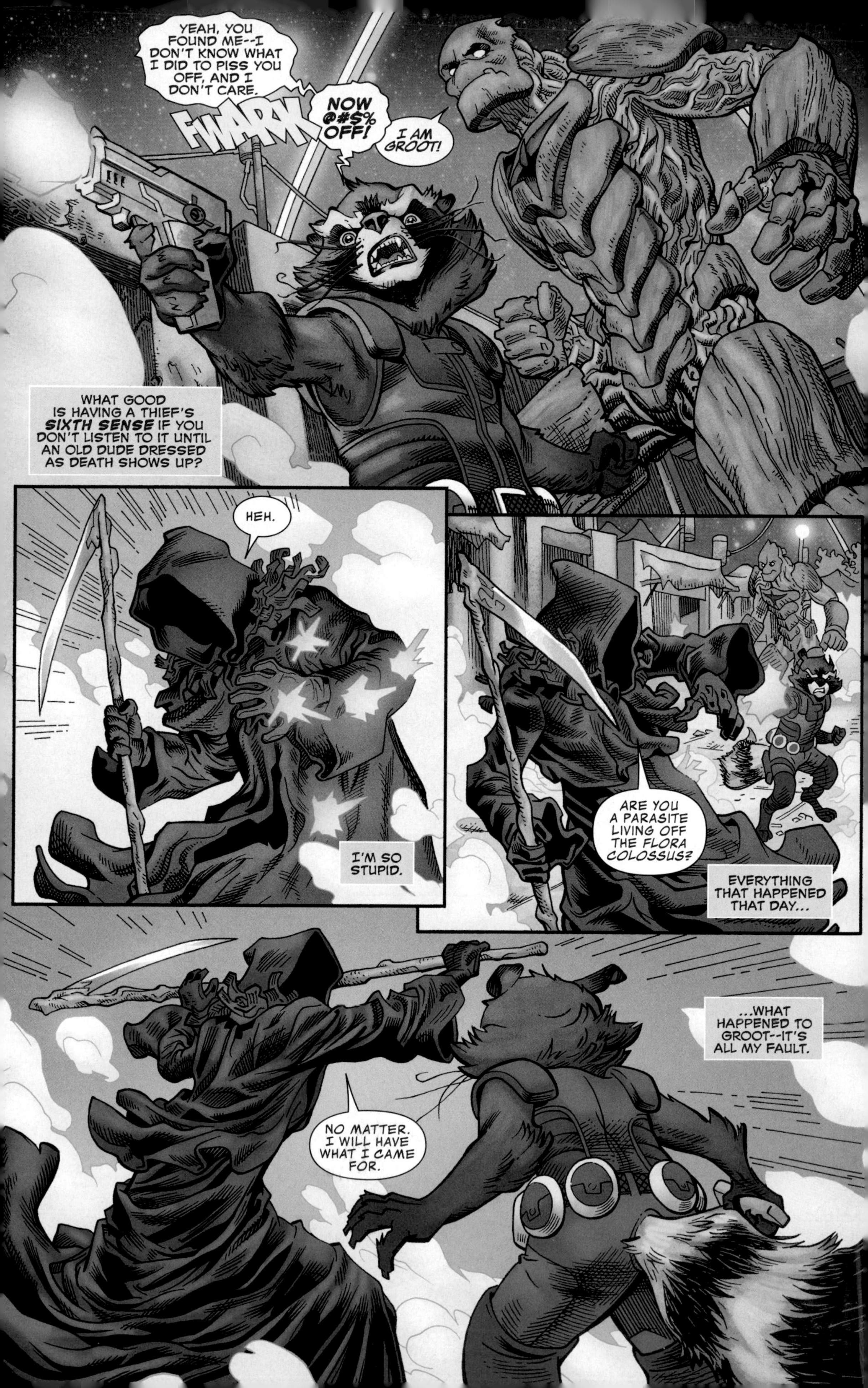
YEAH, YOU FOUND ME--I DON'T KNOW WHAT I DID TO PISS YOU OFF, AND I DON'T CARE.
FWARK
NOW @#$% OFF!
I AM GROOT!
WHAT GOOD IS HAVING A THIEF'S SIXTH SENSE IF YOU DON'T LISTEN TO IT UNTIL AN OLD DUDE DRESSED AS DEATH SHOWS UP?
HEH.
I'M SO STUPID.
ARE YOU A PARASITE LIVING OFF THE FLORA COLOSSUS?
EVERYTHING THAT HAPPENED THAT DAY...
...WHAT HAPPENED TO GROOT--IT'S ALL MY FAULT.
NO MATTER. I WILL HAVE WHAT I CAME FOR.

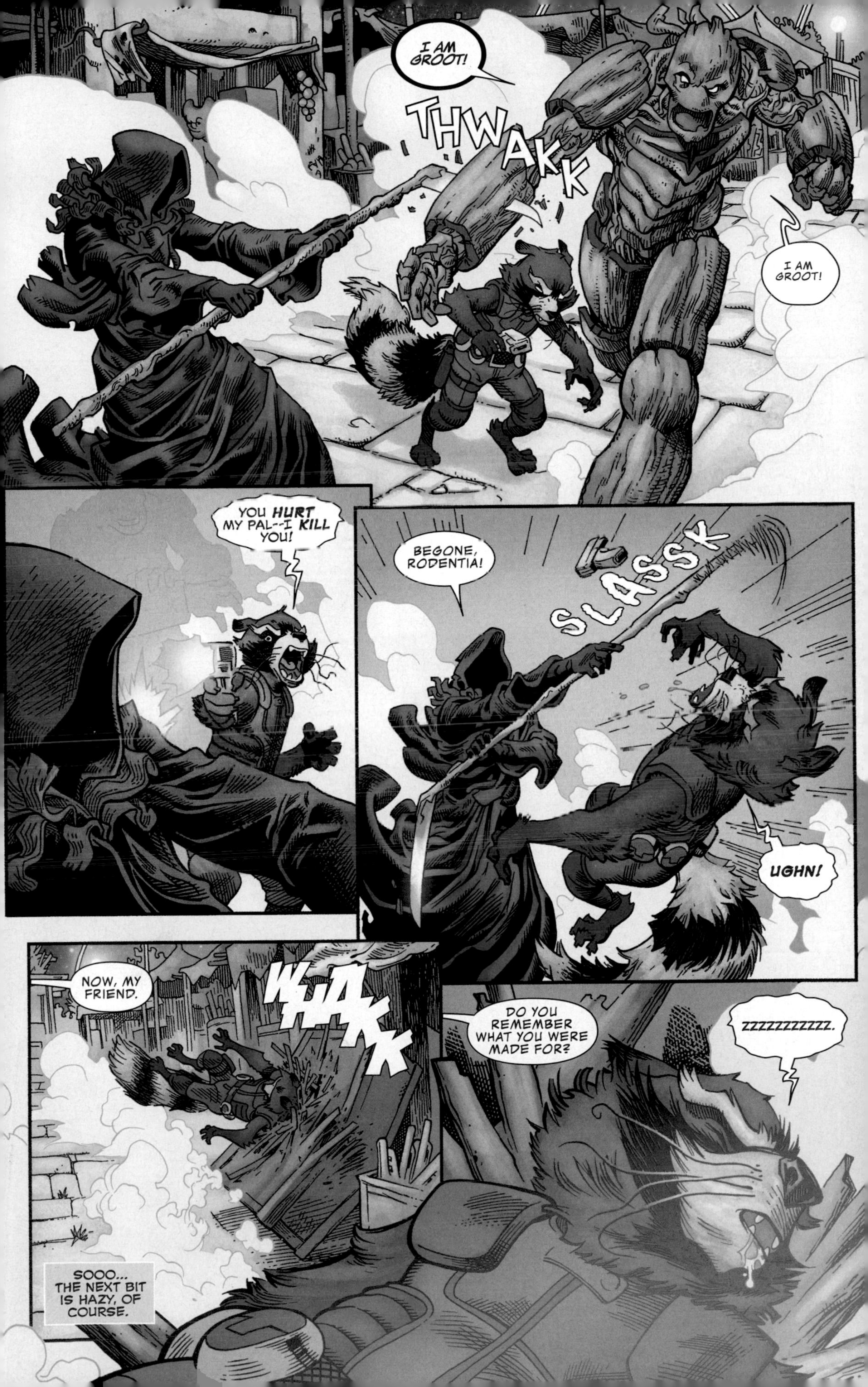
I AM GROOT!
THWAKK
I AM GROOT!
YOU HURT MY PAL--I KILL YOU!
BEGONE, RODENTIA!
SLASSK
UGHN!
NOW, MY FRIEND.
WHAKK
DO YOU REMEMBER WHAT YOU WERE MADE FOR?
ZZZZZZZZZZZ.
SOOO... THE NEXT BIT IS HAZY, OF COURSE.

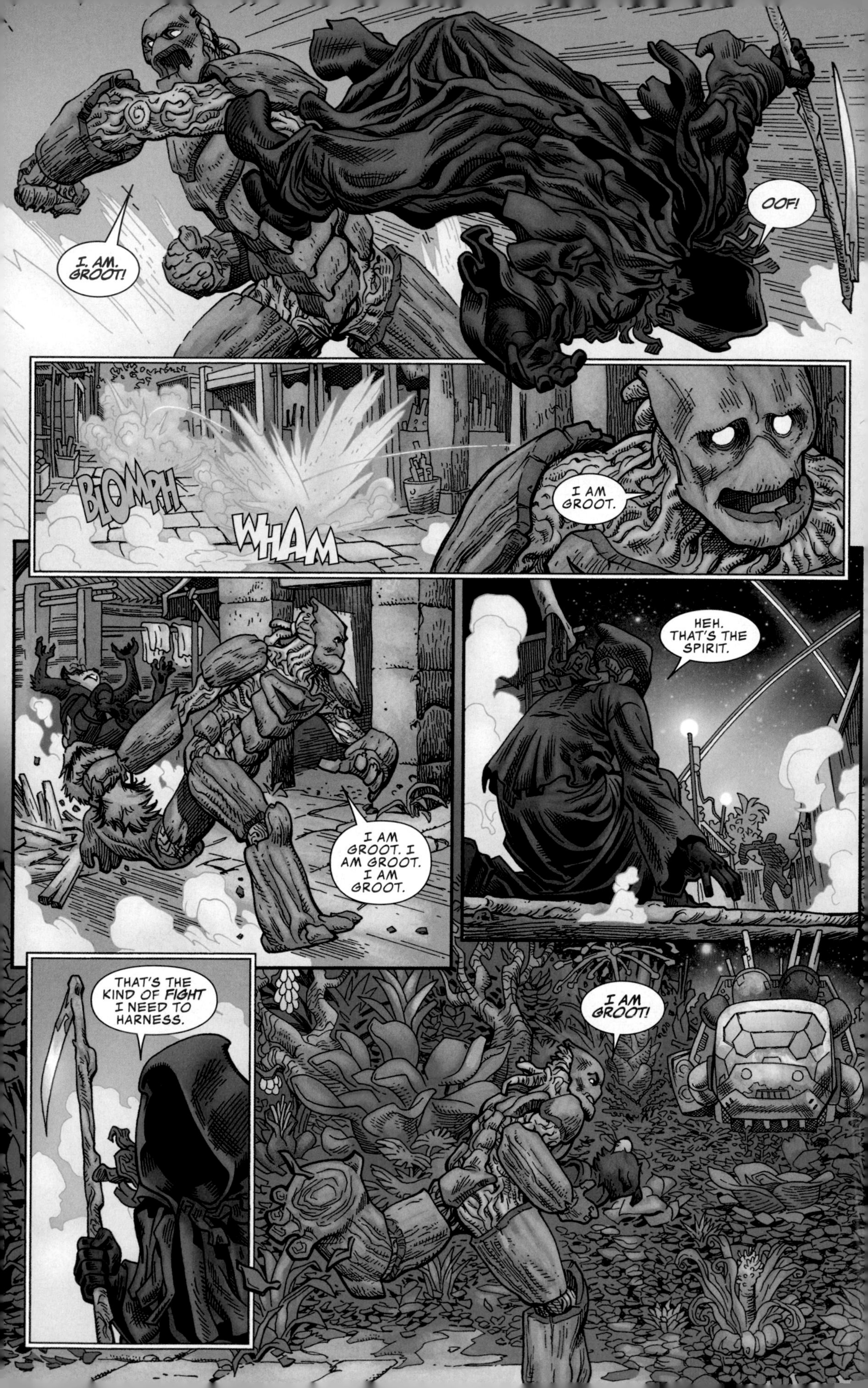
I. AM. GROOT!
OOF!
BLOMPH
WHAM
I AM GROOT.
I AM GROOT. I AM GROOT. I AM GROOT.
HEH. THAT'S THE SPIRIT.
THAT'S THE KIND OF FIGHT I NEED TO HARNESS.
I AM GROOT!

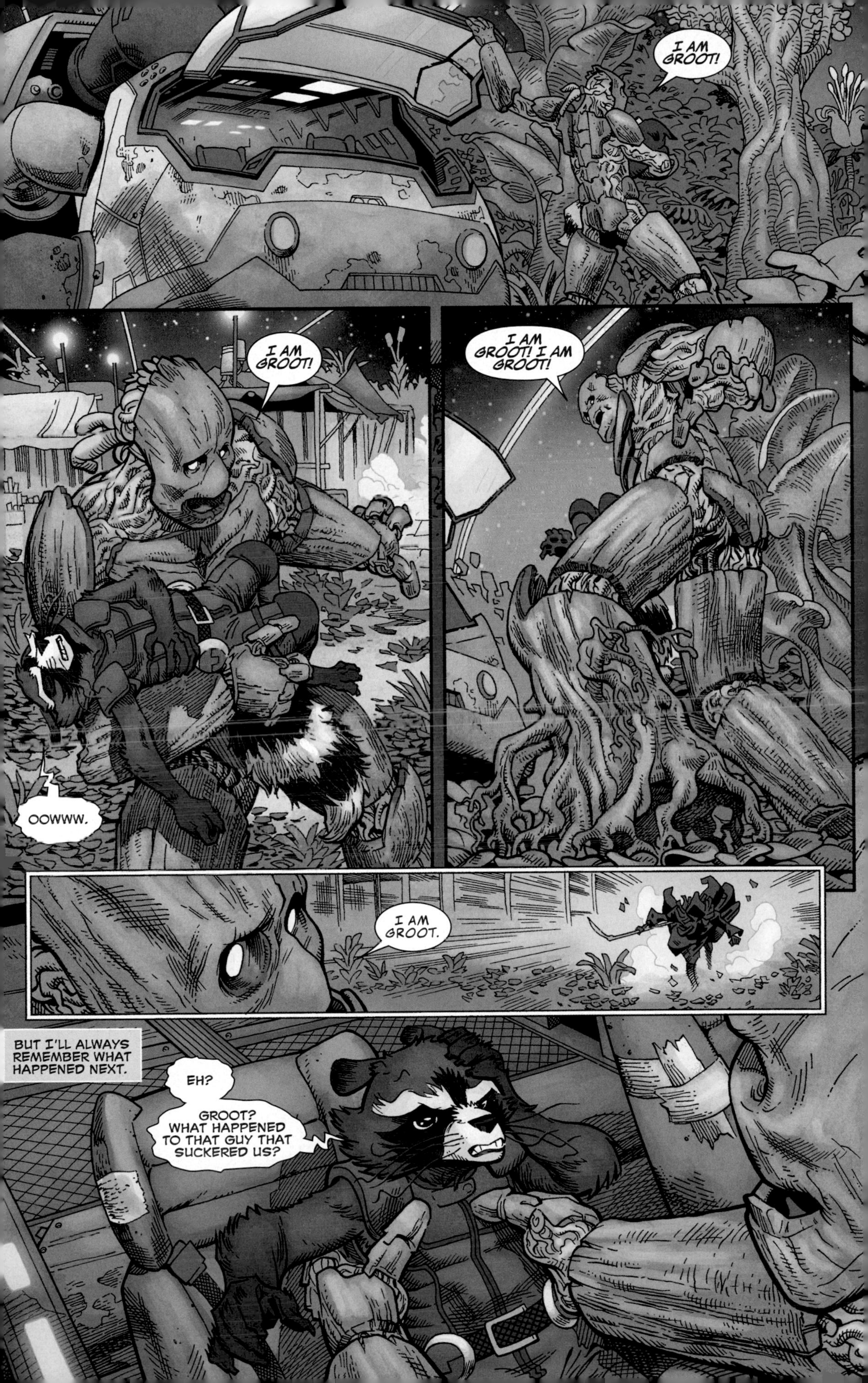
I AM GROOT!
I AM GROOT!
I AM GROOT! I AM GROOT!
OOWWW.
I AM GROOT.
BUT I'LL ALWAYS REMEMBER WHAT HAPPENED NEXT.
EH?
GROOT? WHAT HAPPENED TO THAT GUY THAT SUCKERED US?

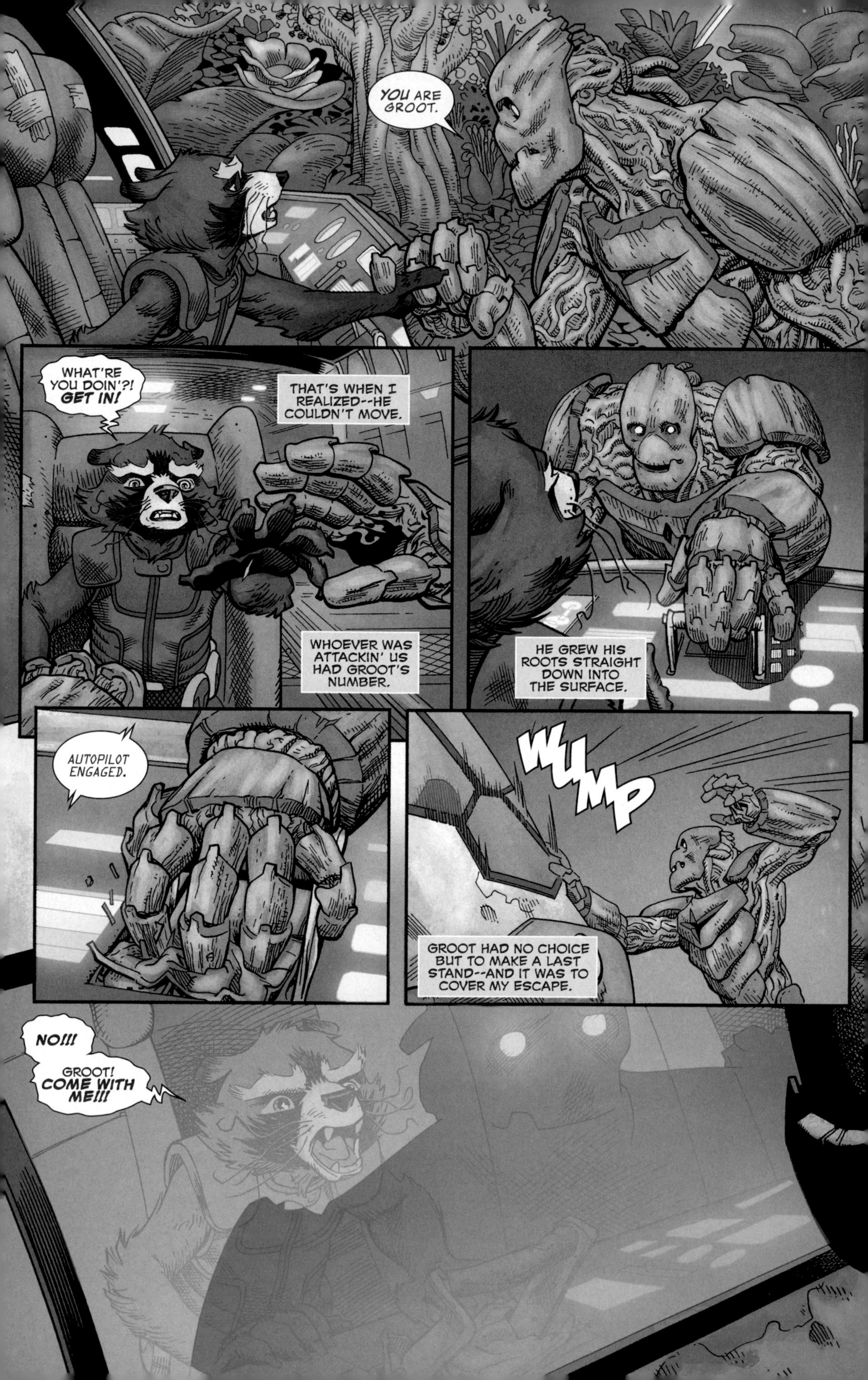
YOU ARE GROOT.
WHAT'RE YOU DOIN'?! GET IN!
THAT'S WHEN I REALIZED--HE COULDN'T MOVE.
WHOEVER WAS ATTACKIN' US HAD GROOT'S NUMBER.
HE GREW HIS ROOTS STRAIGHT DOWN INTO THE SURFACE.
AUTOPILOT ENGAGED.
WUMP
GROOT HAD NO CHOICE BUT TO MAKE A LAST STAND--AND IT WAS TO COVER MY ESCAPE.
NO!!!
GROOT! COME WITH ME!!!

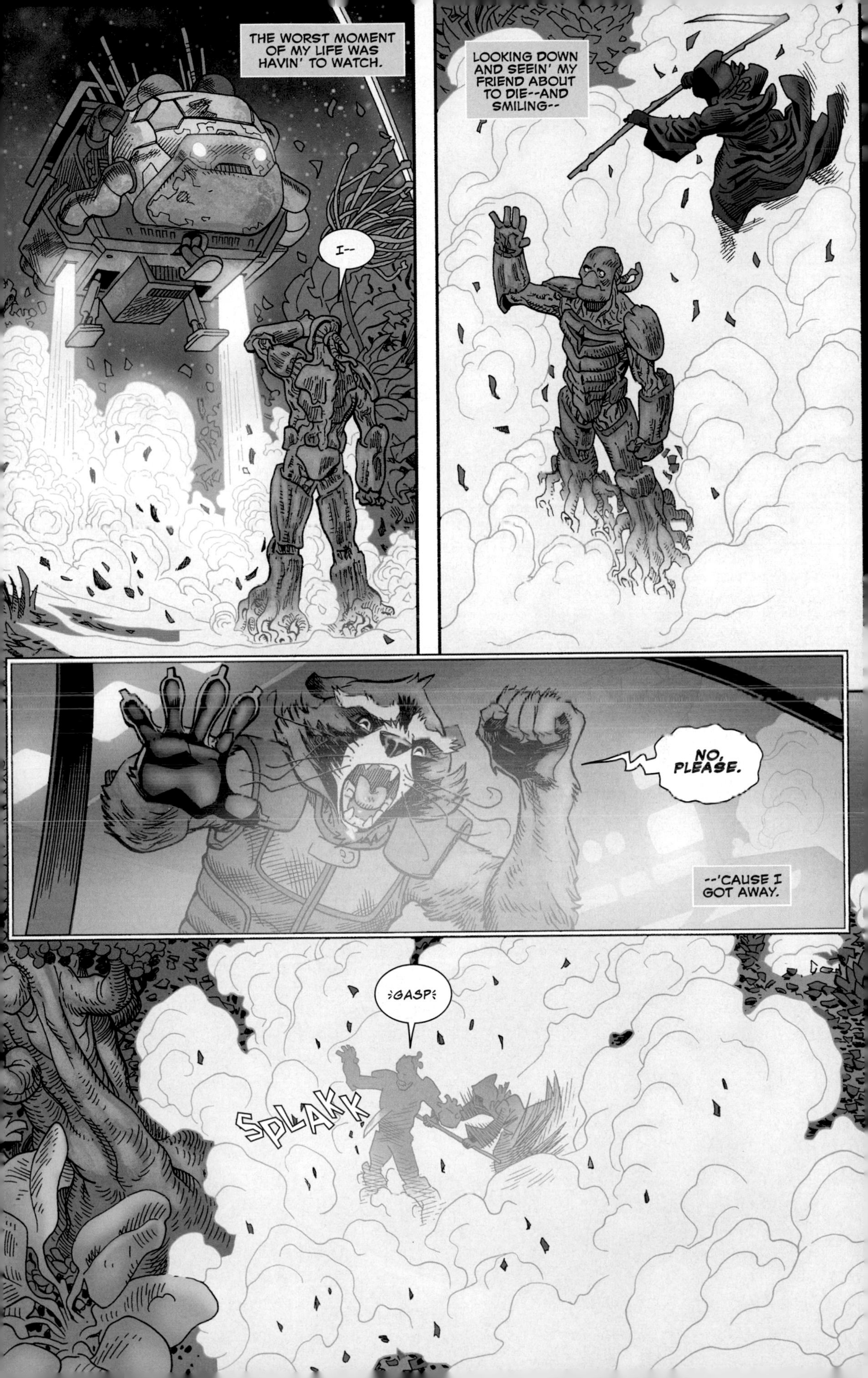
THE WORST MOMENT OF MY LIFE WAS HAVIN' TO WATCH.
I--
LOOKING DOWN AND SEEIN' MY FRIEND ABOUT TO DIE--AND SMILING--
NO, PLEASE.
--'CAUSE I GOT AWAY.
GASP
SPLAKK

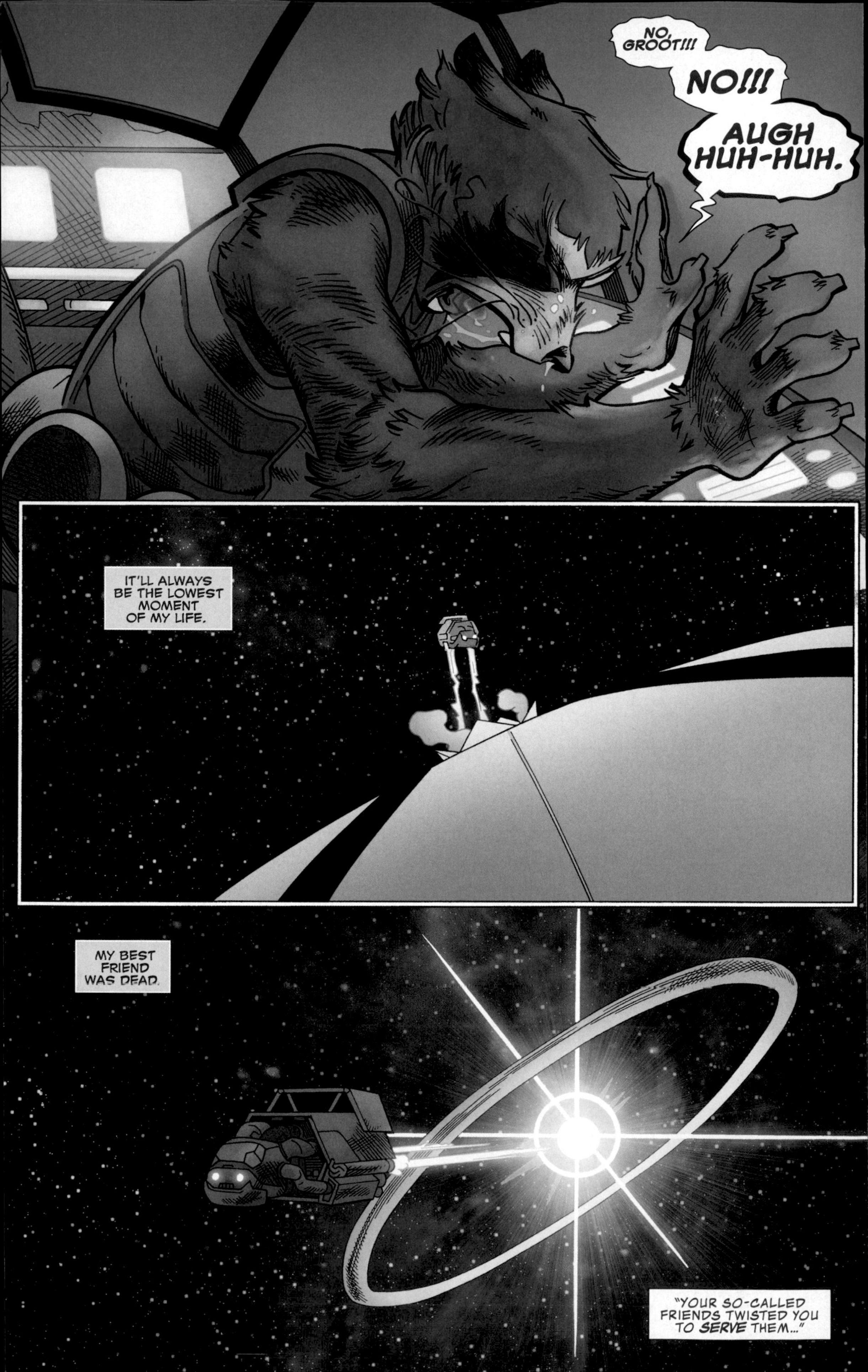
NO, GROOT!!!
NO!!!
AUGH HUH-HUH.
IT'LL ALWAYS BE THE LOWEST MOMENT OF MY LIFE.
MY BEST FRIEND WAS DEAD.
"YOUR SO-CALLED FRIENDS TWISTED YOU TO SERVE THEM..."

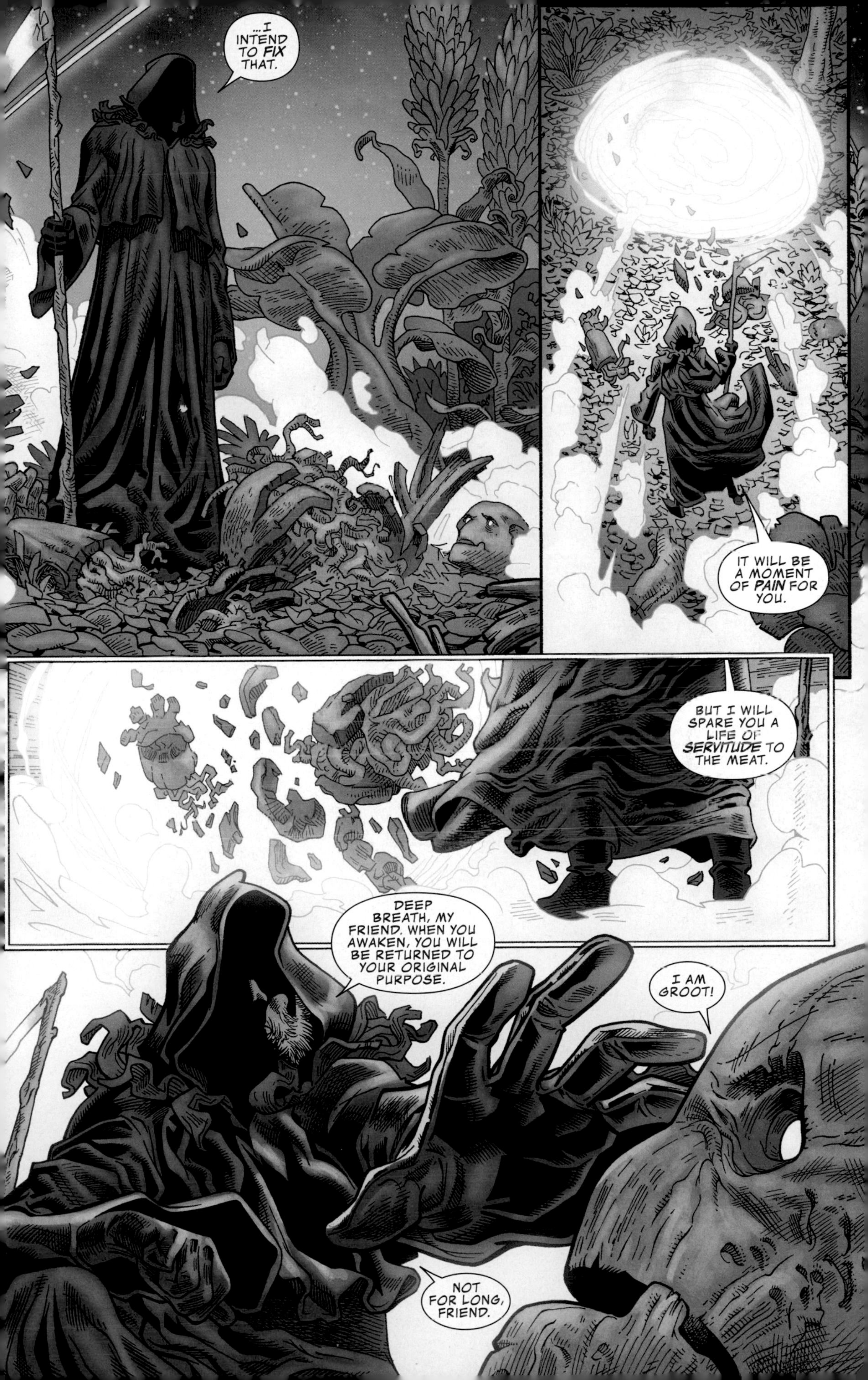
...I INTEND TO FIX THAT.
IT WILL BE A MOMENT OF PAIN FOR YOU.
BUT I WILL SPARE YOU A LIFE OF SERVITUDE TO THE MEAT.
DEEP BREATH, MY FRIEND. WHEN YOU AWAKEN, YOU WILL BE RETURNED TO YOUR ORIGINAL PURPOSE.
I AM GROOT!
NOT FOR LONG, FRIEND.

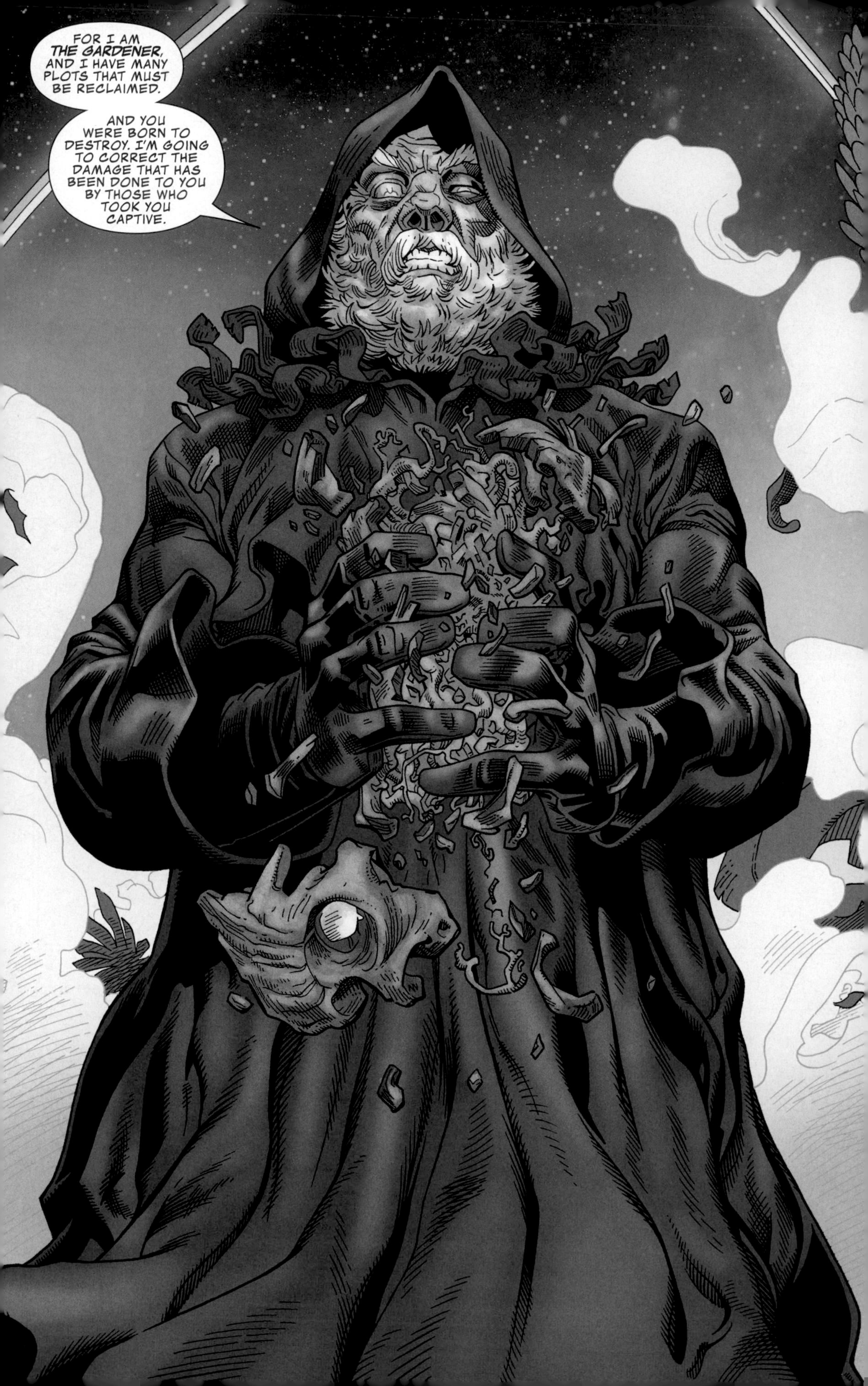

FOR I AM THE GARDENER, AND I HAVE MANY PLOTS THAT MUST BE RECLAIMED.
AND YOU WERE BORN TO DESTROY. I'M GOING TO CORRECT THE DAMAGE THAT HAS BEEN DONE TO YOU BY THOSE WHO TOOK YOU CAPTIVE.

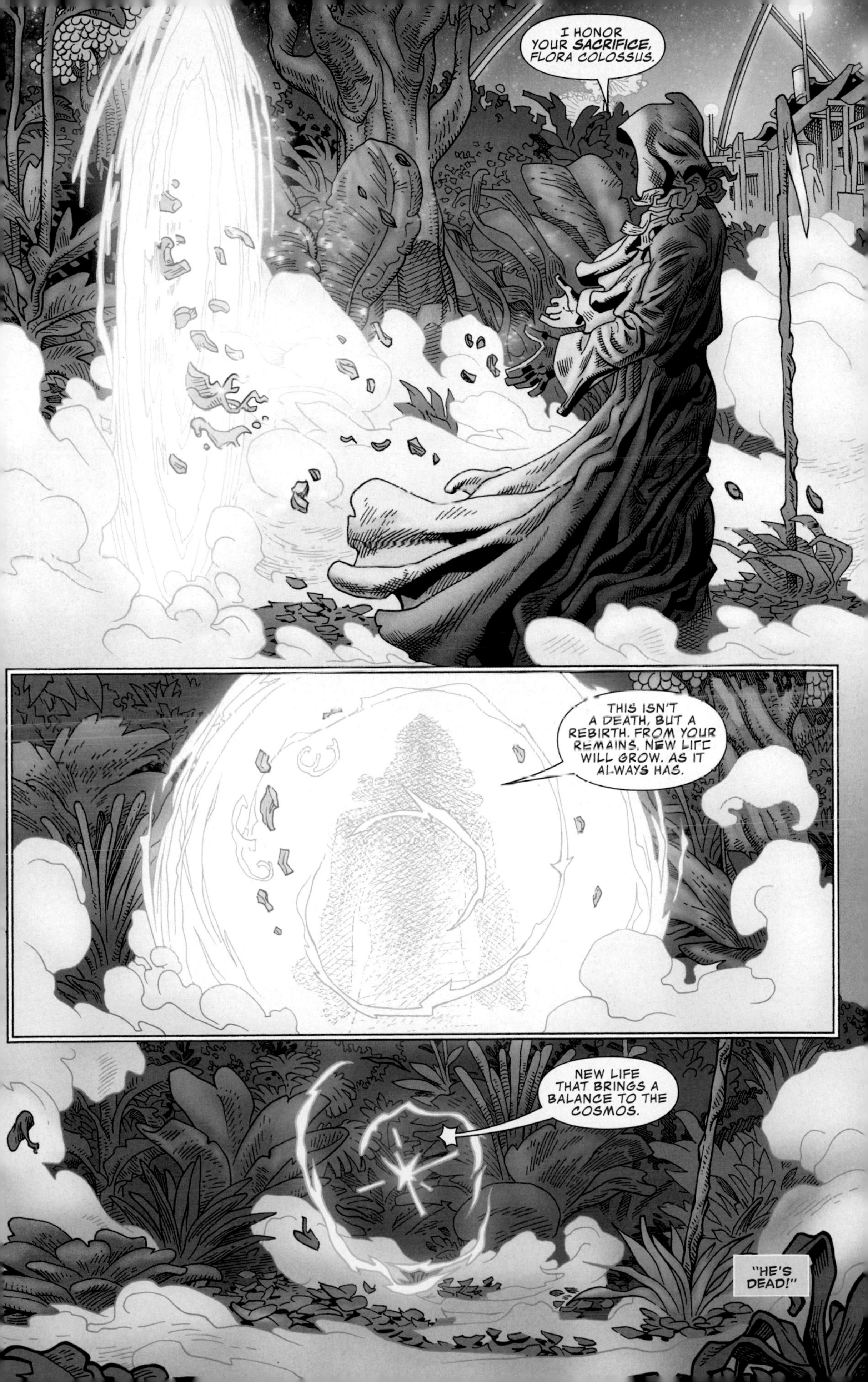
I HONOR YOUR SACRIFICE, FLORA COLOSSUS.
THIS ISN'T A DEATH, BUT A REBIRTH. FROM YOUR REMAINS, NEW LIFE WILL GROW. AS IT ALWAYS HAS.
NEW LIFE THAT BRINGS A BALANCE TO THE COSMOS.
"HE'S DEAD!"

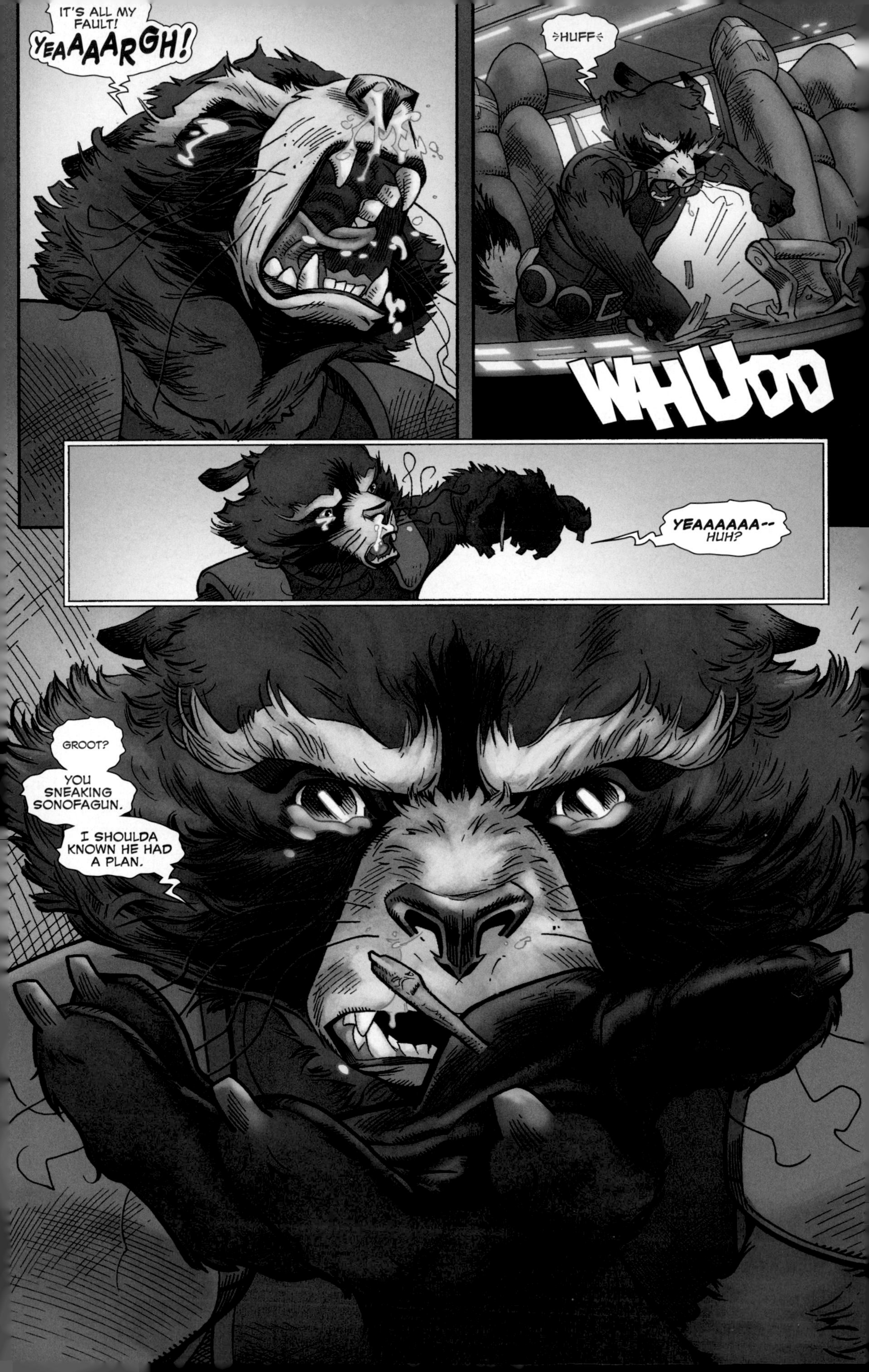
IT'S ALL MY FAULT!
YEAAAARGH!
HUFF
WHUDD
YEAAAAAA-- HUH?
GROOT?
YOU SNEAKING SONOFAGUN.
I SHOULDA KNOWN HE HAD A PLAN.

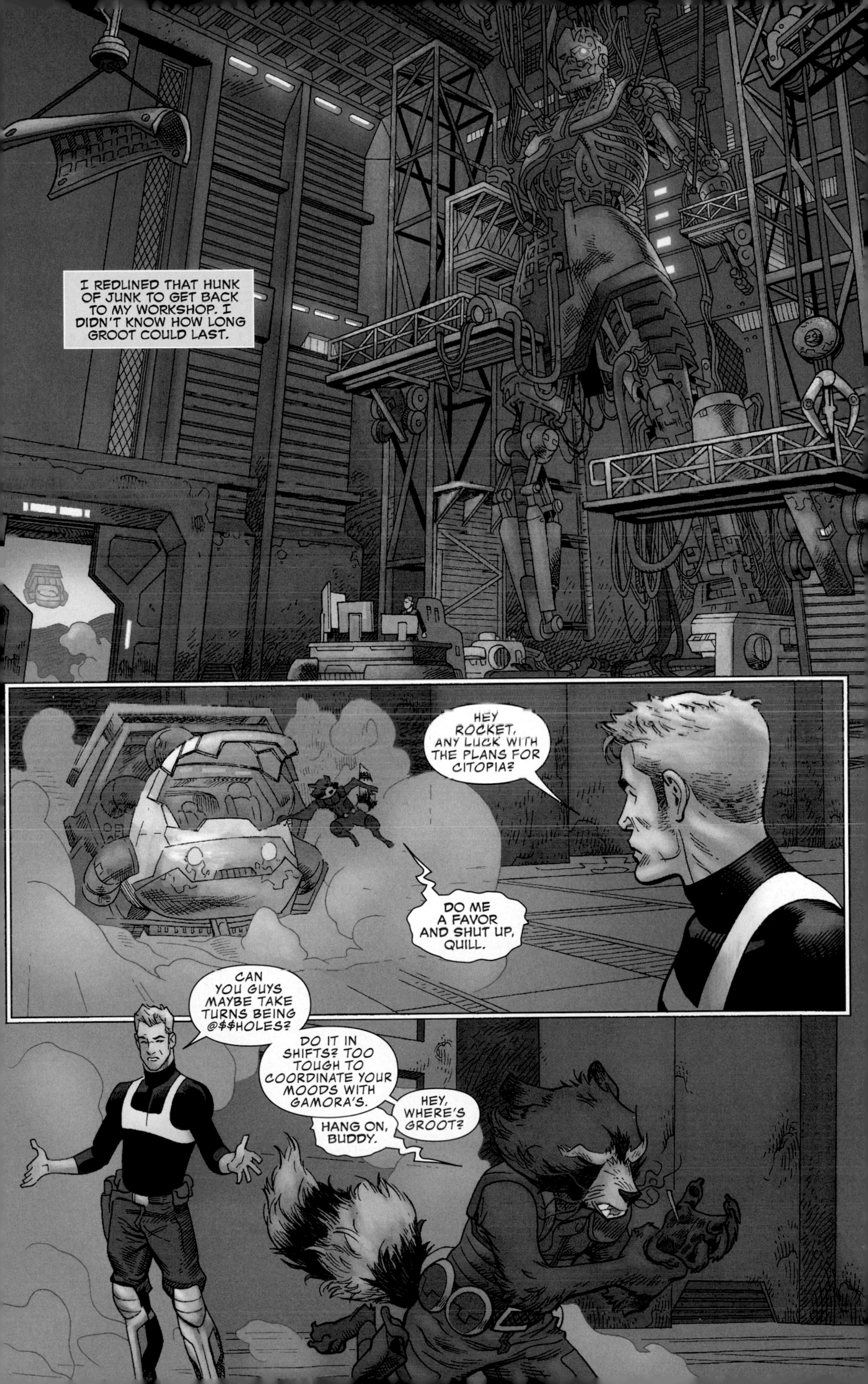
I REDLINED THAT HUNK OF JUNK TO GET BACK TO MY WORKSHOP. I DIDN'T KNOW HOW LONG GROOT COULD LAST.
HEY ROCKET, ANY LUCK WITH THE PLANS FOR CITOPIA?
DO ME A FAVOR AND SHUT UP, QUILL.
CAN YOU GUYS MAYBE TAKE TURNS BEING @$$HOLES?
DO IT IN SHIFTS? TOO TOUGH TO COORDINATE YOUR MOODS WITH GAMORA'S.
HEY, WHERE'S GROOT?
HANG ON, BUDDY.

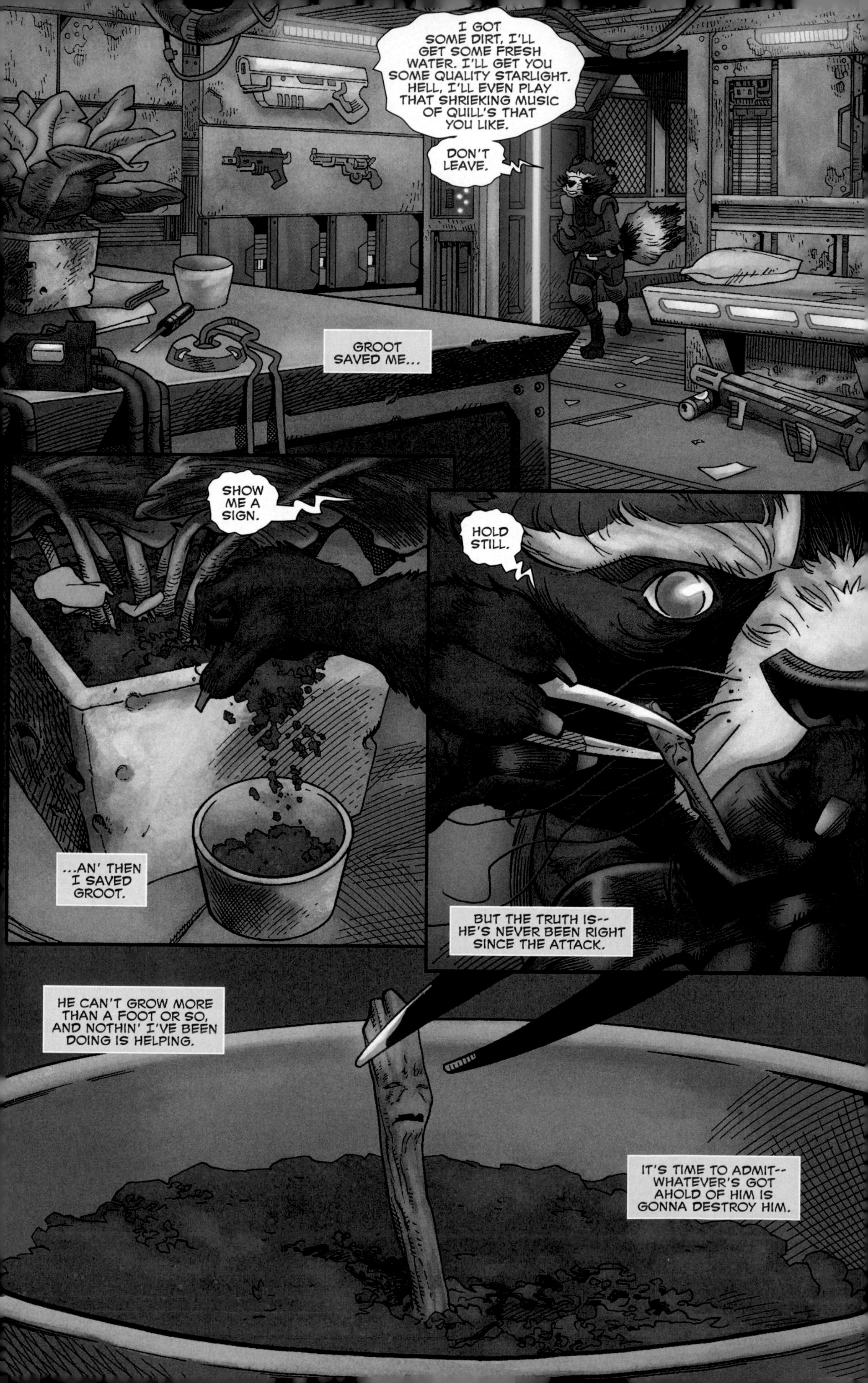
I GOT SOME DIRT, I'LL GET SOME FRESH WATER. I'LL GET YOU SOME QUALITY STARLIGHT. HELL, I'LL EVEN PLAY THAT SHRIEKING MUSIC OF QUILL'S THAT YOU LIKE.
DON'T LEAVE.
GROOT SAVED ME...
SHOW ME A SIGN.
...AN' THEN I SAVED GROOT.
HOLD STILL.
BUT THE TRUTH IS-- HE'S NEVER BEEN RIGHT SINCE THE ATTACK.
HE CAN'T GROW MORE THAN A FOOT OR SO, AND NOTHIN' I'VE BEEN DOING IS HELPING.
IT'S TIME TO ADMIT-- WHATEVER'S GOT AHOLD OF HIM IS GONNA DESTROY HIM.

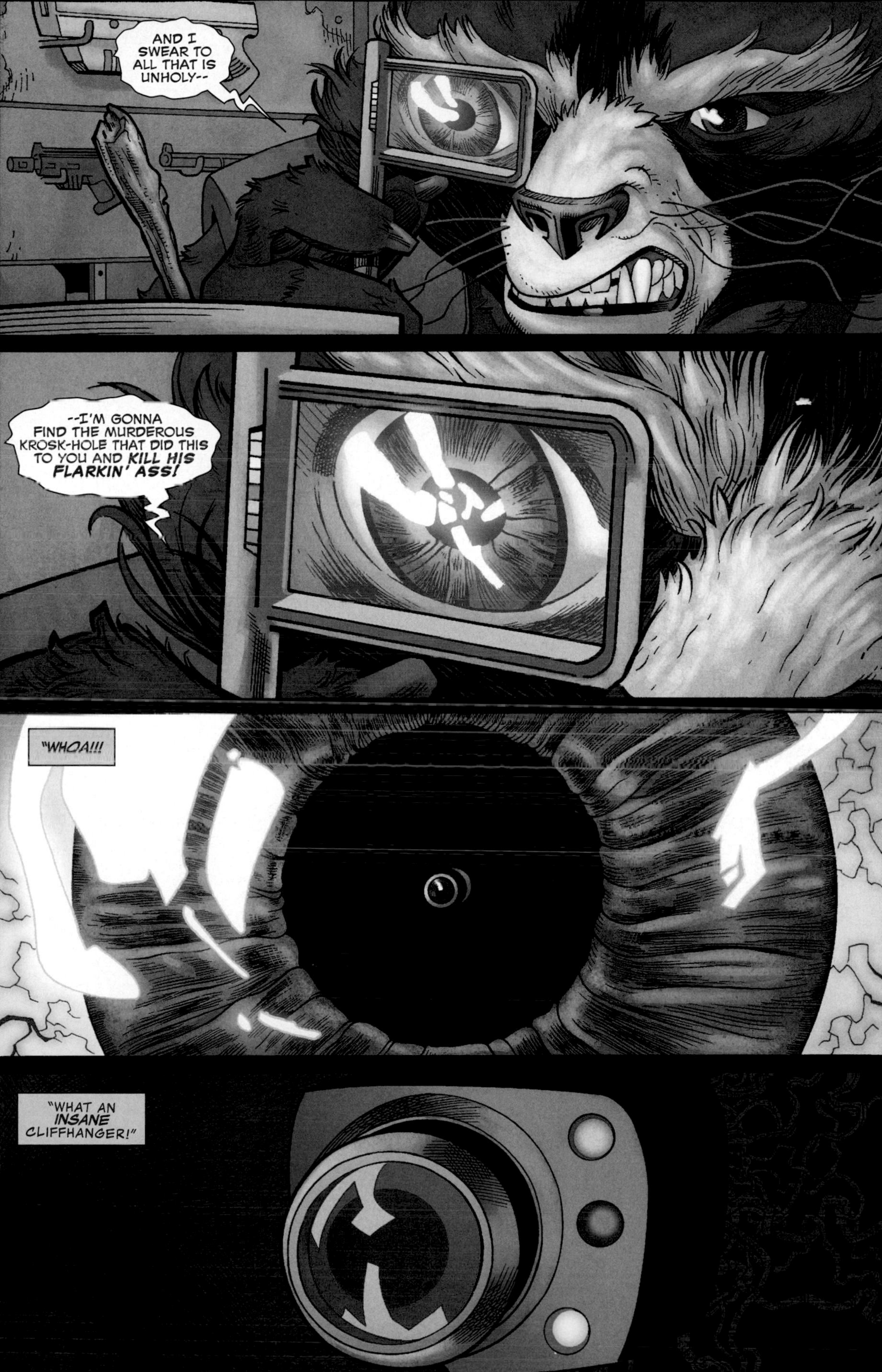
AND I SWEAR TO ALL THAT IS UNHOLY--
--I'M GONNA FIND THE MURDEROUS KROSK-HOLE THAT DID THIS TO YOU AND KILL HIS FLARKIN' ASS!
"WHOA!!!
"WHAT AN INSANE CLIFFHANGER!"

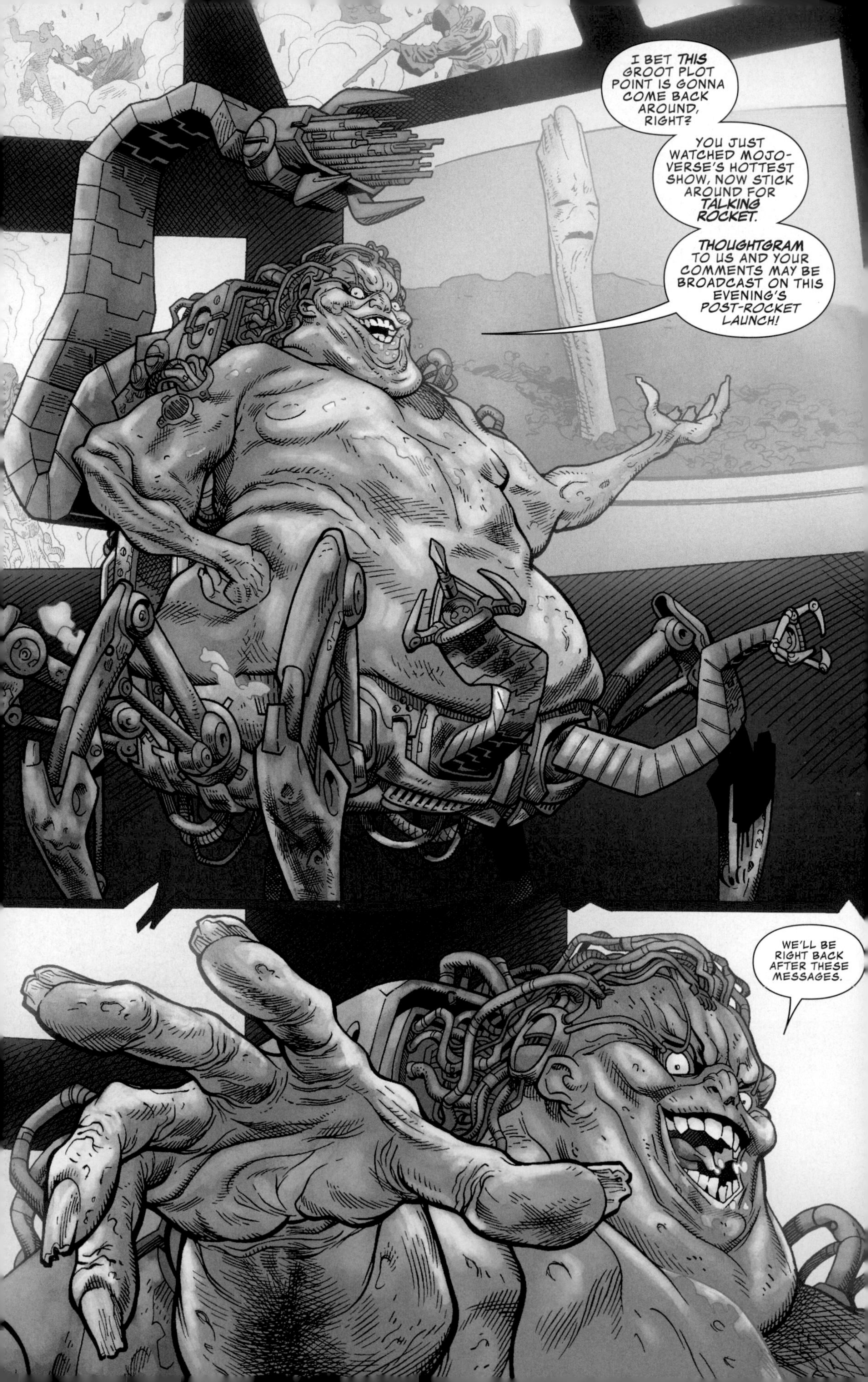
I BET THIS GROOT PLOT POINT IS GONNA COME BACK AROUND, RIGHT?
YOU JUST WATCHED MOJO-VERSE'S HOTTEST SHOW, NOW STICK AROUND FOR TALKING ROCKET.
THOUGHTGRAM TO US AND YOUR COMMENTS MAY BE BROADCAST ON THIS EVENING'S POST-ROCKET LAUNCH!
WE'LL BE RIGHT BACK AFTER THESE MESSAGES.

11

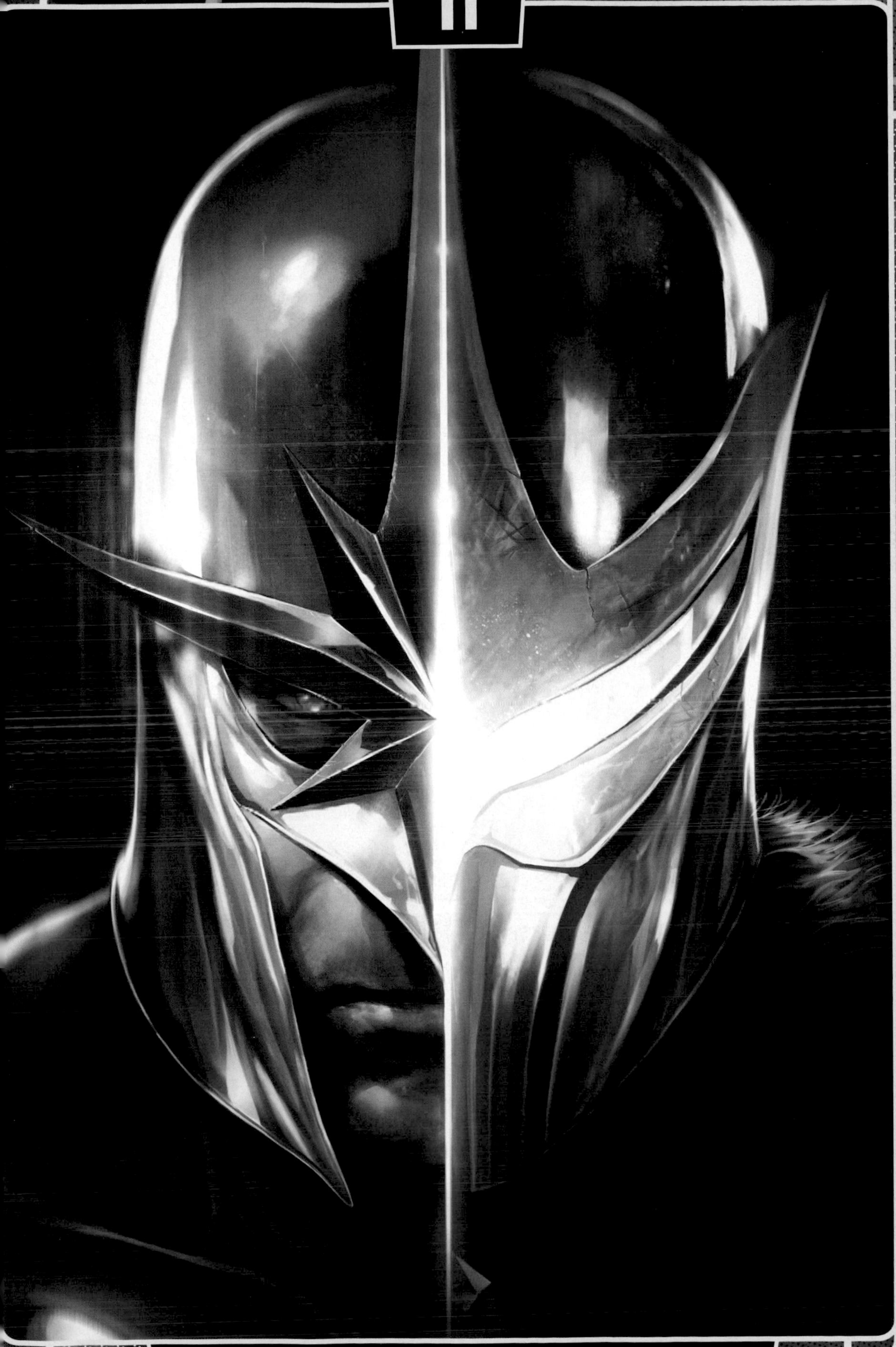

"HIGHWAY PATROLMAN"

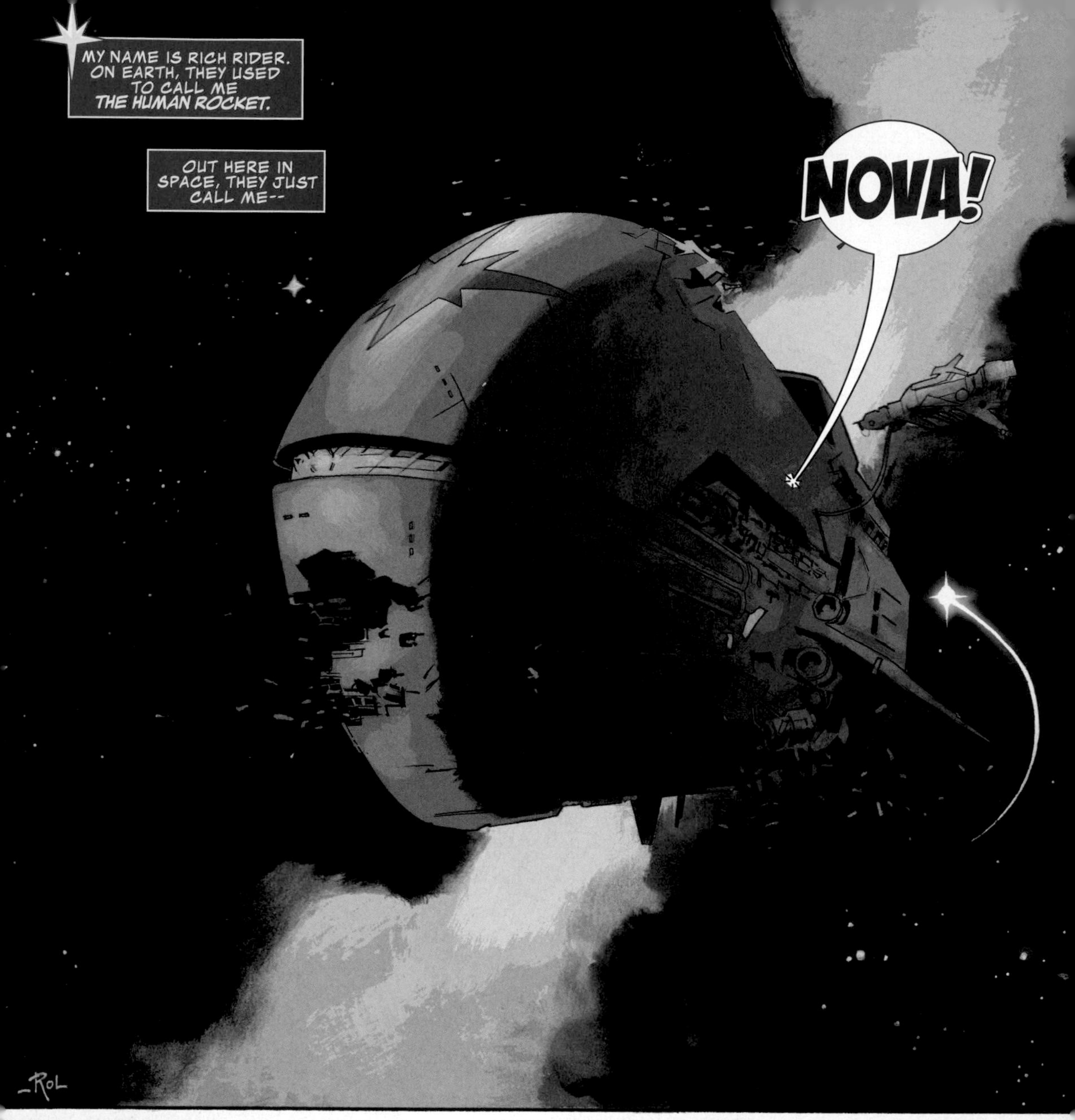
MY NAME IS RICH RIDER. ON EARTH, THEY USED TO CALL ME THE HUMAN ROCKET.
OUT HERE IN SPACE, THEY JUST CALL ME--
NOVA!
-ROL

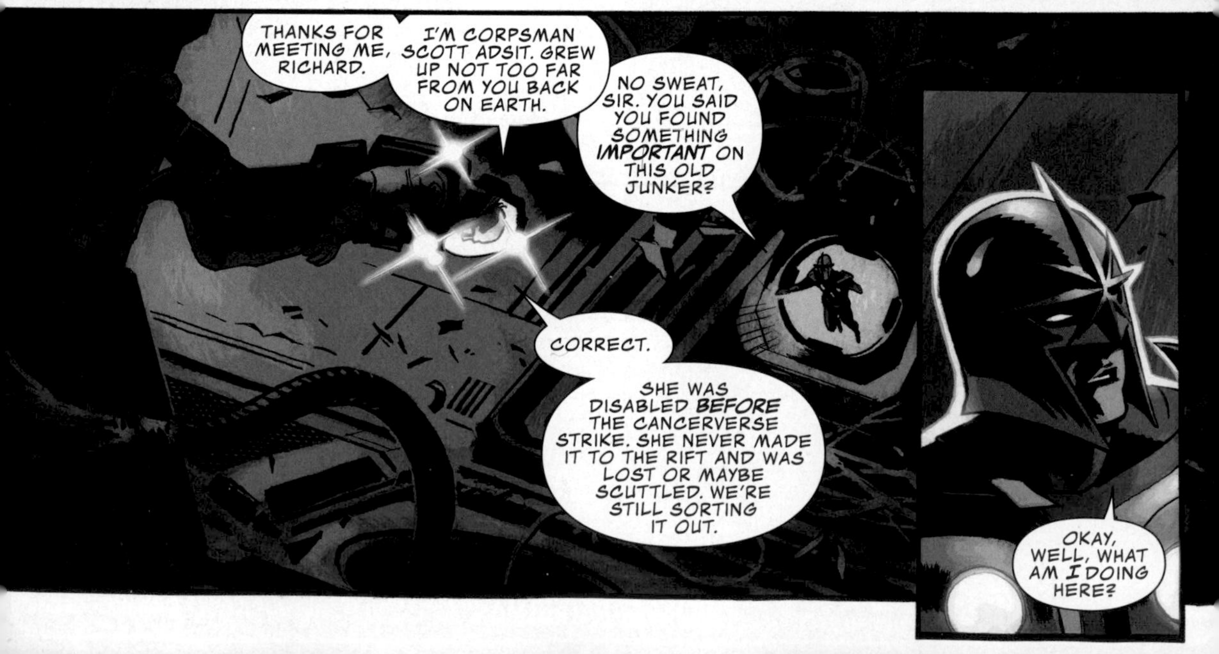
THANKS FOR MEETING ME, RICHARD.
I'M CORPSMAN SCOTT ADSIT. GREW UP NOT TOO FAR FROM YOU BACK ON EARTH.
NO SWEAT, SIR. YOU SAID YOU FOUND SOMETHING IMPORTANT ON THIS OLD JUNKER?
CORRECT.
SHE WAS DISABLED BEFORE THE CANCERVERSE STRIKE. SHE NEVER MADE IT TO THE RIFT AND WAS LOST OR MAYBE SCUTTLED. WE'RE STILL SORTING IT OUT.
OKAY, WELL, WHAT AM I DOING HERE?

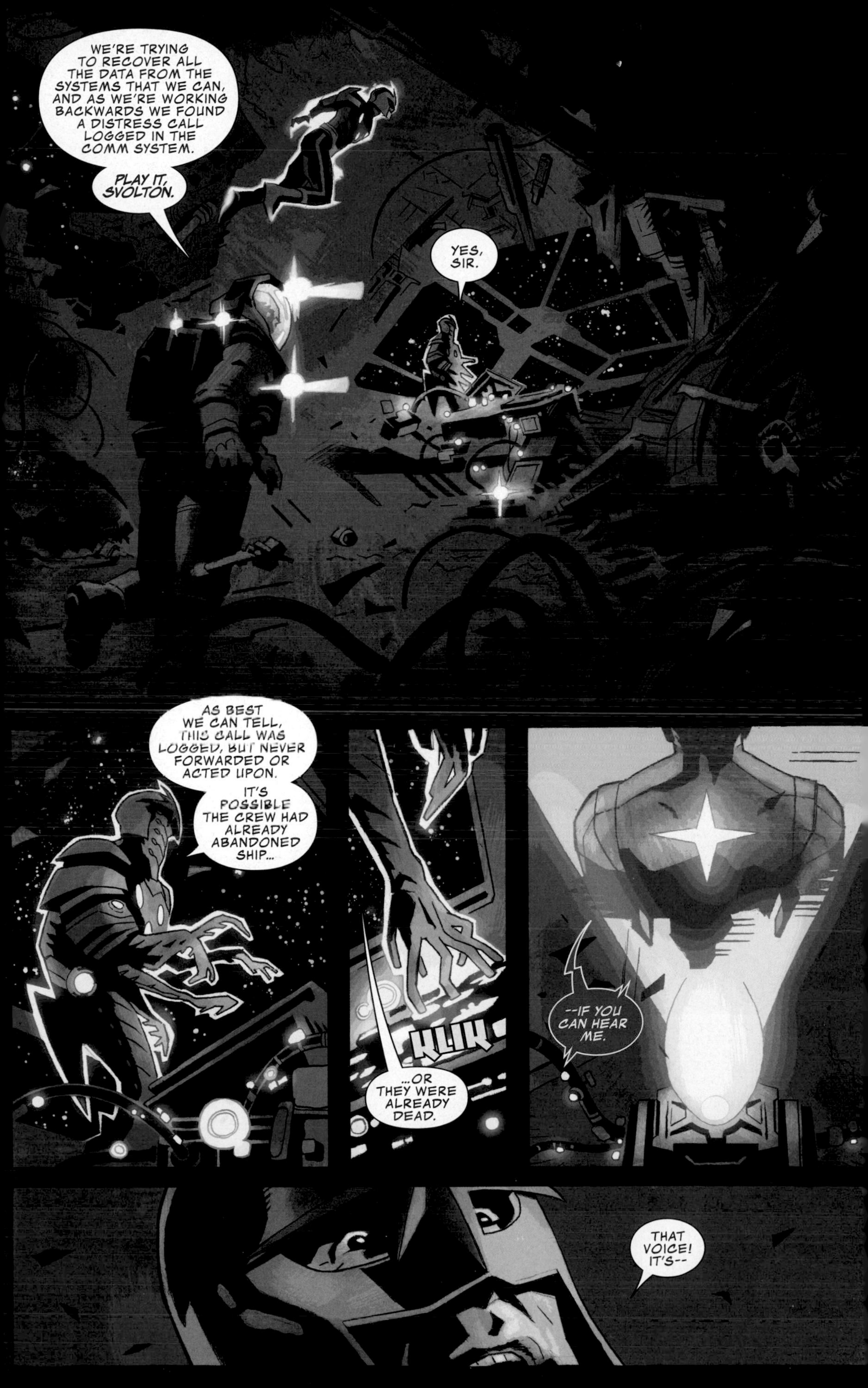
WE'RE TRYING TO RECOVER ALL THE DATA FROM THE SYSTEMS THAT WE CAN, AND AS WE'RE WORKING BACKWARDS WE FOUND A DISTRESS CALL LOGGED IN THE COMM SYSTEM.
PLAY IT, SVOLTON.
YES, SIR.
AS BEST WE CAN TELL, THIS CALL WAS LOGGED, BUT NEVER FORWARDED OR ACTED UPON.
IT'S POSSIBLE THE CREW HAD ALREADY ABANDONED SHIP...
KLIK
...OR THEY WERE ALREADY DEAD.
--IF YOU CAN HEAR ME.
THAT VOICE! IT'S--

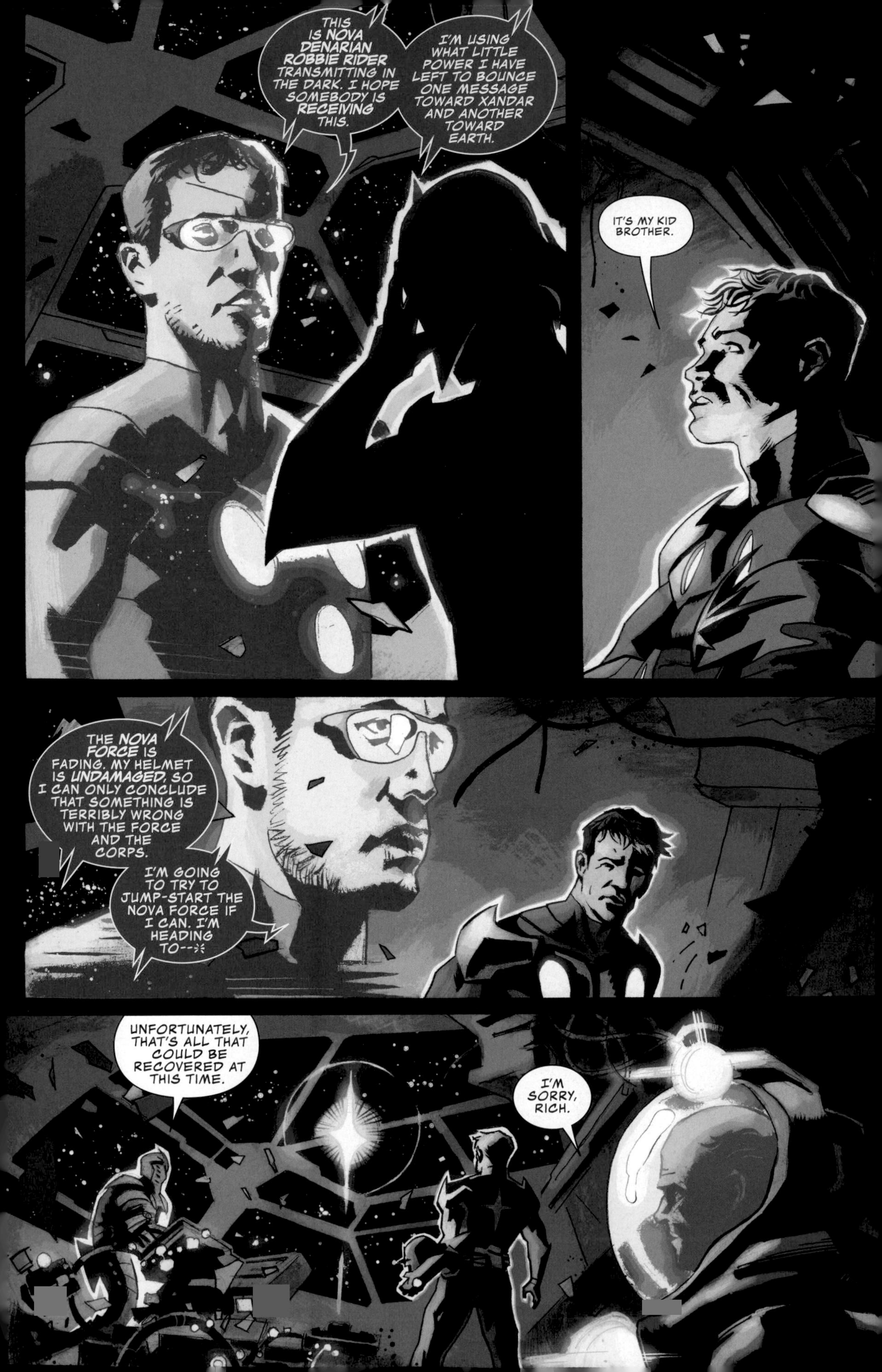
THIS IS NOVA DENARIAN ROBBIE RIDER TRANSMITTING IN THE DARK. I HOPE SOMEBODY IS RECEIVING THIS.
I'M USING WHAT LITTLE POWER I HAVE LEFT TO BOUNCE ONE MESSAGE TOWARD XANDAR AND ANOTHER TOWARD EARTH.
IT'S MY KID BROTHER.
THE NOVA FORCE IS FADING. MY HELMET IS UNDAMAGED, SO I CAN ONLY CONCLUDE THAT SOMETHING IS TERRIBLY WRONG WITH THE FORCE AND THE CORPS.
I'M GOING TO TRY TO JUMP-START THE NOVA FORCE IF I CAN. I'M HEADING TO--
UNFORTUNATELY, THAT'S ALL THAT COULD BE RECOVERED AT THIS TIME.
I'M SORRY, RICH.

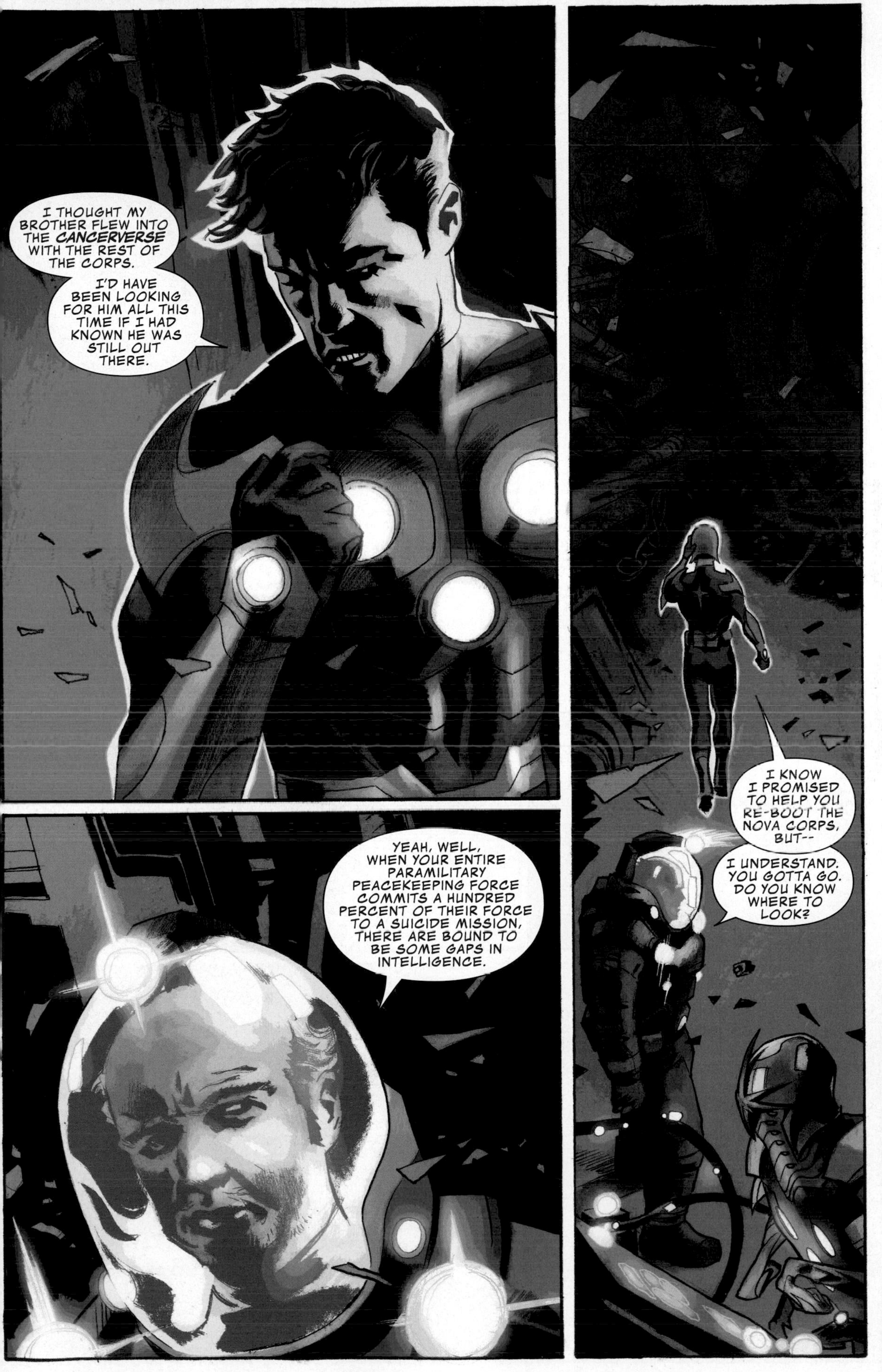
I THOUGHT MY BROTHER FLEW INTO THE *CANCERVERSE* WITH THE REST OF THE CORPS.
I'D HAVE BEEN LOOKING FOR HIM ALL THIS TIME IF I HAD KNOWN HE WAS STILL OUT THERE.
YEAH, WELL, WHEN YOUR ENTIRE PARAMILITARY PEACEKEEPING FORCE COMMITS A HUNDRED PERCENT OF THEIR FORCE TO A SUICIDE MISSION, THERE ARE BOUND TO BE SOME GAPS IN INTELLIGENCE.
I KNOW I PROMISED TO HELP YOU RE-BOOT THE NOVA CORPS, BUT--
I UNDERSTAND. YOU GOTTA GO. DO YOU KNOW WHERE TO LOOK?

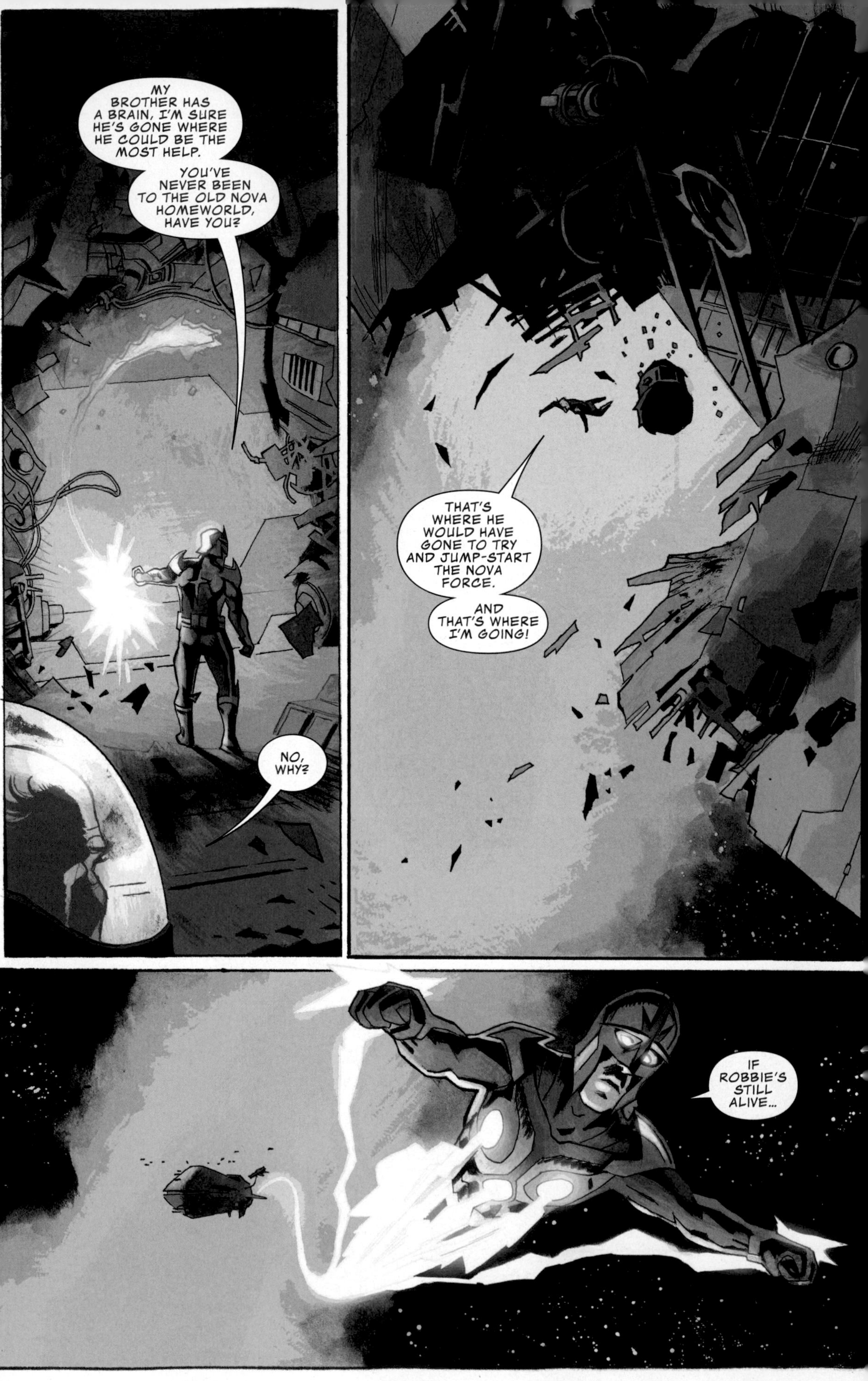
MY BROTHER HAS A BRAIN, I'M SURE HE'S GONE WHERE HE COULD BE THE MOST HELP.
YOU'VE NEVER BEEN TO THE OLD NOVA HOMEWORLD, HAVE YOU?
NO, WHY?
THAT'S WHERE HE WOULD HAVE GONE TO TRY AND JUMP-START THE NOVA FORCE.
AND THAT'S WHERE I'M GOING!
IF ROBBIE'S STILL ALIVE...

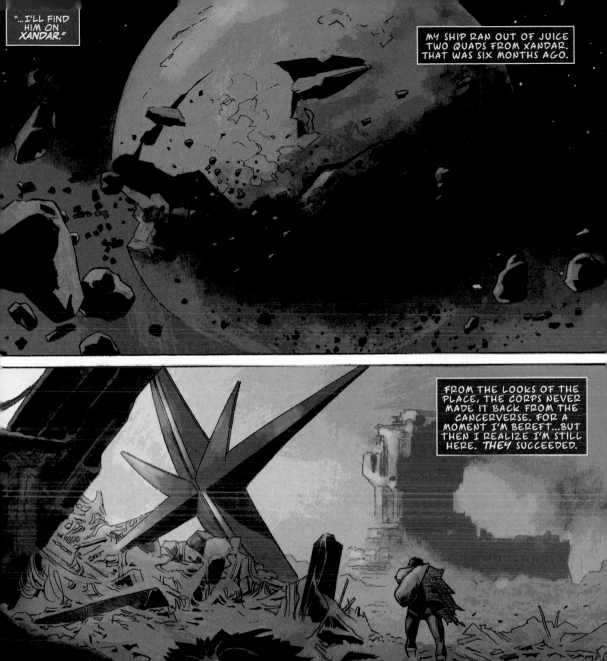

"...I'LL FIND HIM ON *XANDAR*."

MY SHIP RAN OUT OF JUICE TWO QUADS FROM XANDAR. THAT WAS SIX MONTHS AGO.

FROM THE LOOKS OF THE PLACE, THE CORPS NEVER MADE IT BACK FROM THE CANCERVERSE. FOR A MOMENT I'M BEREFT...BUT THEN I REALIZE I'M STILL HERE. *THEY* SUCCEEDED.

THE ONLY REASON I MADE IT WAS BECAUSE I WAS ABLE TO MAKE A HALF-DECENT SOLAR SAIL FROM MY SHIP'S PANELS.

I CAME IN HOT--AND A CONTINENT SHORT.

ANOTHER SEASON LOST WALKING HERE.

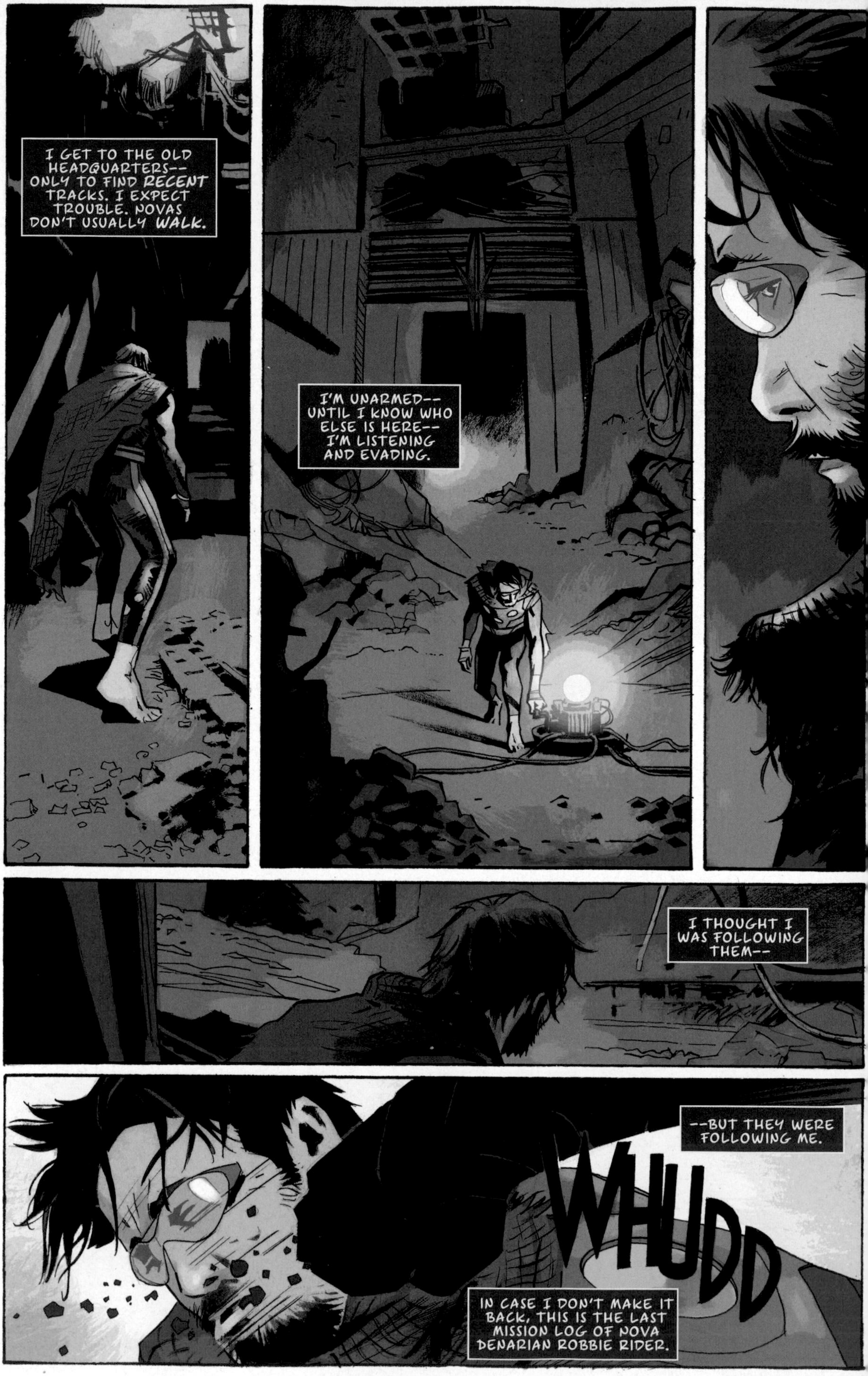
I GET TO THE OLD HEADQUARTERS--ONLY TO FIND RECENT TRACKS. I EXPECT TROUBLE. NOVAS DON'T USUALLY WALK.
I'M UNARMED--UNTIL I KNOW WHO ELSE IS HERE--I'M LISTENING AND EVADING.
I THOUGHT I WAS FOLLOWING THEM--
--BUT THEY WERE FOLLOWING ME.
WHUDD
IN CASE I DON'T MAKE IT BACK, THIS IS THE LAST MISSION LOG OF NOVA DENARIAN ROBBIE RIDER.

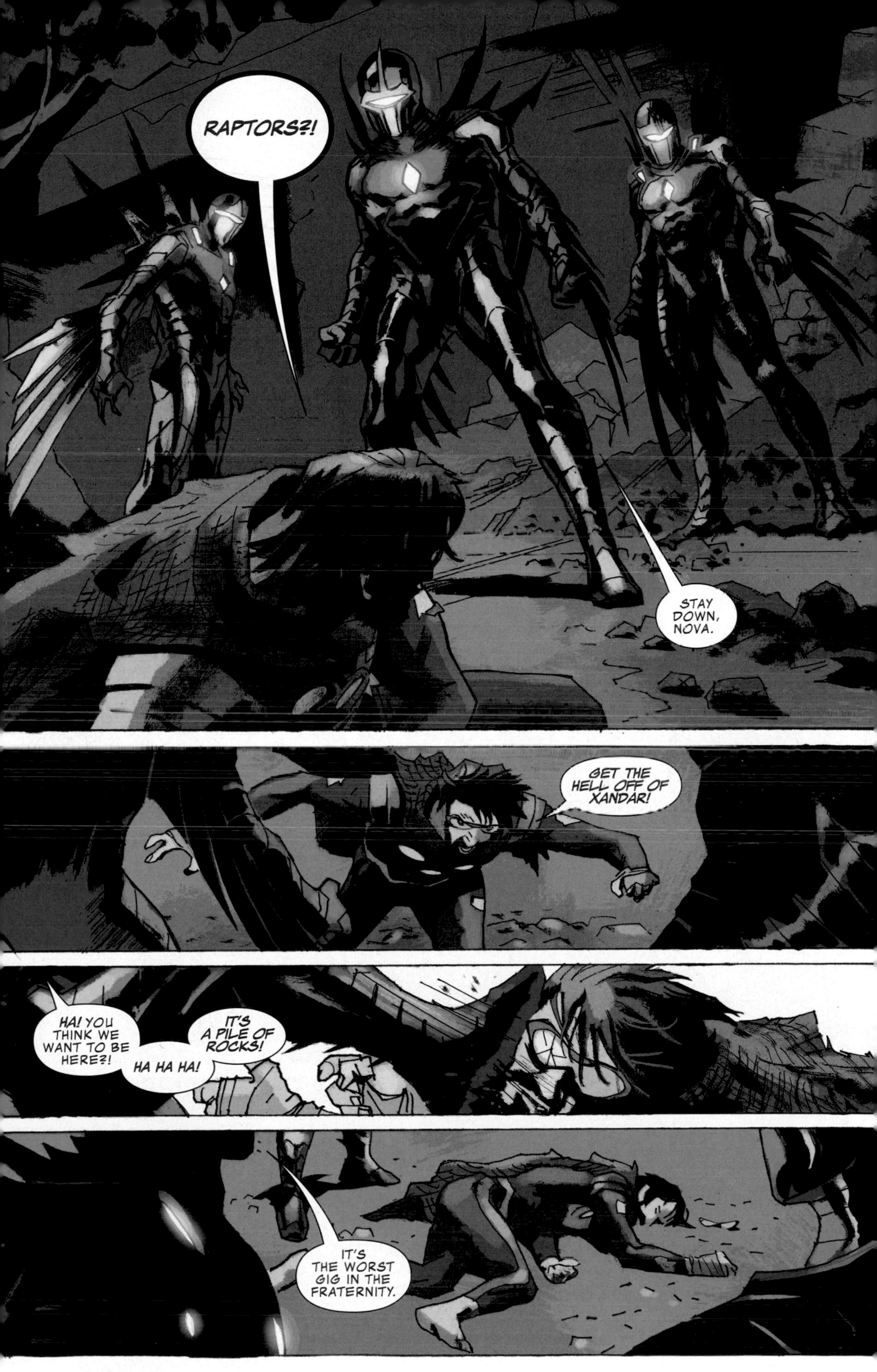
RAPTORS?!
STAY DOWN, NOVA.
GET THE HELL OFF OF XANDAR!
HA! YOU THINK WE WANT TO BE HERE?!
HA HA HA!
IT'S A PILE OF ROCKS!
IT'S THE WORST GIG IN THE FRATERNITY.

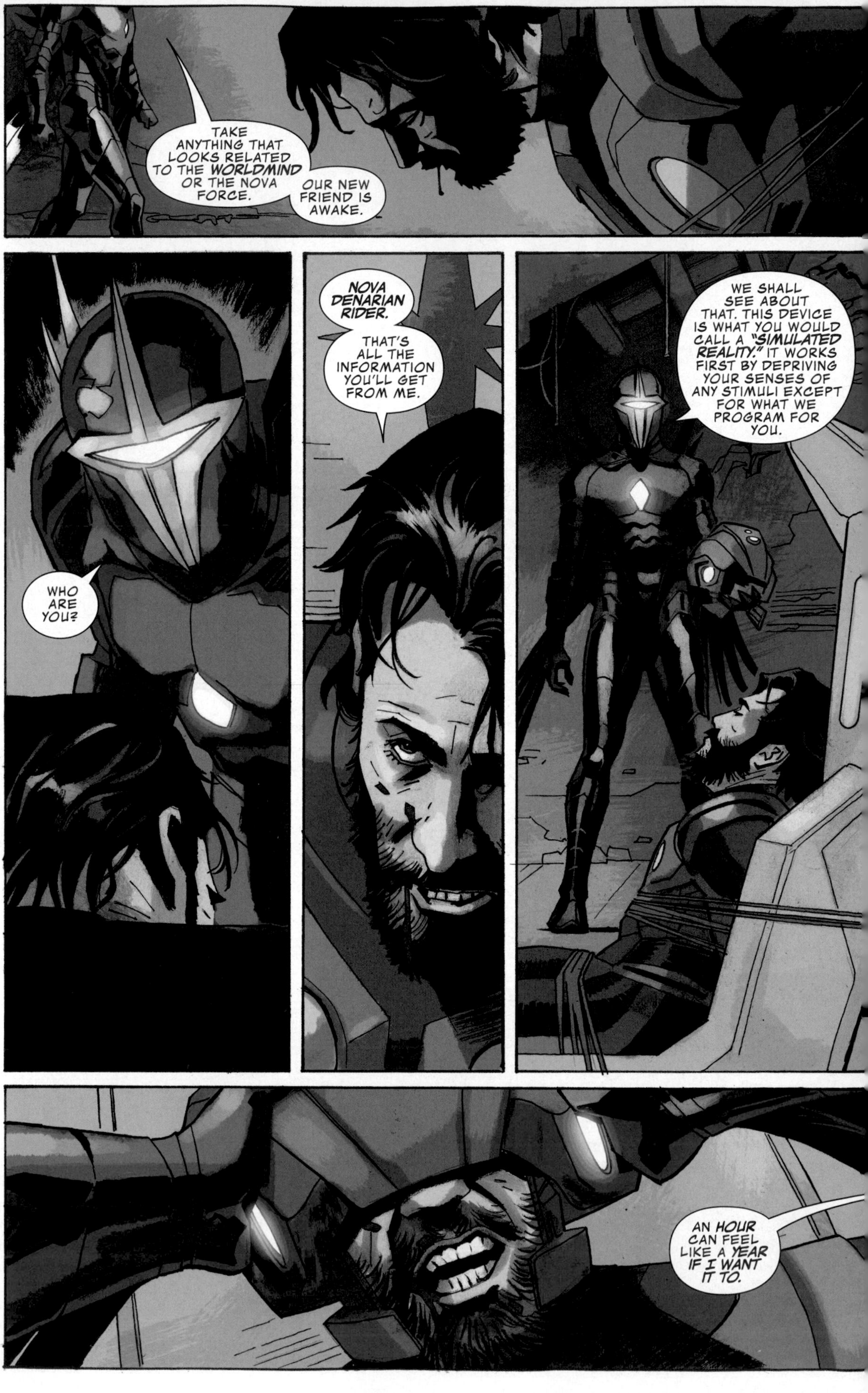
TAKE ANYTHING THAT LOOKS RELATED TO THE WORLDMIND OR THE NOVA FORCE.
OUR NEW FRIEND IS AWAKE.
WHO ARE YOU?
NOVA DENARIAN RIDER.
THAT'S ALL THE INFORMATION YOU'LL GET FROM ME.
WE SHALL SEE ABOUT THAT. THIS DEVICE IS WHAT YOU WOULD CALL A "SIMULATED REALITY." IT WORKS FIRST BY DEPRIVING YOUR SENSES OF ANY STIMULI EXCEPT FOR WHAT WE PROGRAM FOR YOU.
AN HOUR CAN FEEL LIKE A YEAR IF I WANT IT TO.

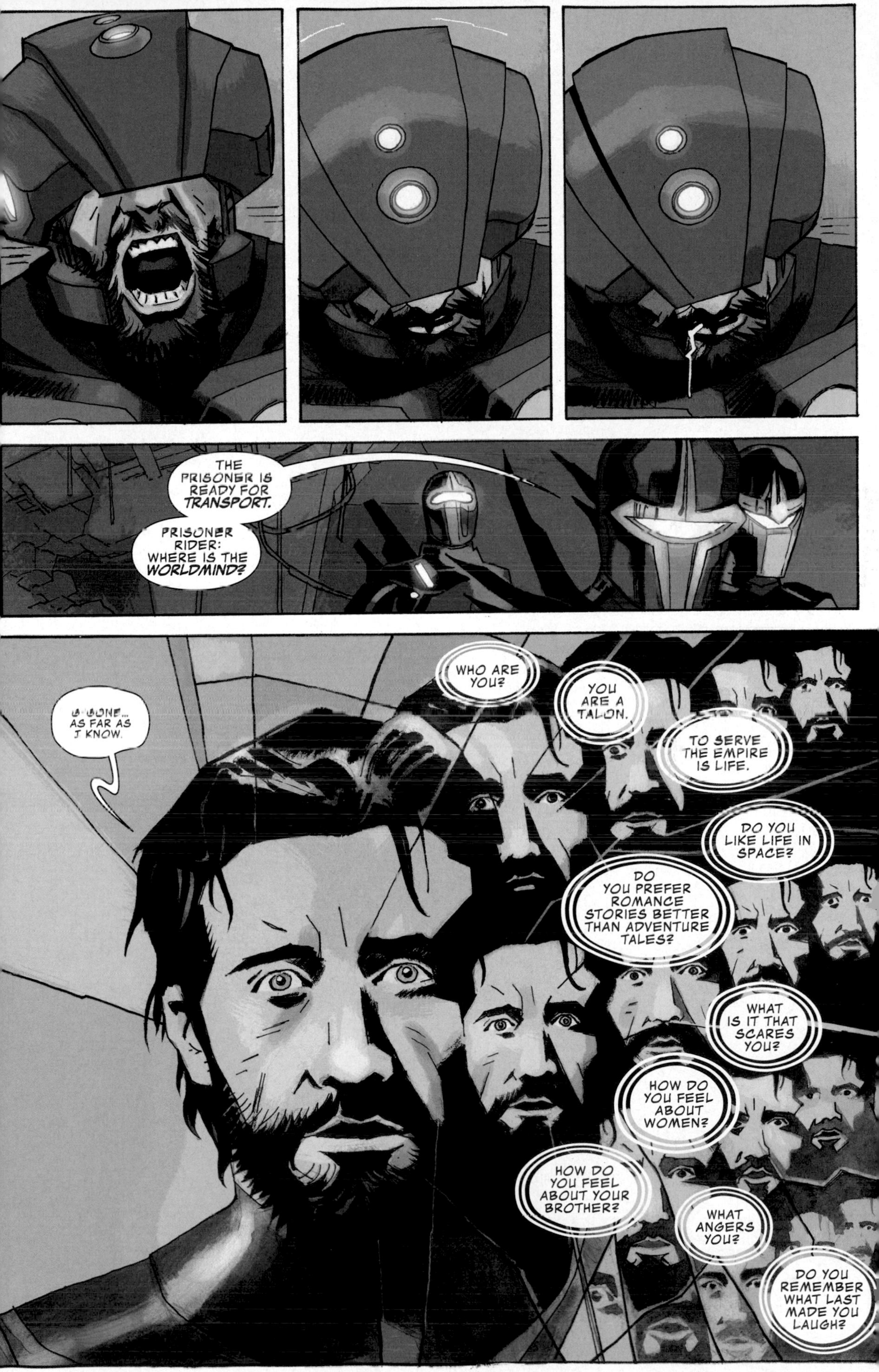
THE PRISONER IS READY FOR TRANSPORT.
PRISONER RIDER: WHERE IS THE WORLDMIND?
G-GONE... AS FAR AS I KNOW.
WHO ARE YOU?
YOU ARE A TALON.
TO SERVE THE EMPIRE IS LIFE.
DO YOU LIKE LIFE IN SPACE?
DO YOU PREFER ROMANCE STORIES BETTER THAN ADVENTURE TALES?
WHAT IS IT THAT SCARES YOU?
HOW DO YOU FEEL ABOUT WOMEN?
HOW DO YOU FEEL ABOUT YOUR BROTHER?
WHAT ANGERS YOU?
DO YOU REMEMBER WHAT LAST MADE YOU LAUGH?

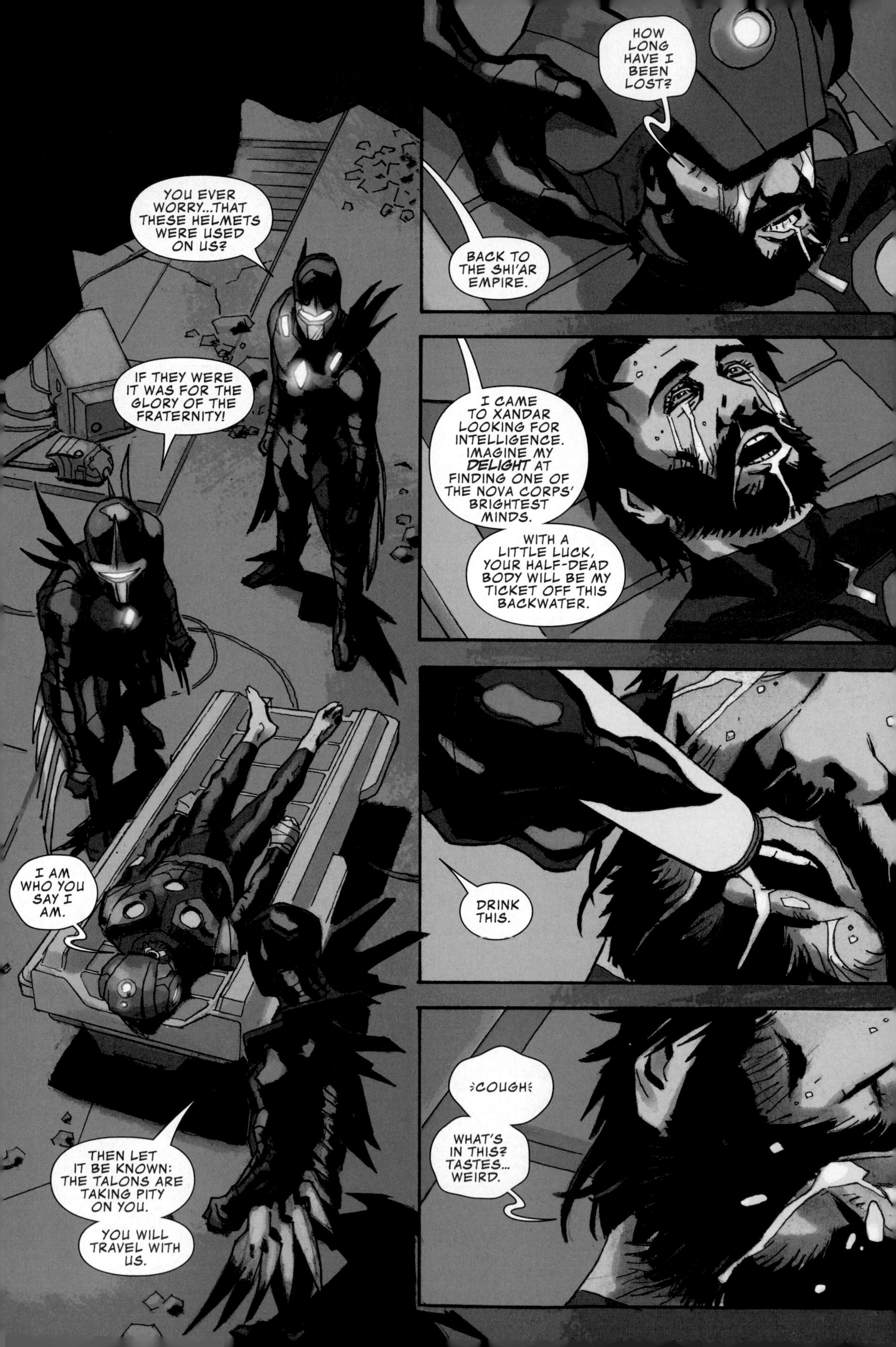
YOU EVER WORRY...THAT THESE HELMETS WERE USED ON US?
IF THEY WERE IT WAS FOR THE GLORY OF THE FRATERNITY!
I AM WHO YOU SAY I AM.
THEN LET IT BE KNOWN: THE TALONS ARE TAKING PITY ON YOU.
YOU WILL TRAVEL WITH US.
HOW LONG HAVE I BEEN LOST?
BACK TO THE SHI'AR EMPIRE.
I CAME TO XANDAR LOOKING FOR INTELLIGENCE. IMAGINE MY DELIGHT AT FINDING ONE OF THE NOVA CORPS' BRIGHTEST MINDS.
WITH A LITTLE LUCK, YOUR HALF-DEAD BODY WILL BE MY TICKET OFF THIS BACKWATER.
DRINK THIS.
COUGH
WHAT'S IN THIS? TASTES... WEIRD.

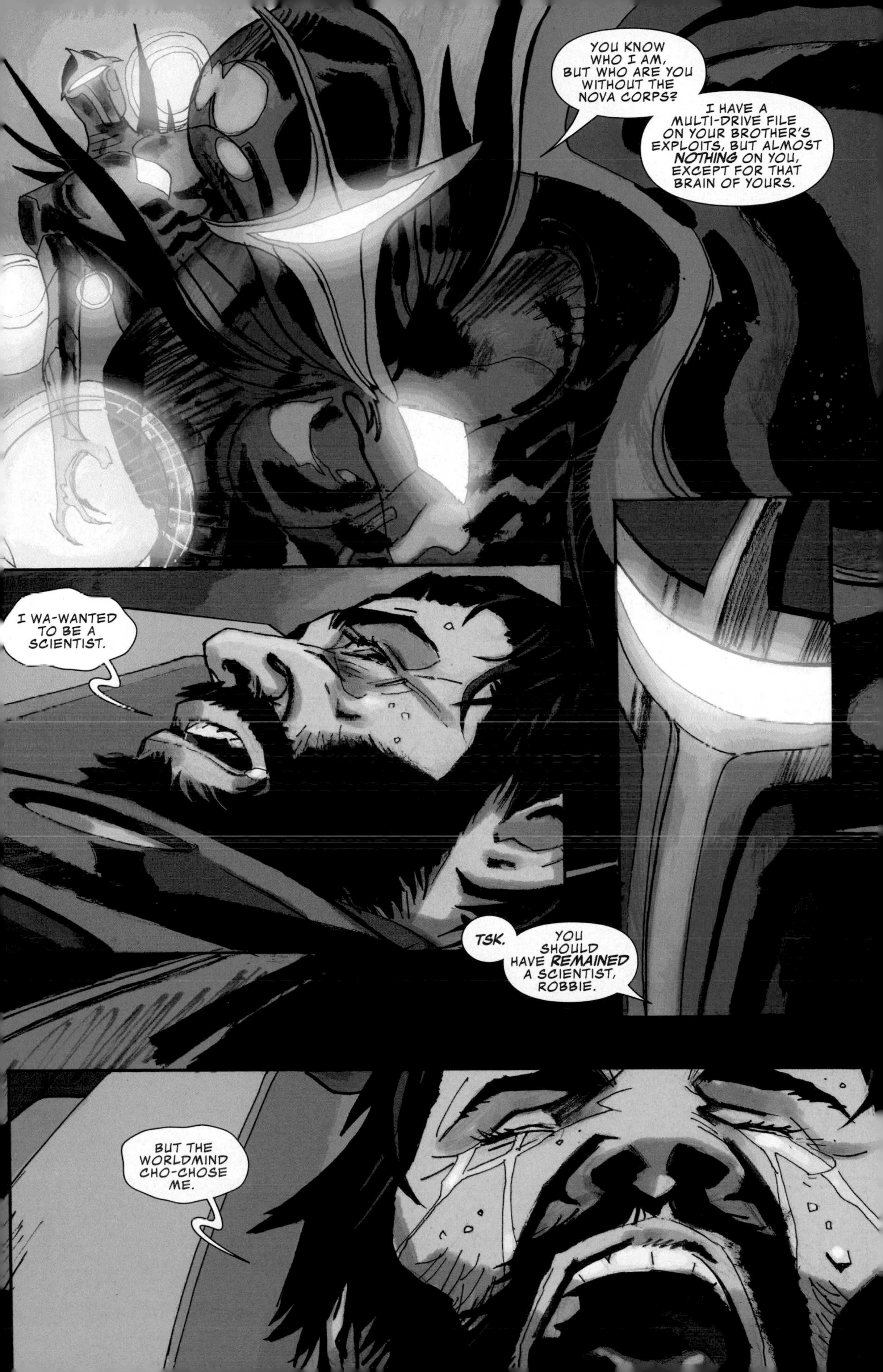
YOU KNOW WHO I AM, BUT WHO ARE YOU WITHOUT THE NOVA CORPS?
I HAVE A MULTI-DRIVE FILE ON YOUR BROTHER'S EXPLOITS, BUT ALMOST NOTHING ON YOU, EXCEPT FOR THAT BRAIN OF YOURS.
I WA-WANTED TO BE A SCIENTIST.
TSK.
YOU SHOULD HAVE REMAINED A SCIENTIST, ROBBIE.
BUT THE WORLDMIND CHO-CHOSE ME.

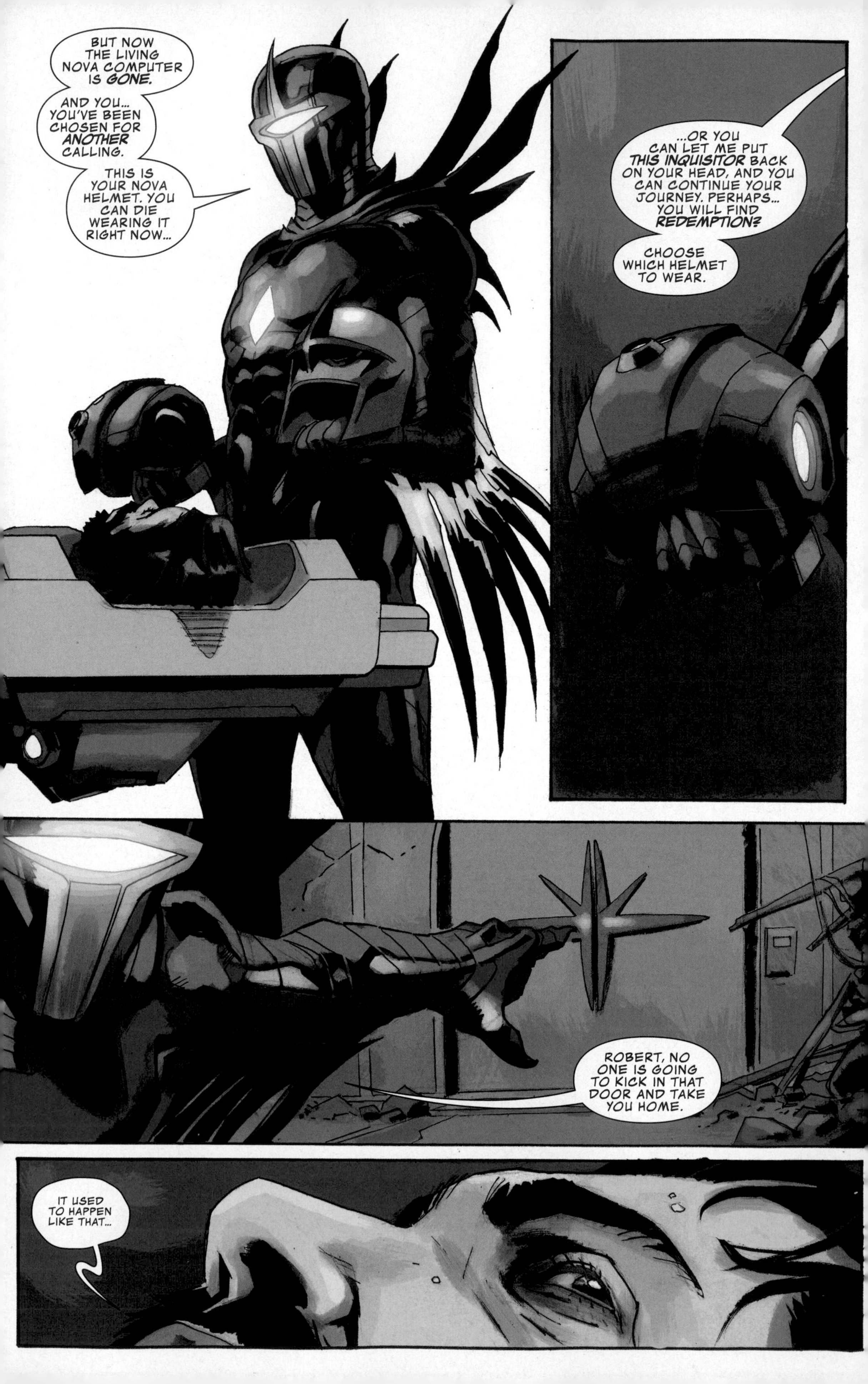
BUT NOW THE LIVING NOVA COMPUTER IS GONE.
AND YOU... YOU'VE BEEN CHOSEN FOR ANOTHER CALLING.
THIS IS YOUR NOVA HELMET. YOU CAN DIE WEARING IT RIGHT NOW...
...OR YOU CAN LET ME PUT THIS INQUISITOR BACK ON YOUR HEAD, AND YOU CAN CONTINUE YOUR JOURNEY. PERHAPS... YOU WILL FIND REDEMPTION?
CHOOSE WHICH HELMET TO WEAR.
ROBERT, NO ONE IS GOING TO KICK IN THAT DOOR AND TAKE YOU HOME.
IT USED TO HAPPEN LIKE THAT...

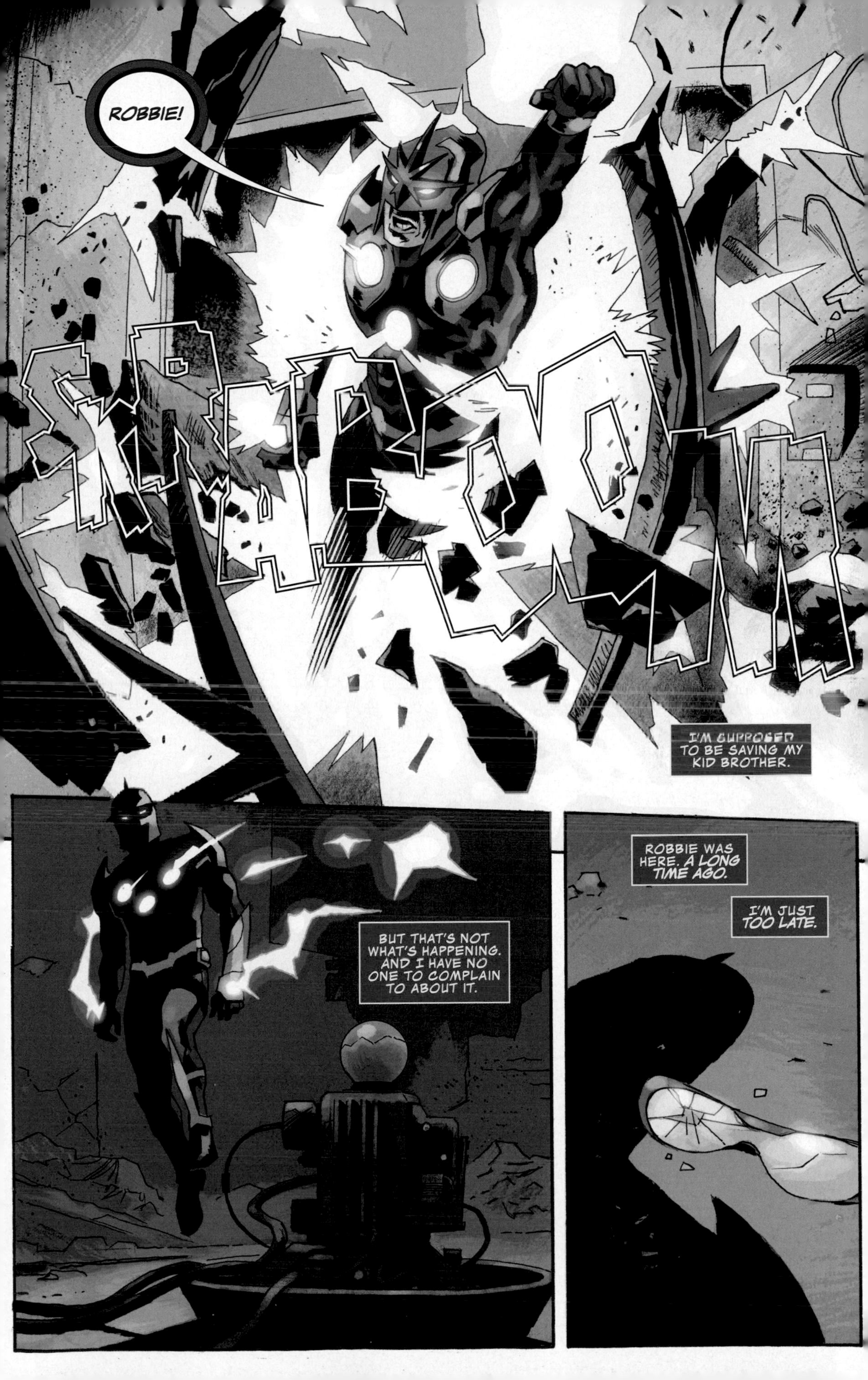
ROBBIE!
I'M SUPPOSED TO BE SAVING MY KID BROTHER.
BUT THAT'S NOT WHAT'S HAPPENING. AND I HAVE NO ONE TO COMPLAIN TO ABOUT IT.
ROBBIE WAS HERE. A LONG TIME AGO.
I'M JUST TOO LATE.

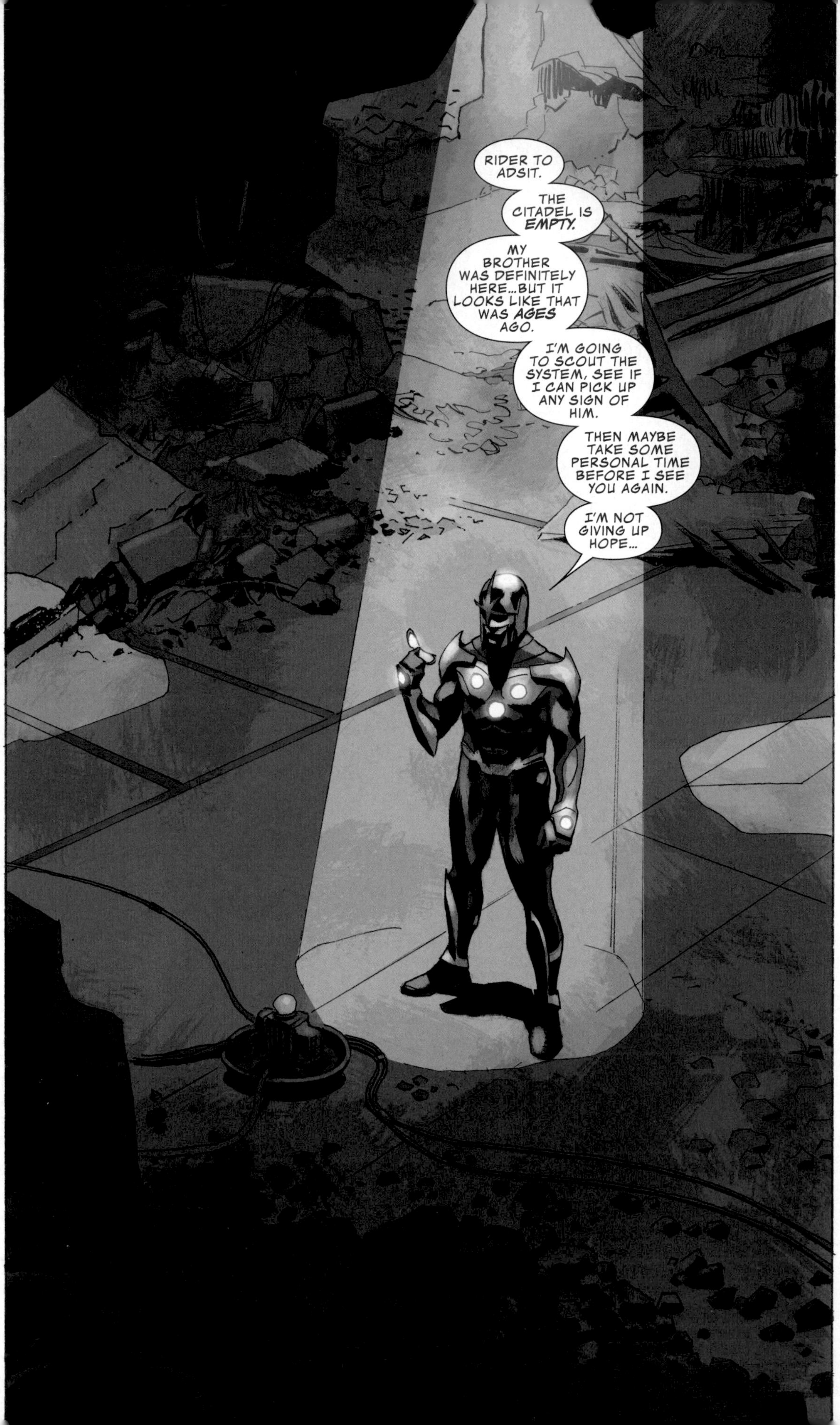
RIDER TO ADSIT.
THE CITADEL IS *EMPTY.*
MY BROTHER WAS DEFINITELY HERE...BUT IT LOOKS LIKE THAT WAS *AGES* AGO.
I'M GOING TO SCOUT THE SYSTEM, SEE IF I CAN PICK UP ANY SIGN OF HIM.
THEN MAYBE TAKE SOME PERSONAL TIME BEFORE I SEE YOU AGAIN.
I'M NOT GIVING UP HOPE...

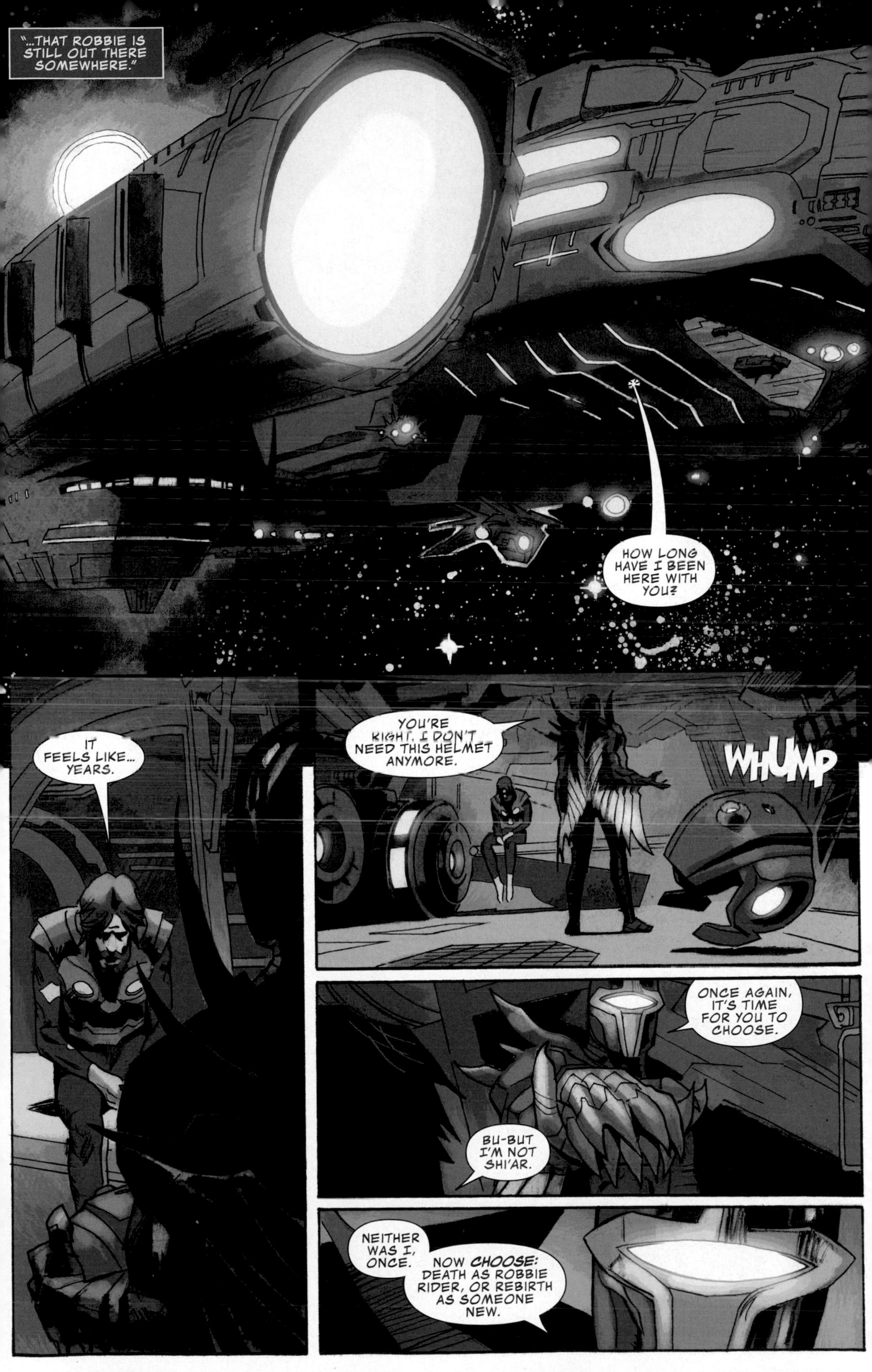
"...THAT ROBBIE IS STILL OUT THERE SOMEWHERE."
HOW LONG HAVE I BEEN HERE WITH YOU?
IT FEELS LIKE... YEARS.
YOU'RE RIGHT. I DON'T NEED THIS HELMET ANYMORE.
WHUMP
ONCE AGAIN, IT'S TIME FOR YOU TO CHOOSE.
BU-BUT I'M NOT SHI'AR.
NEITHER WAS I, ONCE.
NOW *CHOOSE:* DEATH AS ROBBIE RIDER, OR REBIRTH AS SOMEONE NEW.

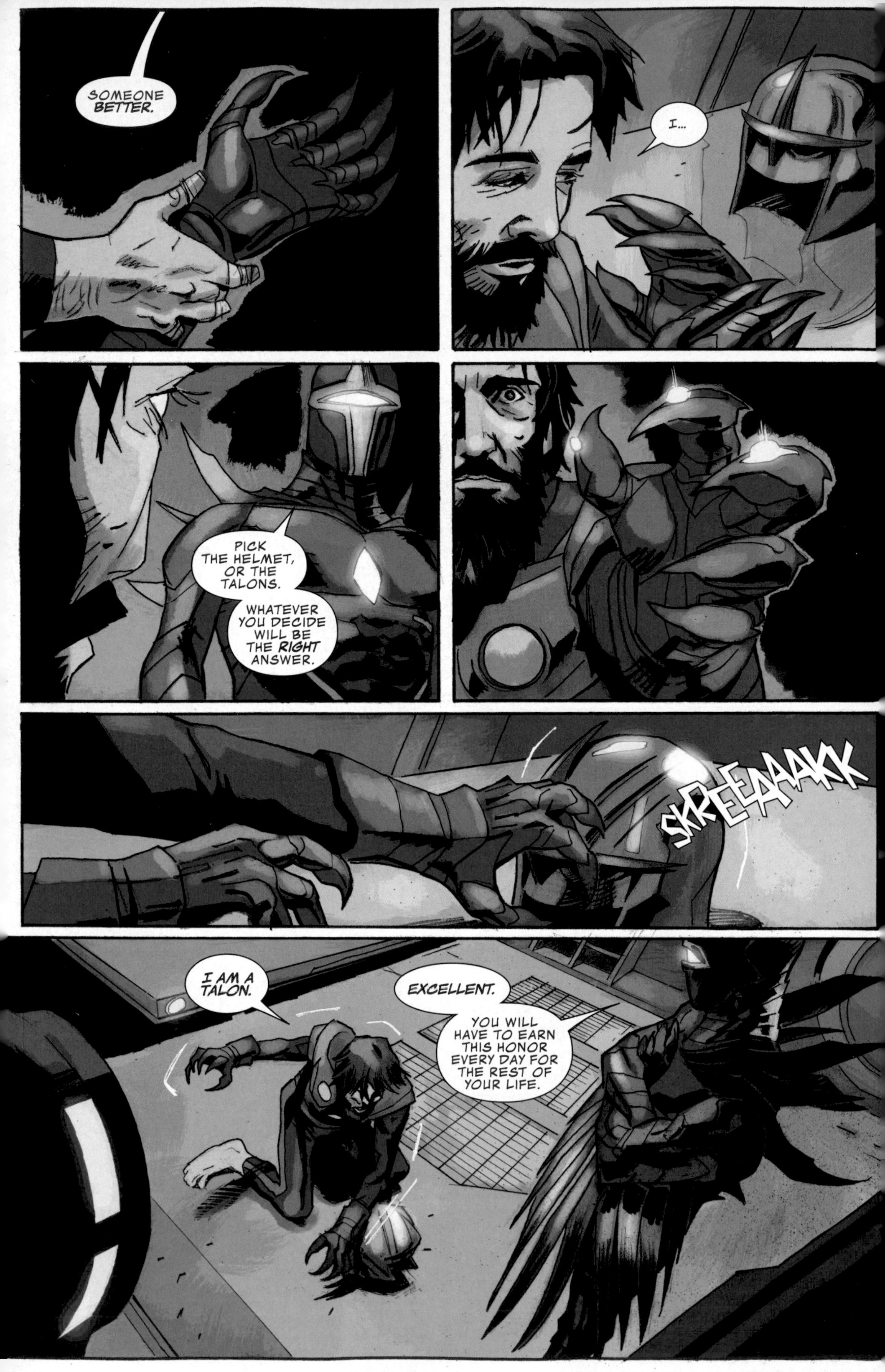
SOMEONE BETTER.
I...
PICK THE HELMET, OR THE TALONS.
WHATEVER YOU DECIDE WILL BE THE RIGHT ANSWER.
SKREEAAAKK
I AM A TALON.
EXCELLENT.
YOU WILL HAVE TO EARN THIS HONOR EVERY DAY FOR THE REST OF YOUR LIFE.

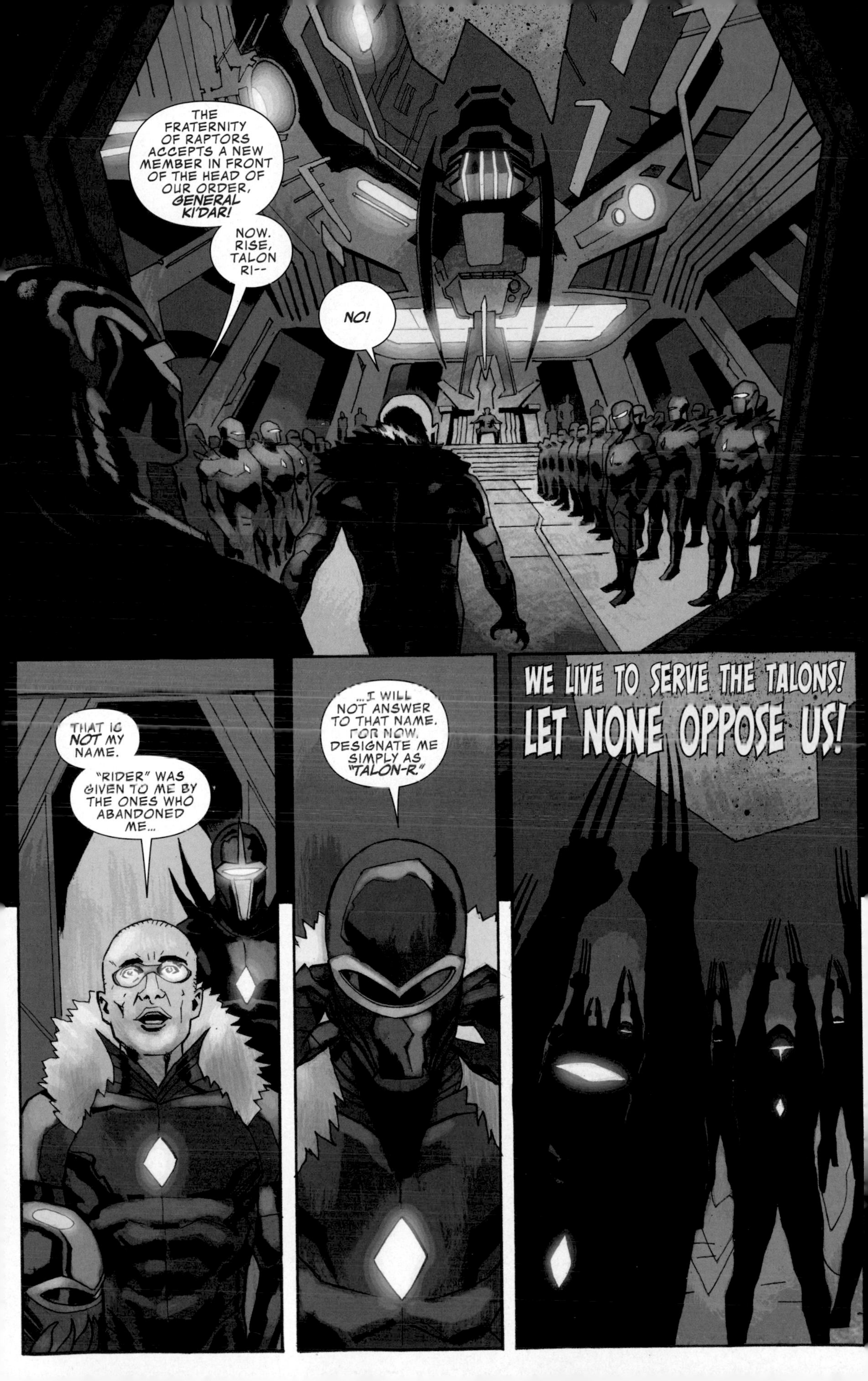
THE FRATERNITY OF RAPTORS ACCEPTS A NEW MEMBER IN FRONT OF THE HEAD OF OUR ORDER, GENERAL KI'DAR!
NOW. RISE, TALON RI--
NO!
THAT IS NOT MY NAME.
"RIDER" WAS GIVEN TO ME BY THE ONES WHO ABANDONED ME...
...I WILL NOT ANSWER TO THAT NAME. FOR NOW. DESIGNATE ME SIMPLY AS "TALON-R."
WE LIVE TO SERVE THE TALONS!
LET NONE OPPOSE US!

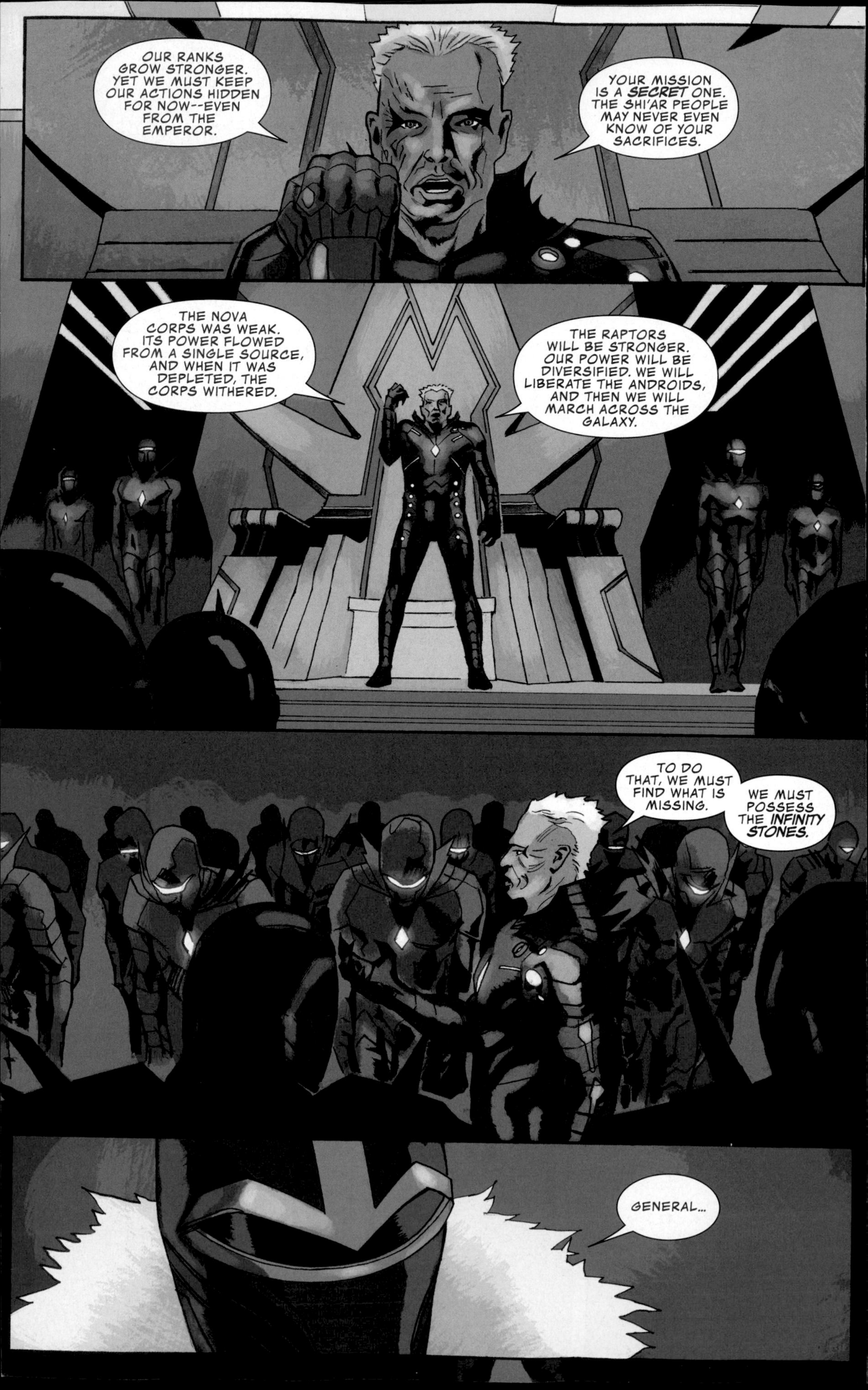
OUR RANKS GROW STRONGER. YET WE MUST KEEP OUR ACTIONS HIDDEN FOR NOW--EVEN FROM THE EMPEROR.
YOUR MISSION IS A SECRET ONE. THE SHI'AR PEOPLE MAY NEVER EVEN KNOW OF YOUR SACRIFICES.
THE NOVA CORPS WAS WEAK. ITS POWER FLOWED FROM A SINGLE SOURCE, AND WHEN IT WAS DEPLETED, THE CORPS WITHERED.
THE RAPTORS WILL BE STRONGER. OUR POWER WILL BE DIVERSIFIED. WE WILL LIBERATE THE ANDROIDS, AND THEN WE WILL MARCH ACROSS THE GALAXY.
TO DO THAT, WE MUST FIND WHAT IS MISSING.
WE MUST POSSESS THE INFINITY STONES.
GENERAL...

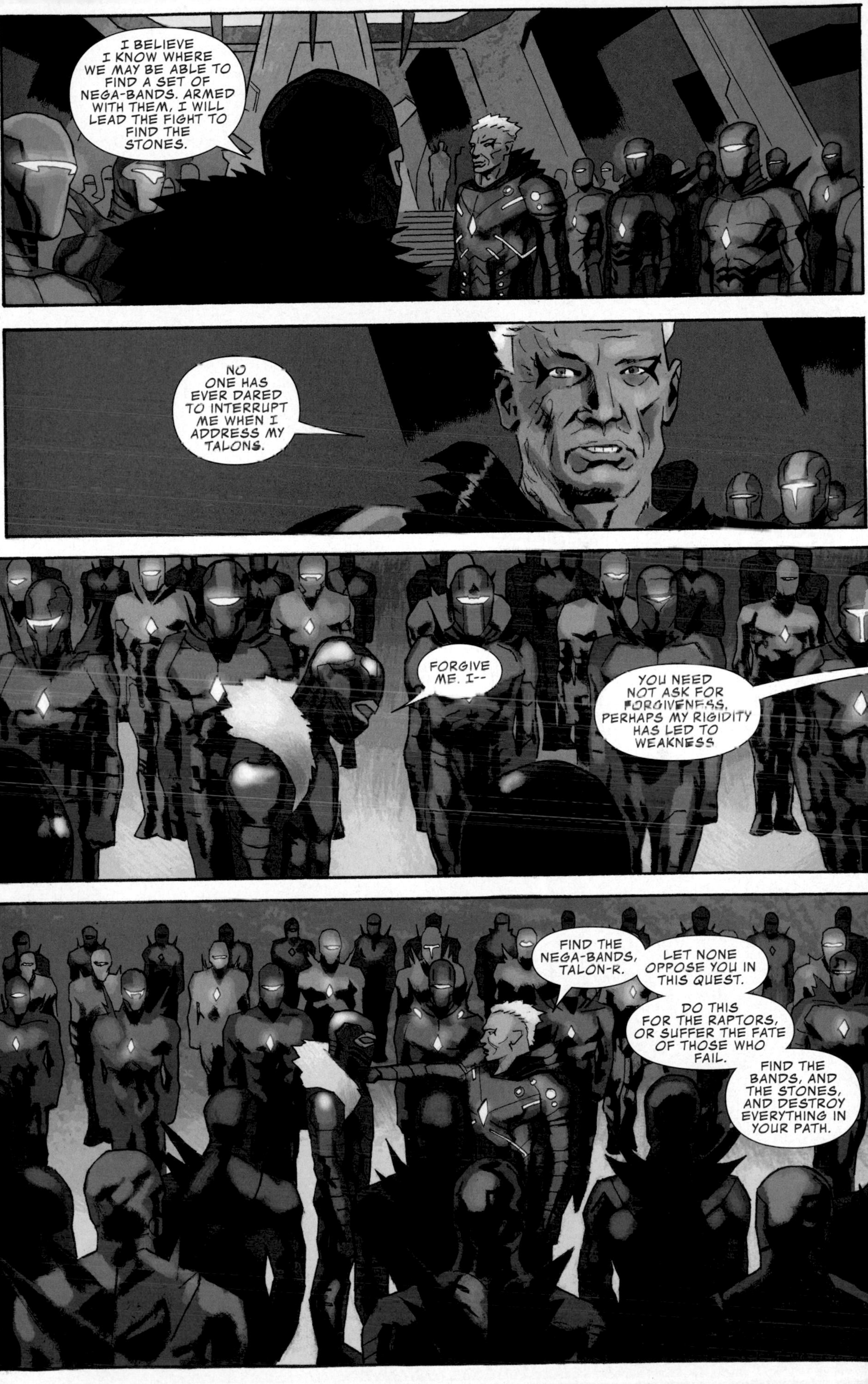
I BELIEVE I KNOW WHERE WE MAY BE ABLE TO FIND A SET OF NEGA-BANDS. ARMED WITH THEM, I WILL LEAD THE FIGHT TO FIND THE STONES.
NO ONE HAS EVER DARED TO INTERRUPT ME WHEN I ADDRESS MY TALONS.
FORGIVE ME. I--
YOU NEED NOT ASK FOR FORGIVENESS. PERHAPS MY RIGIDITY HAS LED TO WEAKNESS
FIND THE NEGA-BANDS, TALON-R.
LET NONE OPPOSE YOU IN THIS QUEST.
DO THIS FOR THE RAPTORS, OR SUFFER THE FATE OF THOSE WHO FAIL.
FIND THE BANDS, AND THE STONES, AND DESTROY EVERYTHING IN YOUR PATH.

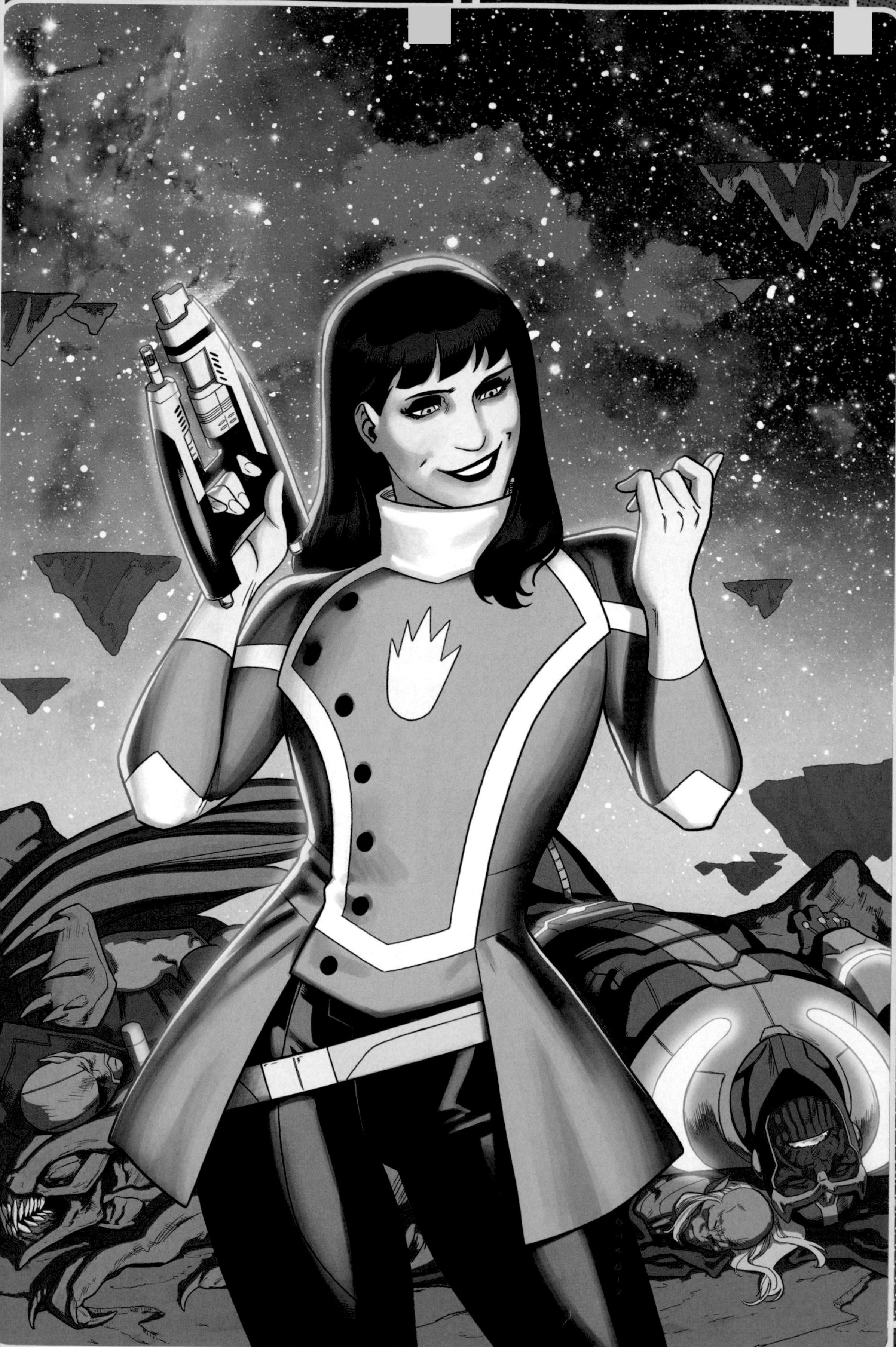

#3 MARY JANE VARIANT BY KRIS ANKA

12

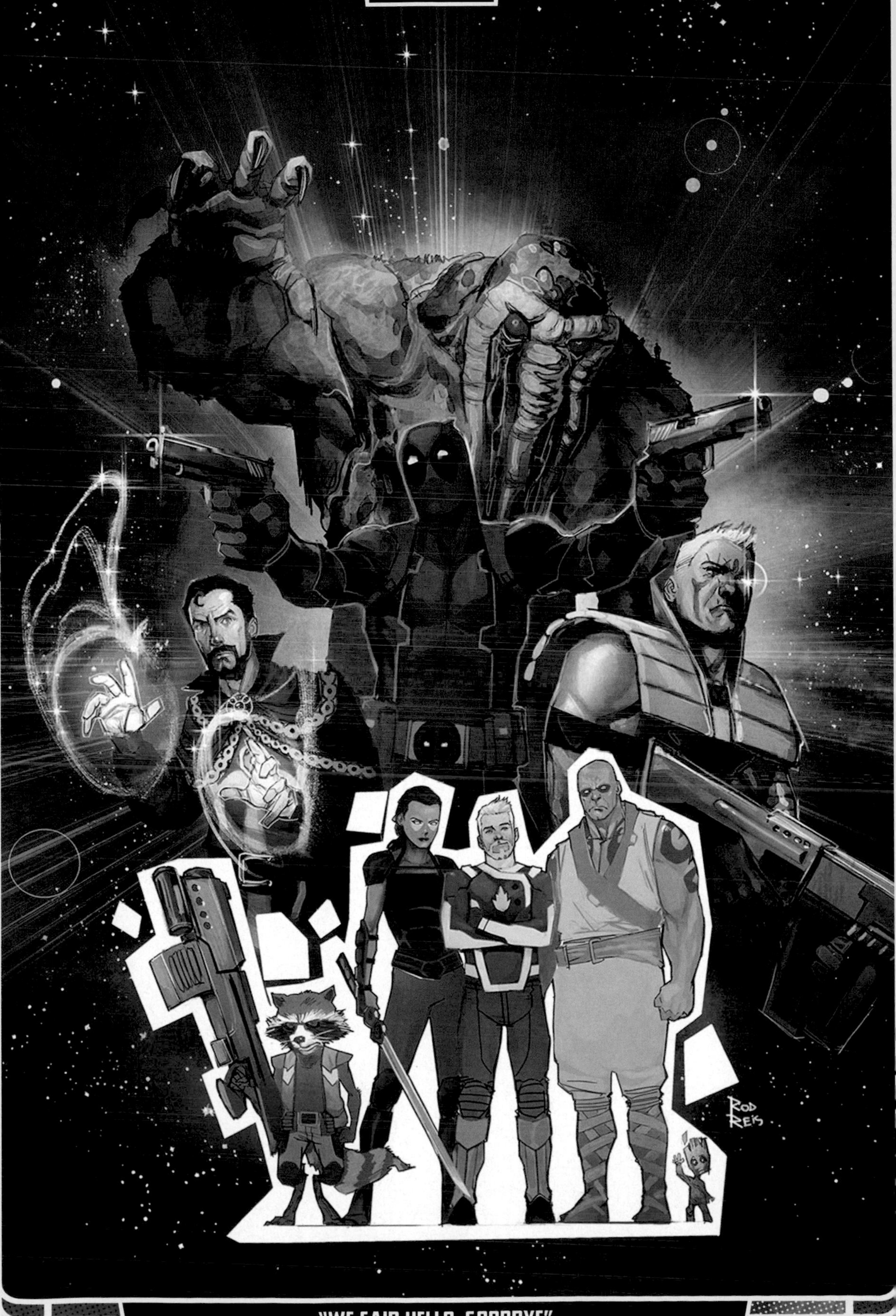
ROD REIS

"WE SAID HELLO, GOODBYE"

TWO ELDERS OF THE UNIVERSE HAVE CHARGED THE GANG WITH A MISSION
WORTHY OF THE GUARDIANS OF THE GALAXY: FIND AND PROTECT THE SIX INFINITY
STONES, WHICH HAVE BEEN MISSING SINCE, ACCORDING TO THE GRANDMASTER,
THE ENTIRE UNIVERSE CHANGED INDISCERNIBLY.

THE STONES' ABSENCE CORRESPONDS WITH SOME BAD LUCK - PART OF GAMORA
IS TRAPPED IN THE SOUL STONE AND THE GARDENER (WHO, ALONG WITH OTHER
ELDERS, IS MISSING) HAS SOMETHING TO DO WITH GROOT'S UNUSUALLY SMALL
STATURE. SO, OKAY, THERE ARE SOME SELF-SERVING MOTIVATIONS, BUT THE
SEARCH IS STILL A TOTALLY NOBLE QUEST, WHICH MAY BE FRAUGHT WITH DANGER!

OH, AND NO ONE KNOWS IT YET, BUT LOKI IS THE ONE WHO DROVE THE GARDENER
INSANE DURING HIS OWN SEARCH FOR THE STONES...

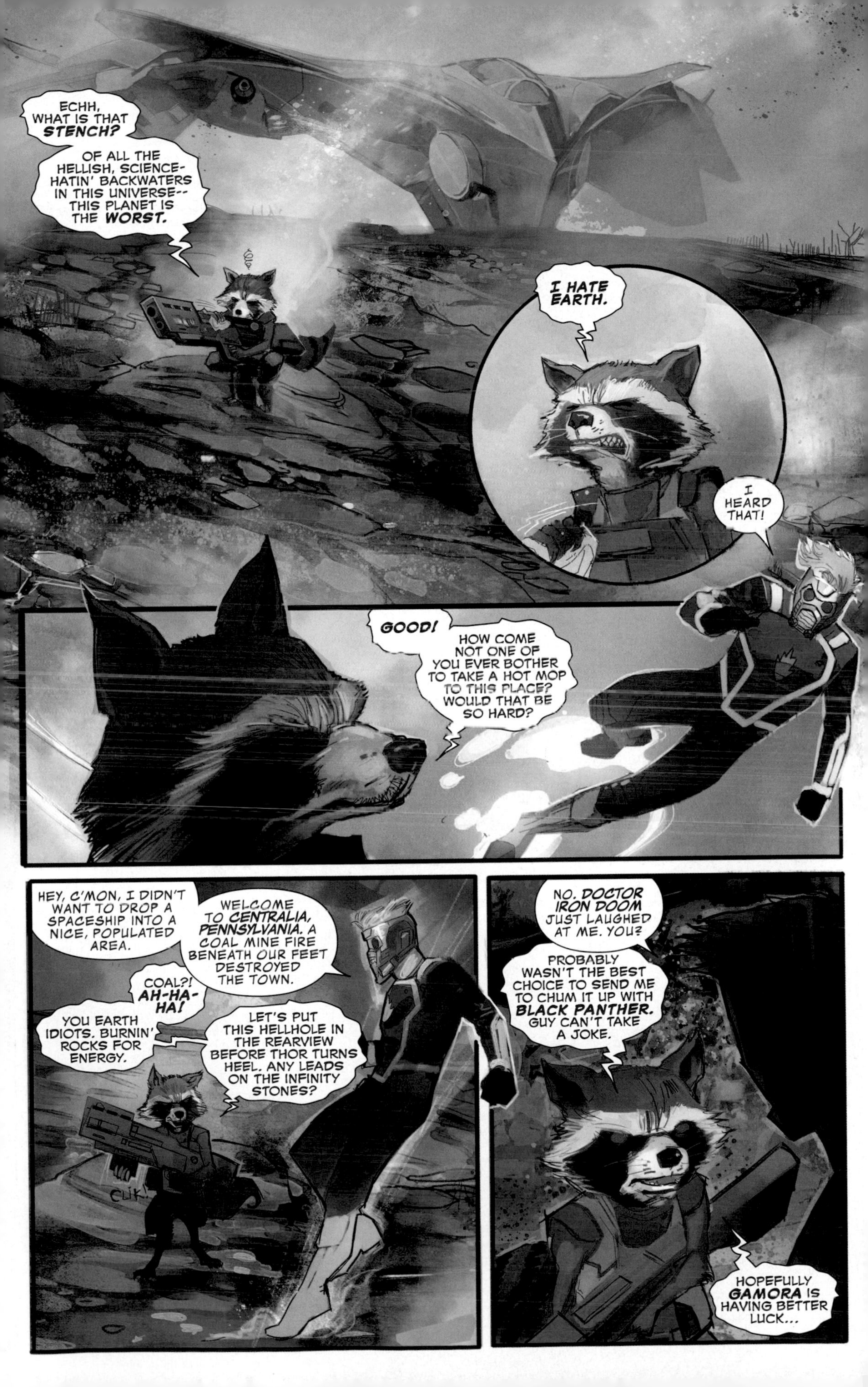
ECHH, WHAT IS THAT STENCH?
OF ALL THE HELLISH, SCIENCE-HATIN' BACKWATERS IN THIS UNIVERSE--THIS PLANET IS THE WORST.
I HATE EARTH.
I HEARD THAT!
GOOD!
HOW COME NOT ONE OF YOU EVER BOTHER TO TAKE A HOT MOP TO THIS PLACE? WOULD THAT BE SO HARD?
HEY, C'MON, I DIDN'T WANT TO DROP A SPACESHIP INTO A NICE, POPULATED AREA.
WELCOME TO CENTRALIA, PENNSYLVANIA. A COAL MINE FIRE BENEATH OUR FEET DESTROYED THE TOWN.
COAL?! AH-HA-HA!
YOU EARTH IDIOTS. BURNIN' ROCKS FOR ENERGY.
LET'S PUT THIS HELLHOLE IN THE REARVIEW BEFORE THOR TURNS HEEL. ANY LEADS ON THE INFINITY STONES?
CLIK!
NO. DOCTOR IRON DOOM JUST LAUGHED AT ME. YOU?
PROBABLY WASN'T THE BEST CHOICE TO SEND ME TO CHUM IT UP WITH BLACK PANTHER. GUY CAN'T TAKE A JOKE.
HOPEFULLY GAMORA IS HAVING BETTER LUCK...

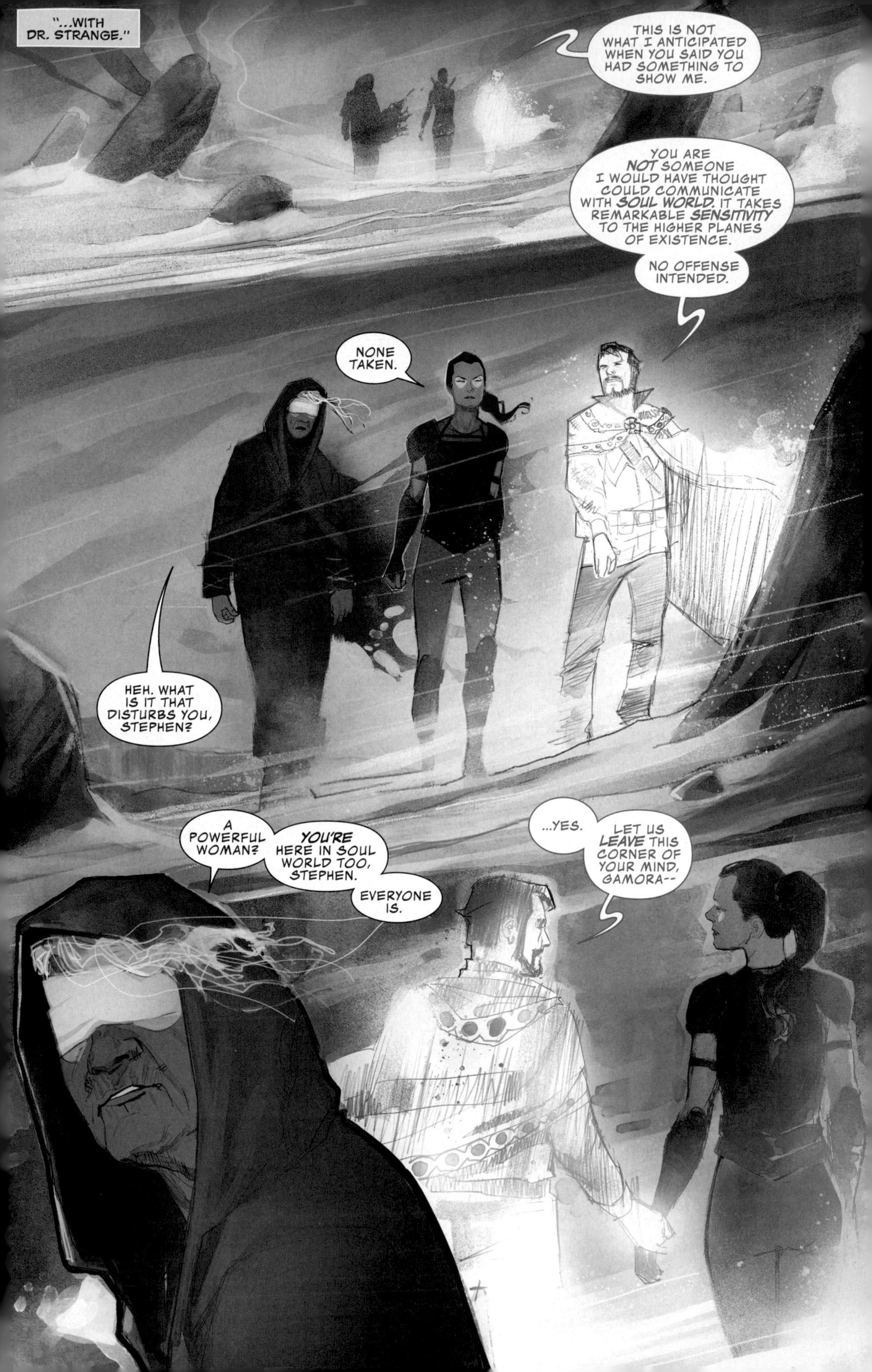
"...WITH DR. STRANGE."
THIS IS NOT WHAT I ANTICIPATED WHEN YOU SAID YOU HAD SOMETHING TO SHOW ME.
YOU ARE NOT SOMEONE I WOULD HAVE THOUGHT COULD COMMUNICATE WITH SOUL WORLD. IT TAKES REMARKABLE SENSITIVITY TO THE HIGHER PLANES OF EXISTENCE.
NO OFFENSE INTENDED.
NONE TAKEN.
HEH. WHAT IS IT THAT DISTURBS YOU, STEPHEN?
A POWERFUL WOMAN?
YOU'RE HERE IN SOUL WORLD TOO, STEPHEN.
EVERYONE IS.
...YES.
LET US LEAVE THIS CORNER OF YOUR MIND, GAMORA--

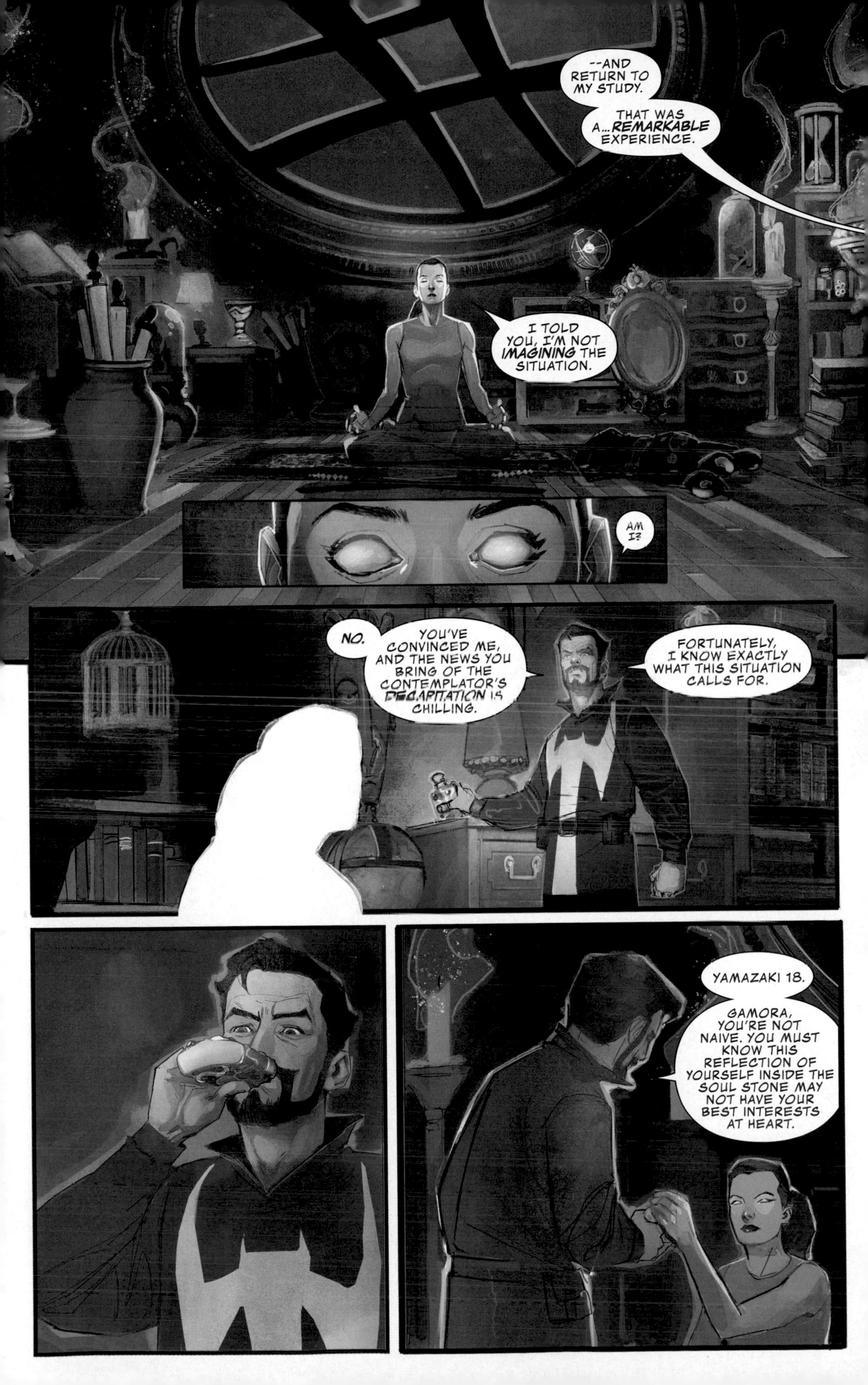
--AND RETURN TO MY STUDY.
THAT WAS A...REMARKABLE EXPERIENCE.
I TOLD YOU, I'M NOT IMAGINING THE SITUATION.
AM I?
NO.
YOU'VE CONVINCED ME, AND THE NEWS YOU BRING OF THE CONTEMPLATOR'S DECAPITATION IS CHILLING.
FORTUNATELY, I KNOW EXACTLY WHAT THIS SITUATION CALLS FOR.
YAMAZAKI 18.
GAMORA, YOU'RE NOT NAIVE. YOU MUST KNOW THIS REFLECTION OF YOURSELF INSIDE THE SOUL STONE MAY NOT HAVE YOUR BEST INTERESTS AT HEART.

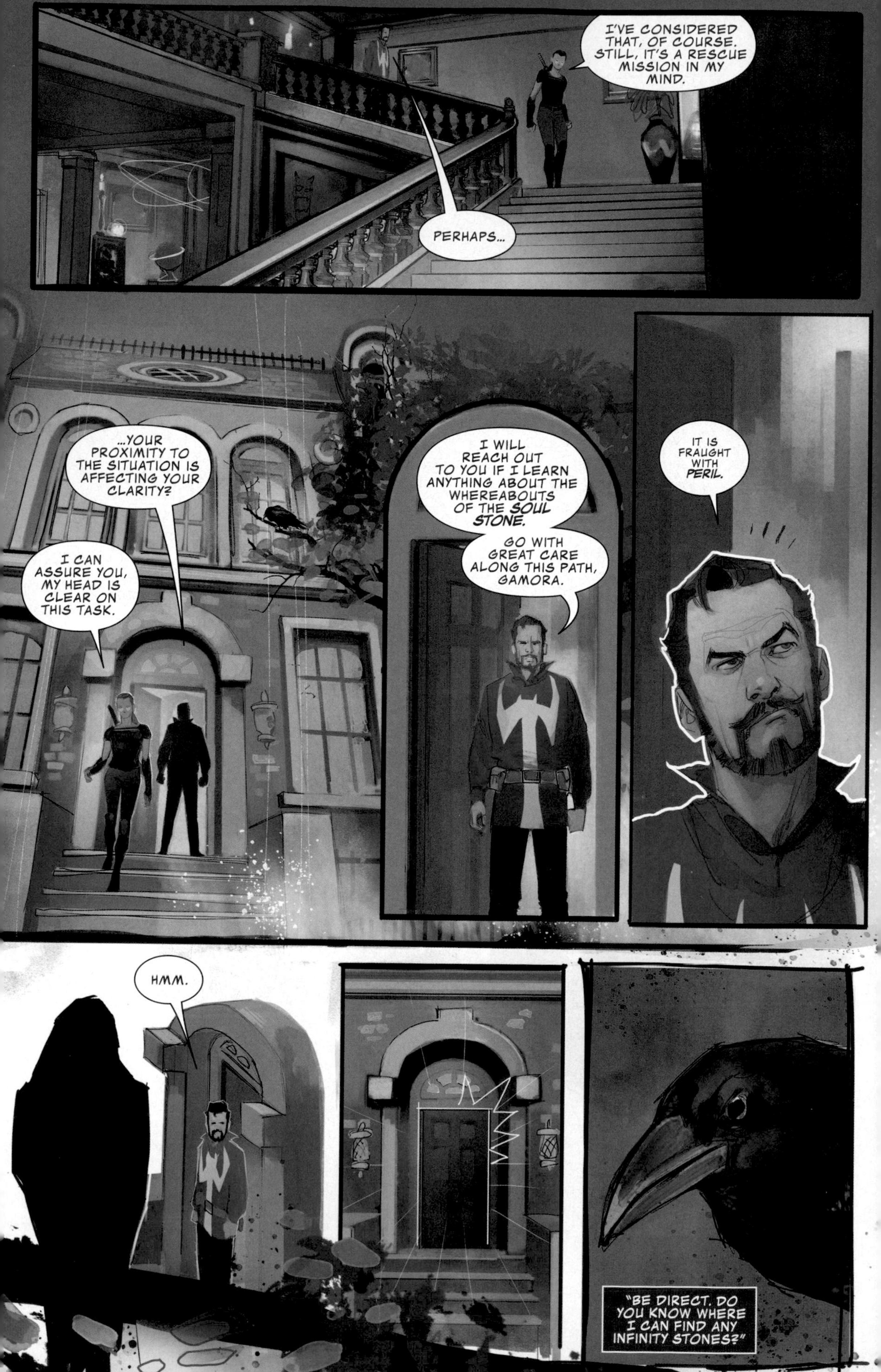
I'VE CONSIDERED THAT, OF COURSE. STILL, IT'S A RESCUE MISSION IN MY MIND.
PERHAPS...
...YOUR PROXIMITY TO THE SITUATION IS AFFECTING YOUR CLARITY?
I CAN ASSURE YOU, MY HEAD IS CLEAR ON THIS TASK.
I WILL REACH OUT TO YOU IF I LEARN ANYTHING ABOUT THE WHEREABOUTS OF THE SOUL STONE.
GO WITH GREAT CARE ALONG THIS PATH, GAMORA.
IT IS FRAUGHT WITH PERIL.
HMM.
"BE DIRECT. DO YOU KNOW WHERE I CAN FIND ANY INFINITY STONES?"

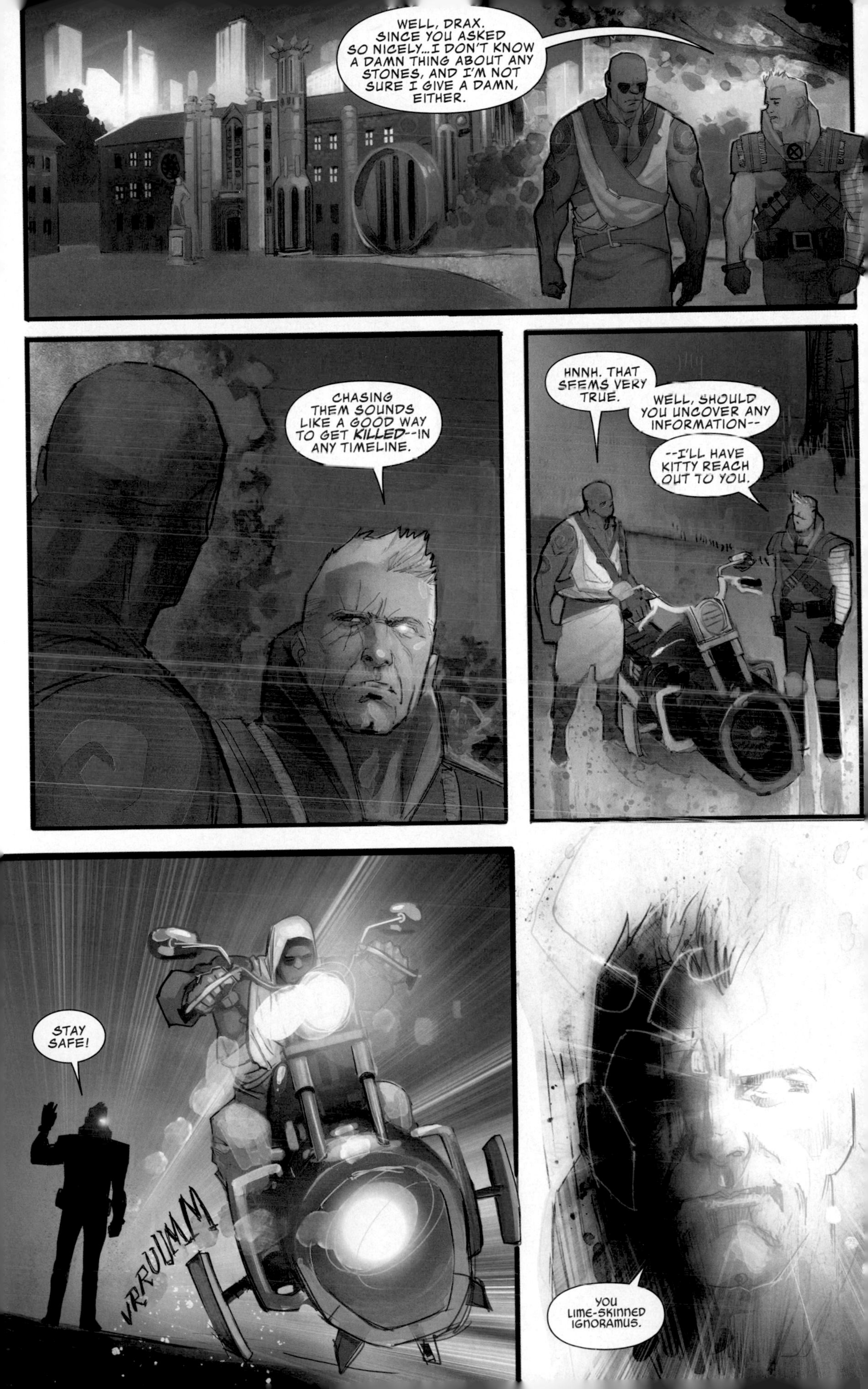
WELL, DRAX. SINCE YOU ASKED SO NICELY...I DON'T KNOW A DAMN THING ABOUT ANY STONES, AND I'M NOT SURE I GIVE A DAMN, EITHER.
CHASING THEM SOUNDS LIKE A GOOD WAY TO GET KILLED--IN ANY TIMELINE.
HNNH. THAT SEEMS VERY TRUE.
WELL, SHOULD YOU UNCOVER ANY INFORMATION--
--I'LL HAVE KITTY REACH OUT TO YOU.
STAY SAFE!
VRRUUMM
YOU LIME-SKINNED IGNORAMUS.

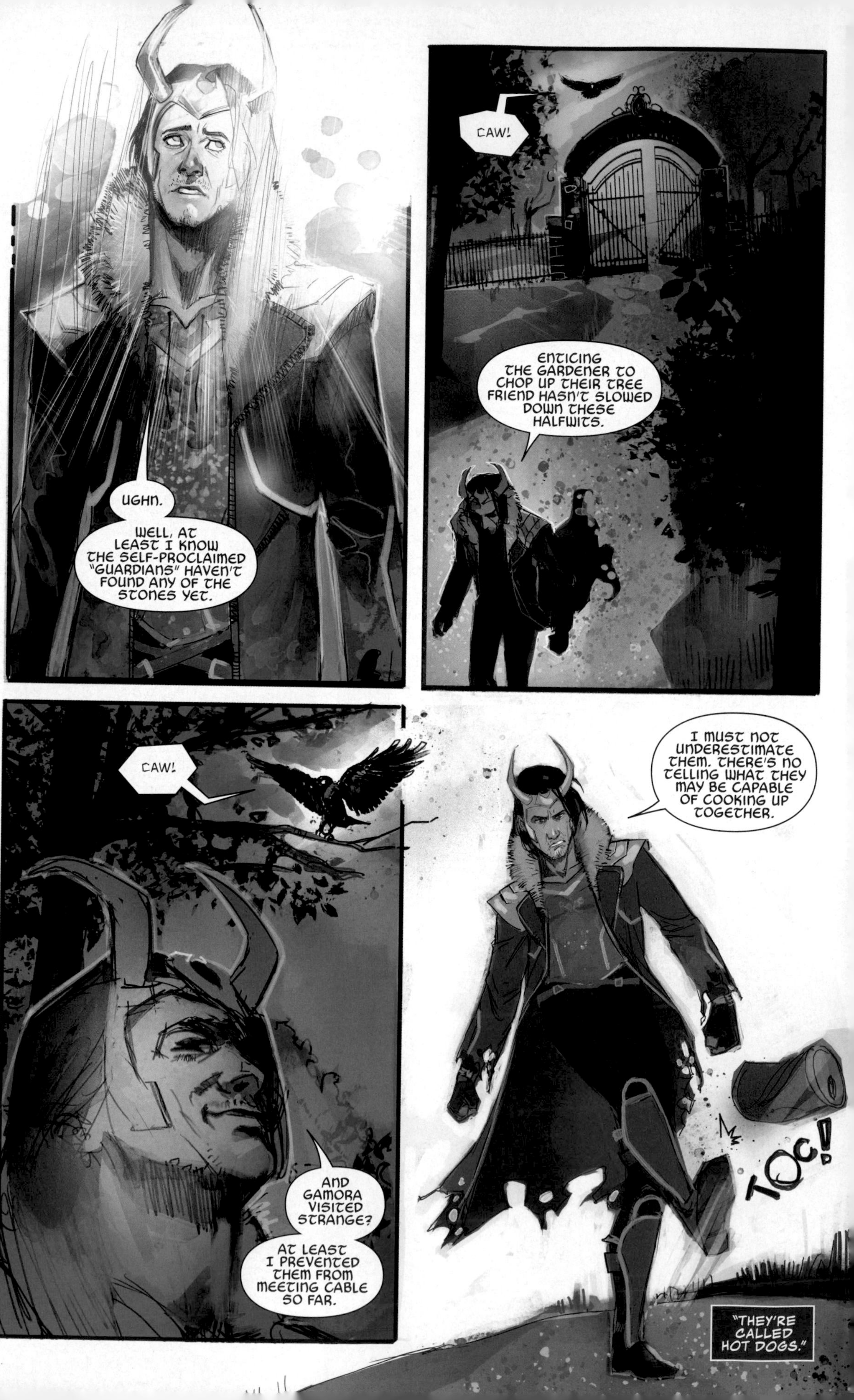
UGHN.
WELL, AT LEAST I KNOW THE SELF-PROCLAIMED "GUARDIANS" HAVEN'T FOUND ANY OF THE STONES YET.
CAW!
ENTICING THE GARDENER TO CHOP UP THEIR TREE FRIEND HASN'T SLOWED DOWN THESE HALFWITS.
CAW!
AND GAMORA VISITED STRANGE?
AT LEAST I PREVENTED THEM FROM MEETING CABLE SO FAR.
I MUST NOT UNDERESTIMATE THEM. THERE'S NO TELLING WHAT THEY MAY BE CAPABLE OF COOKING UP TOGETHER.
TOC!
"THEY'RE CALLED HOT DOGS."

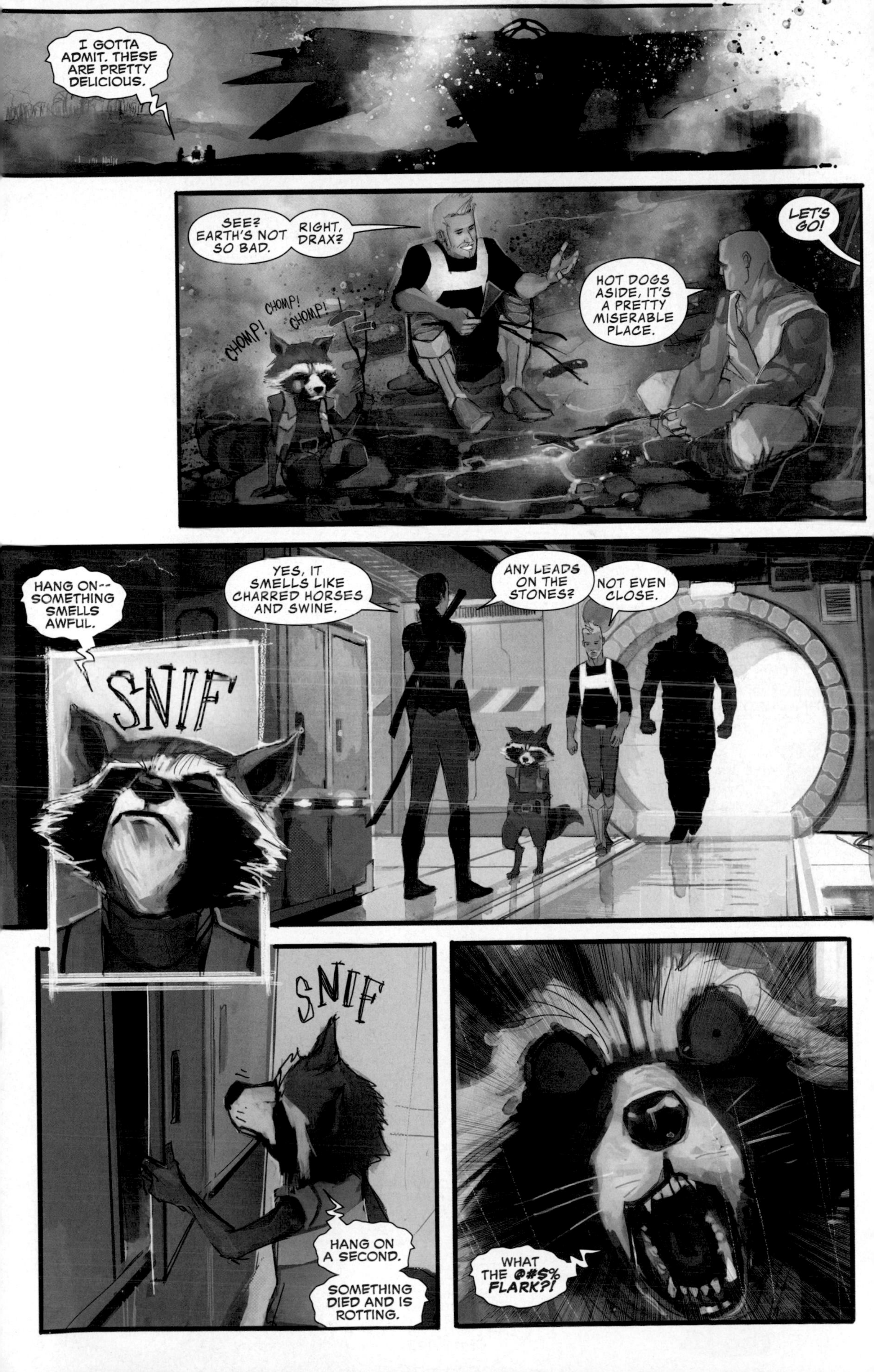

I GOTTA ADMIT. THESE ARE PRETTY DELICIOUS.
SEE? EARTH'S NOT SO BAD.
RIGHT, DRAX?
CHOMP! CHOMP! CHOMP!
HOT DOGS ASIDE, IT'S A PRETTY MISERABLE PLACE.
LET'S GO!
HANG ON-- SOMETHING SMELLS AWFUL.
SNIF
YES, IT SMELLS LIKE CHARRED HORSES AND SWINE.
ANY LEADS ON THE STONES?
NOT EVEN CLOSE.
SNIF
HANG ON A SECOND.
SOMETHING DIED AND IS ROTTING.
WHAT THE @#$% FLARK?!

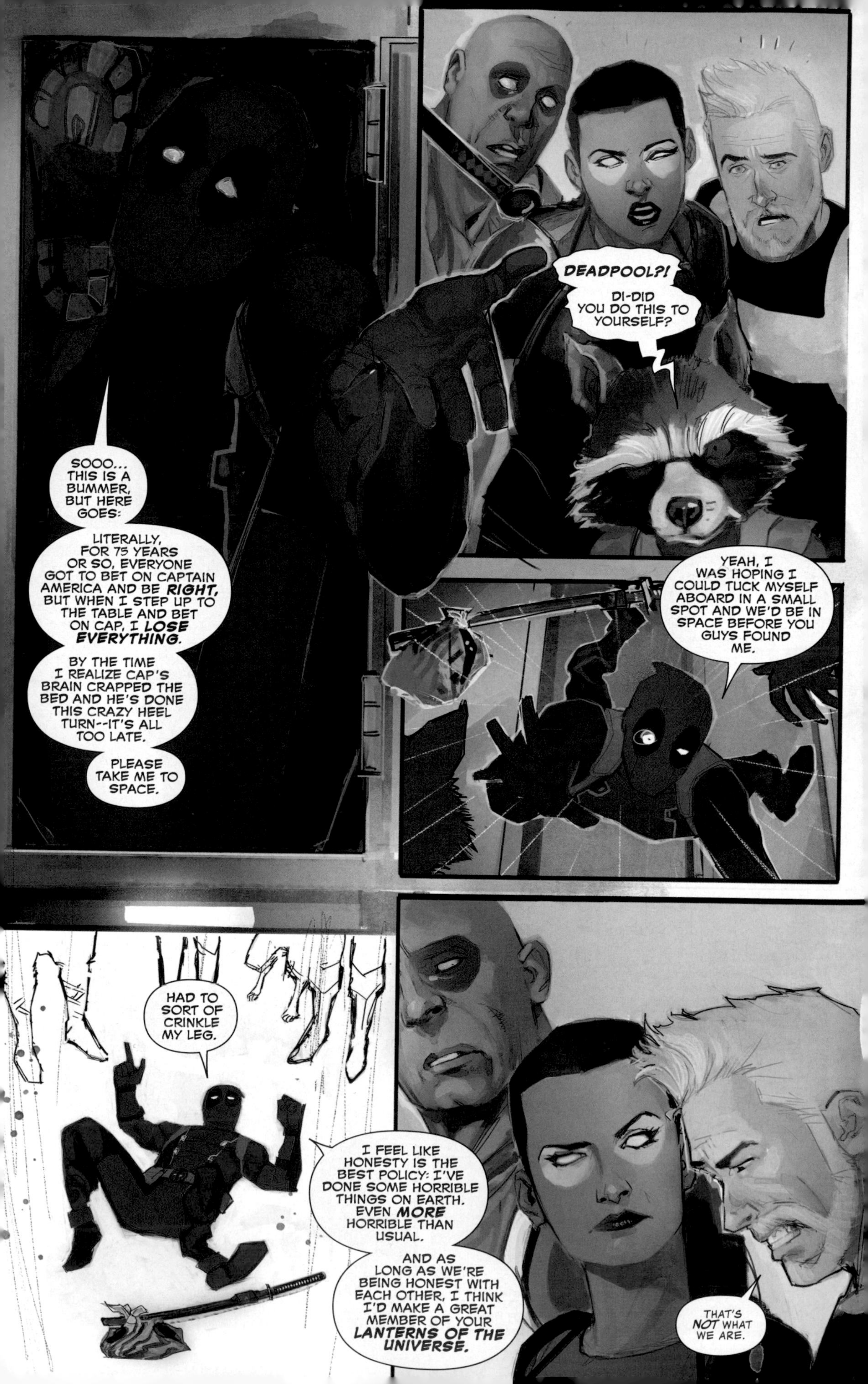
DEADPOOL?!
DI-DID YOU DO THIS TO YOURSELF?
SOOO... THIS IS A BUMMER, BUT HERE GOES:
LITERALLY, FOR 75 YEARS OR SO, EVERYONE GOT TO BET ON CAPTAIN AMERICA AND BE RIGHT, BUT WHEN I STEP UP TO THE TABLE AND BET ON CAP, I LOSE EVERYTHING.
BY THE TIME I REALIZE CAP'S BRAIN CRAPPED THE BED AND HE'S DONE THIS CRAZY HEEL TURN--IT'S ALL TOO LATE.
PLEASE TAKE ME TO SPACE.
YEAH, I WAS HOPING I COULD TUCK MYSELF ABOARD IN A SMALL SPOT AND WE'D BE IN SPACE BEFORE YOU GUYS FOUND ME.
HAD TO SORT OF CRINKLE MY LEG.
I FEEL LIKE HONESTY IS THE BEST POLICY: I'VE DONE SOME HORRIBLE THINGS ON EARTH. EVEN MORE HORRIBLE THAN USUAL.
AND AS LONG AS WE'RE BEING HONEST WITH EACH OTHER, I THINK I'D MAKE A GREAT MEMBER OF YOUR LANTERNS OF THE UNIVERSE.
THAT'S NOT WHAT WE ARE.

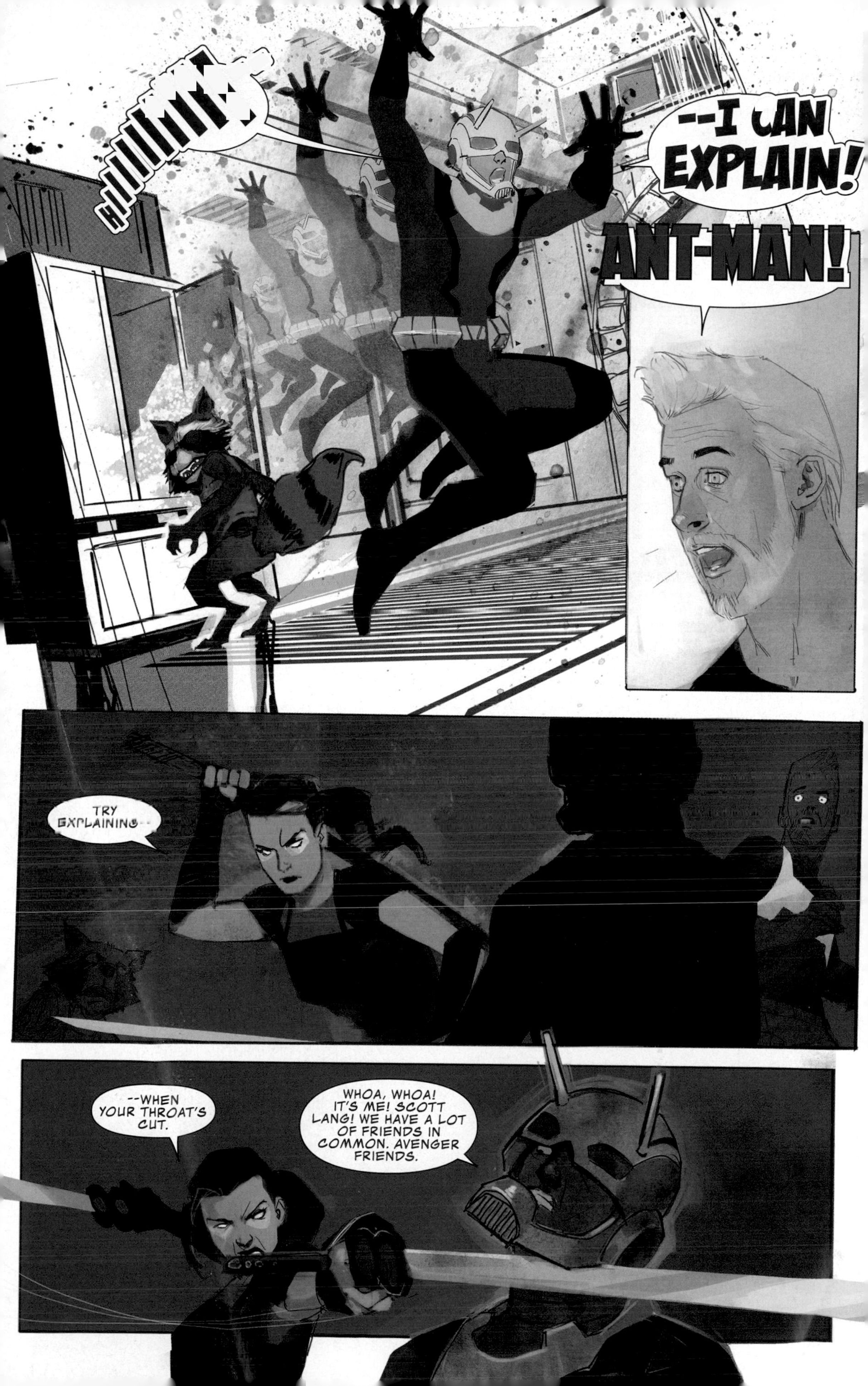
--I CAN EXPLAIN!
ANT-MAN!
TRY EXPLAINING--
--WHEN YOUR THROAT'S CUT.
WHOA, WHOA! IT'S ME! SCOTT LANG! WE HAVE A LOT OF FRIENDS IN COMMON. AVENGER FRIENDS.

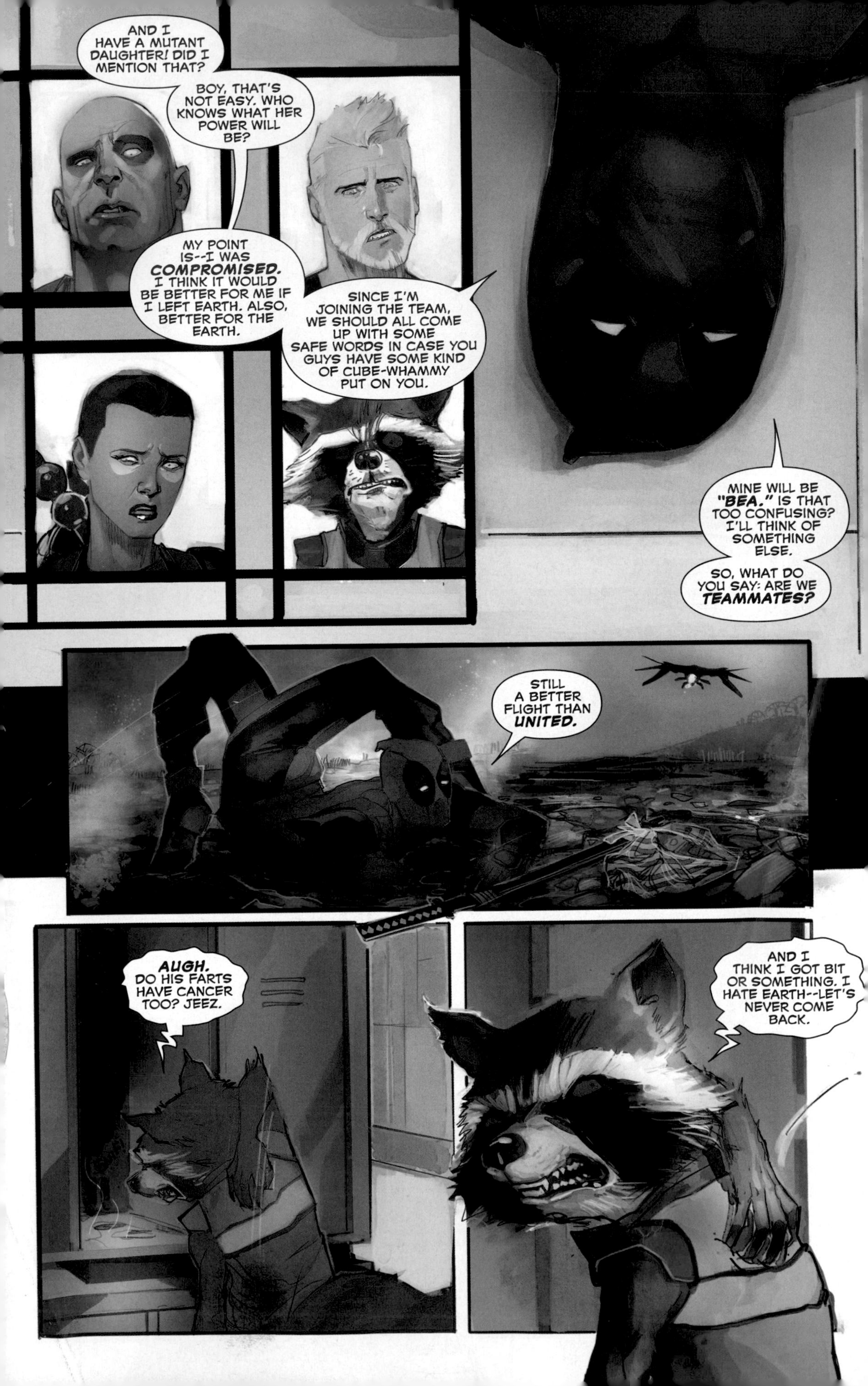
AND I HAVE A MUTANT DAUGHTER! DID I MENTION THAT?
BOY, THAT'S NOT EASY. WHO KNOWS WHAT HER POWER WILL BE?
MY POINT IS--I WAS **COMPROMISED.** I THINK IT WOULD BE BETTER FOR ME IF I LEFT EARTH. ALSO, BETTER FOR THE EARTH.
SINCE I'M JOINING THE TEAM, WE SHOULD ALL COME UP WITH SOME SAFE WORDS IN CASE YOU GUYS HAVE SOME KIND OF CUBE-WHAMMY PUT ON YOU.
MINE WILL BE **"BEA."** IS THAT TOO CONFUSING? I'LL THINK OF SOMETHING ELSE.
SO, WHAT DO YOU SAY: ARE WE ***TEAMMATES?***
STILL A BETTER FLIGHT THAN ***UNITED.***
AUGH. DO HIS FARTS HAVE CANCER TOO? JEEZ.
AND I THINK I GOT BIT OR SOMETHING. I HATE EARTH--LET'S NEVER COME BACK.

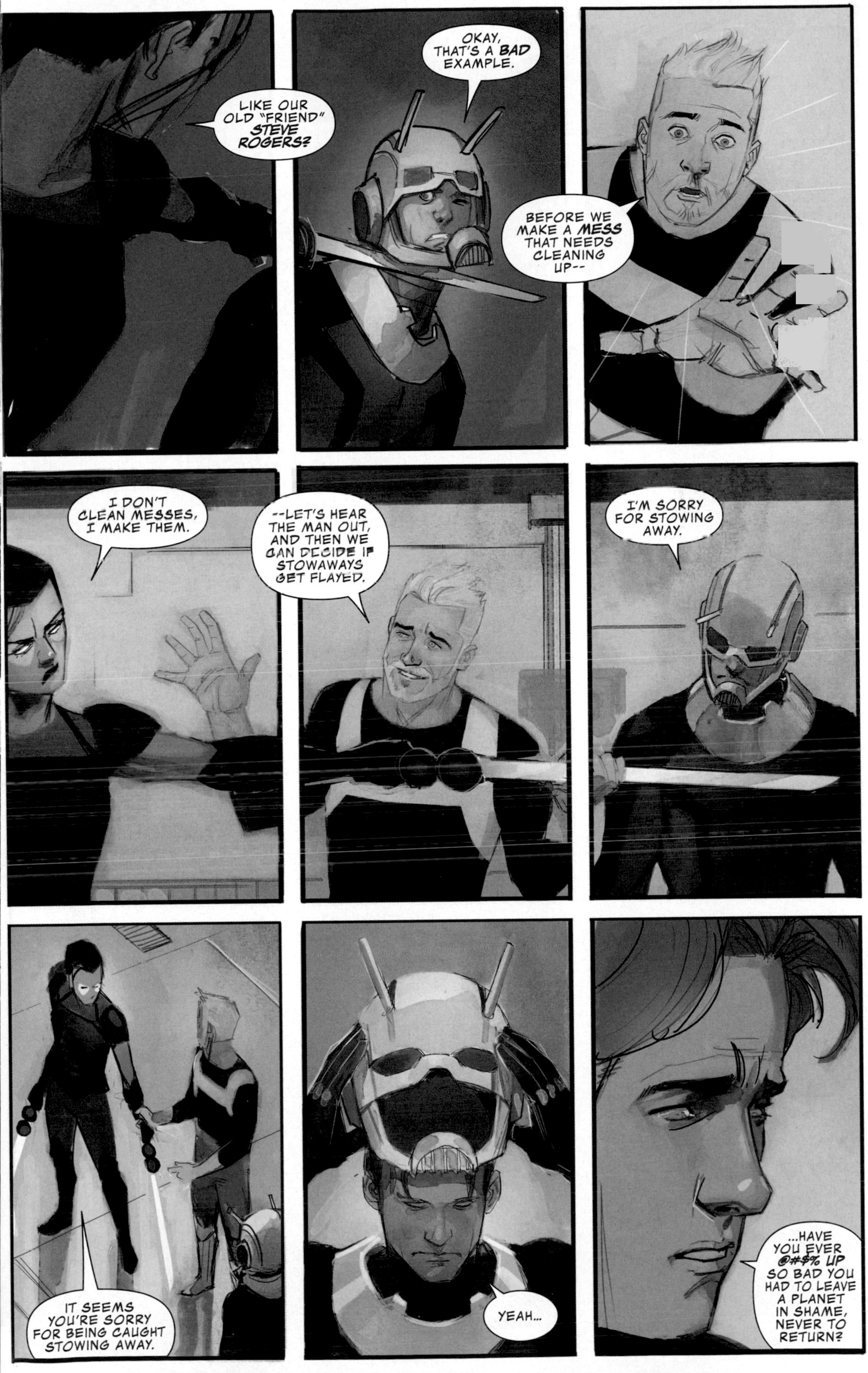
LIKE OUR OLD "FRIEND" STEVE ROGERS?
OKAY, THAT'S A BAD EXAMPLE.
BEFORE WE MAKE A MESS THAT NEEDS CLEANING UP--
I DON'T CLEAN MESSES, I MAKE THEM.
--LET'S HEAR THE MAN OUT, AND THEN WE CAN DECIDE IF STOWAWAYS GET FLAYED.
I'M SORRY FOR STOWING AWAY.
IT SEEMS YOU'RE SORRY FOR BEING CAUGHT STOWING AWAY.
YEAH...
...HAVE YOU EVER @#$% UP SO BAD YOU HAD TO LEAVE A PLANET IN SHAME, NEVER TO RETURN?

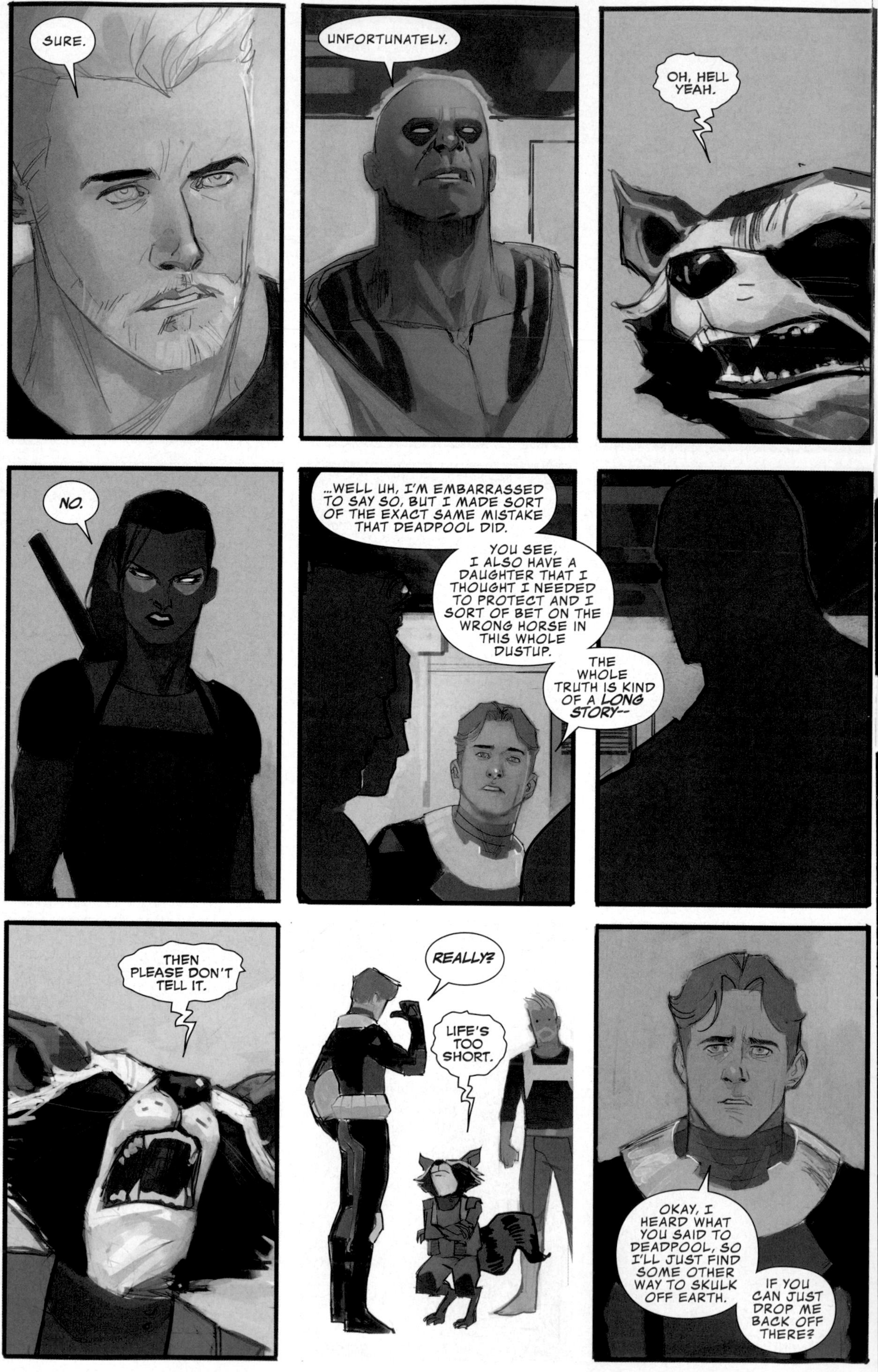
SURE.
UNFORTUNATELY.
OH, HELL YEAH.
NO.
...WELL UH, I'M EMBARRASSED TO SAY SO, BUT I MADE SORT OF THE EXACT SAME MISTAKE THAT DEADPOOL DID.
YOU SEE, I ALSO HAVE A DAUGHTER THAT I THOUGHT I NEEDED TO PROTECT AND I SORT OF BET ON THE WRONG HORSE IN THIS WHOLE DUSTUP.
THE WHOLE TRUTH IS KIND OF A LONG STORY--
THEN PLEASE DON'T TELL IT.
REALLY?
LIFE'S TOO SHORT.
OKAY, I HEARD WHAT YOU SAID TO DEADPOOL, SO I'LL JUST FIND SOME OTHER WAY TO SKULK OFF EARTH.
IF YOU CAN JUST DROP ME BACK OFF THERE?

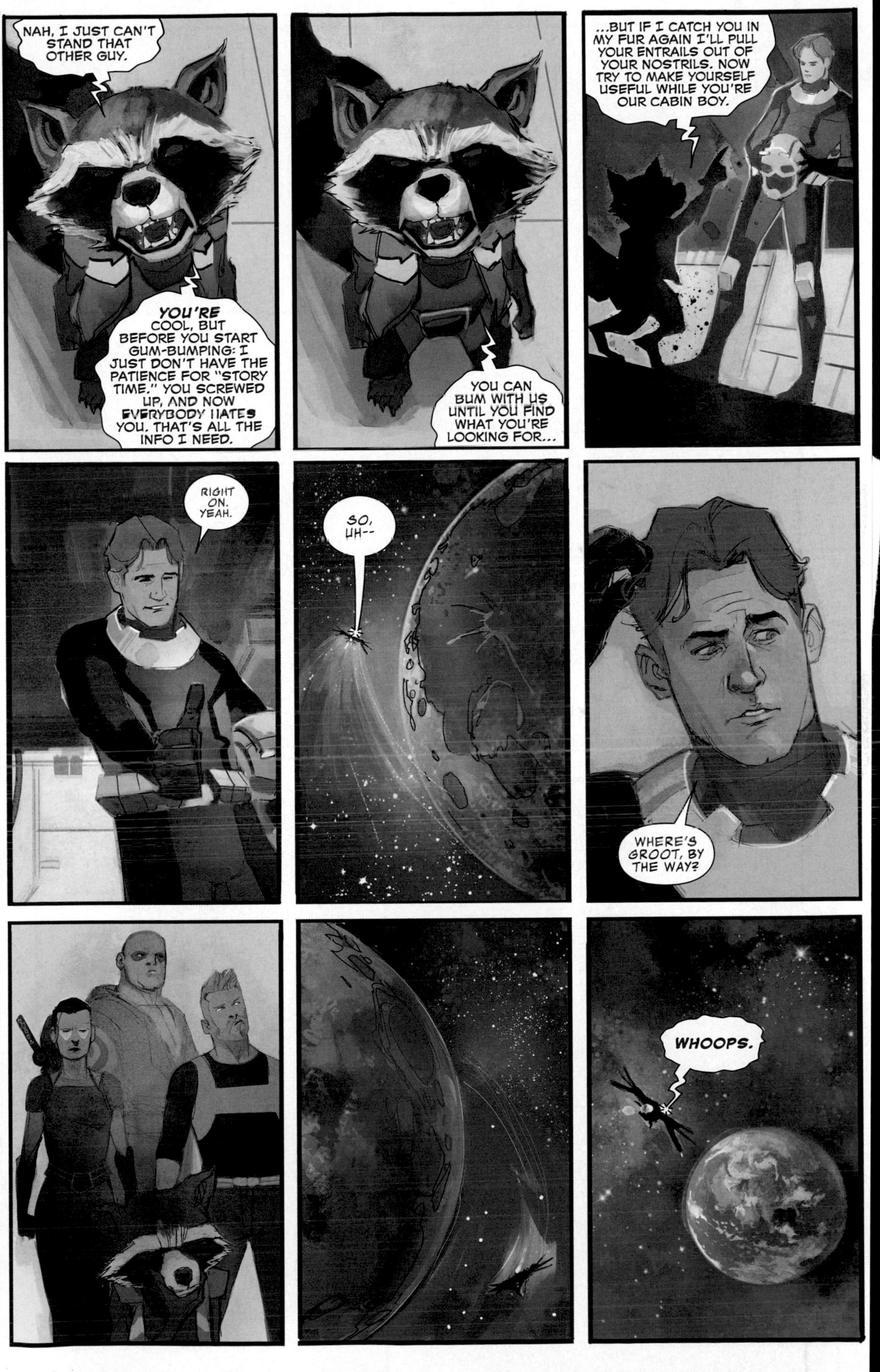
NAH, I JUST CAN'T STAND THAT OTHER GUY.
YOU'RE COOL, BUT BEFORE YOU START GUM-BUMPING: I JUST DON'T HAVE THE PATIENCE FOR "STORY TIME." YOU SCREWED UP, AND NOW EVERYBODY HATES YOU. THAT'S ALL THE INFO I NEED.
YOU CAN BUM WITH US UNTIL YOU FIND WHAT YOU'RE LOOKING FOR...
...BUT IF I CATCH YOU IN MY FUR AGAIN I'LL PULL YOUR ENTRAILS OUT OF YOUR NOSTRILS. NOW TRY TO MAKE YOURSELF USEFUL WHILE YOU'RE OUR CABIN BOY.
RIGHT ON. YEAH.
SO, UH--
WHERE'S GROOT, BY THE WAY?
WHOOPS.

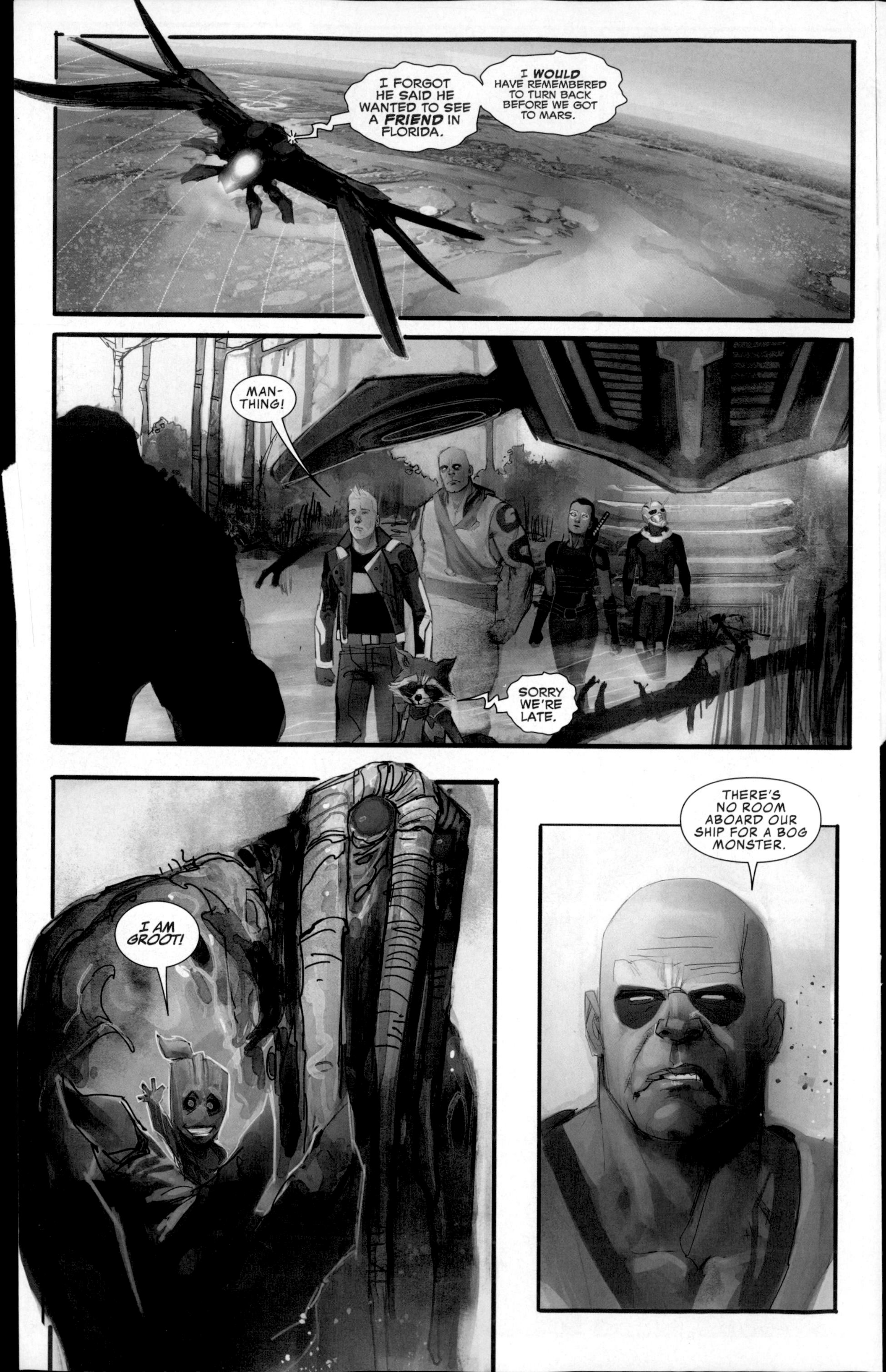
I FORGOT HE SAID HE WANTED TO SEE A FRIEND IN FLORIDA.
I WOULD HAVE REMEMBERED TO TURN BACK BEFORE WE GOT TO MARS.
MAN-THING!
SORRY WE'RE LATE.
I AM GROOT!
THERE'S NO ROOM ABOARD OUR SHIP FOR A BOG MONSTER.

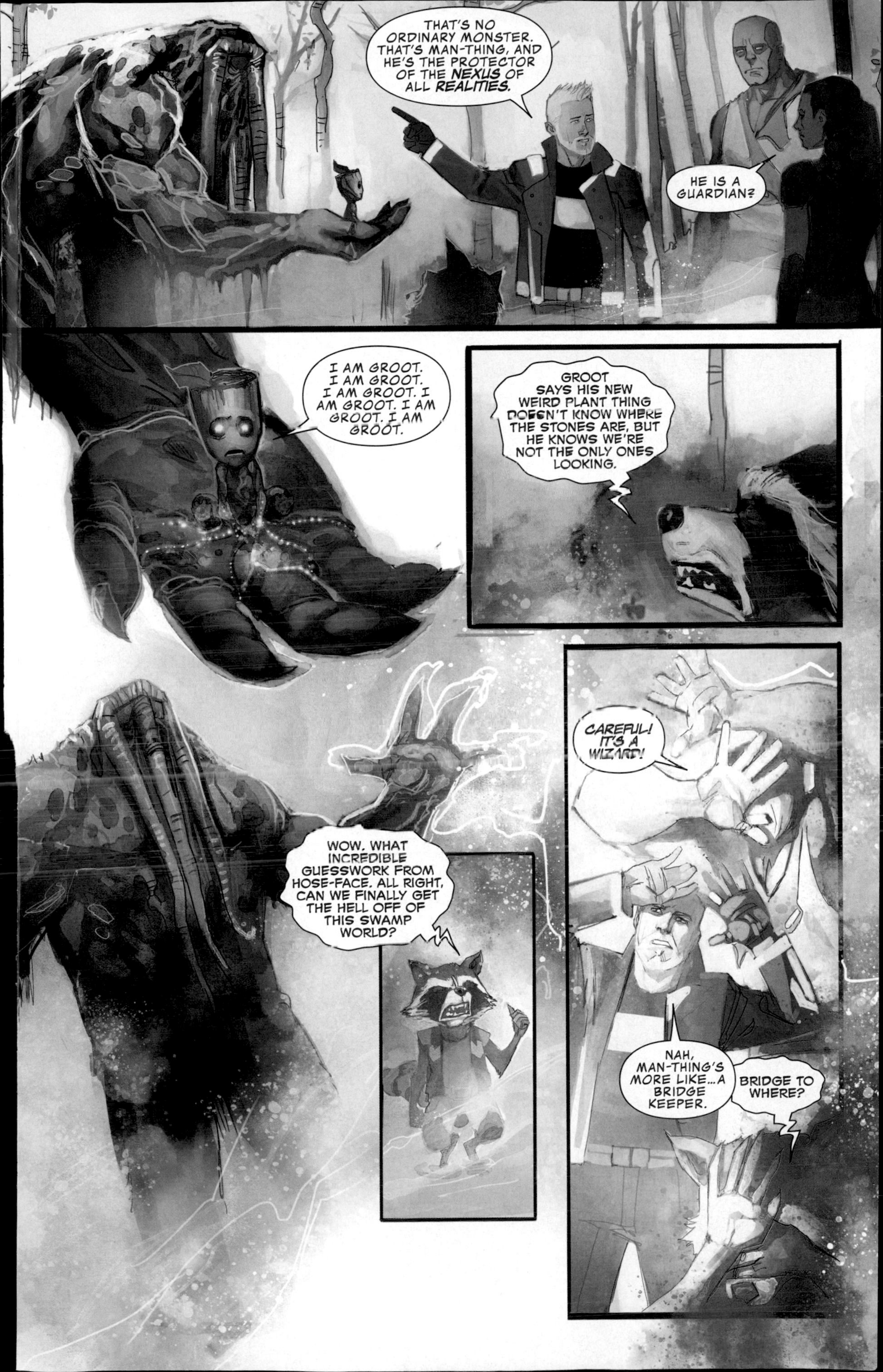
THAT'S NO ORDINARY MONSTER. THAT'S MAN-THING, AND HE'S THE PROTECTOR OF THE NEXUS OF ALL REALITIES.
HE IS A GUARDIAN?
I AM GROOT. I AM GROOT. I AM GROOT. I AM GROOT. I AM GROOT. I AM GROOT.
GROOT SAYS HIS NEW WEIRD PLANT THING DOESN'T KNOW WHERE THE STONES ARE, BUT HE KNOWS WE'RE NOT THE ONLY ONES LOOKING.
CAREFUL! IT'S A WIZARD!
WOW. WHAT INCREDIBLE GUESSWORK FROM HOSE-FACE. ALL RIGHT, CAN WE FINALLY GET THE HELL OFF OF THIS SWAMP WORLD?
NAH, MAN-THING'S MORE LIKE...A BRIDGE KEEPER.
BRIDGE TO WHERE?

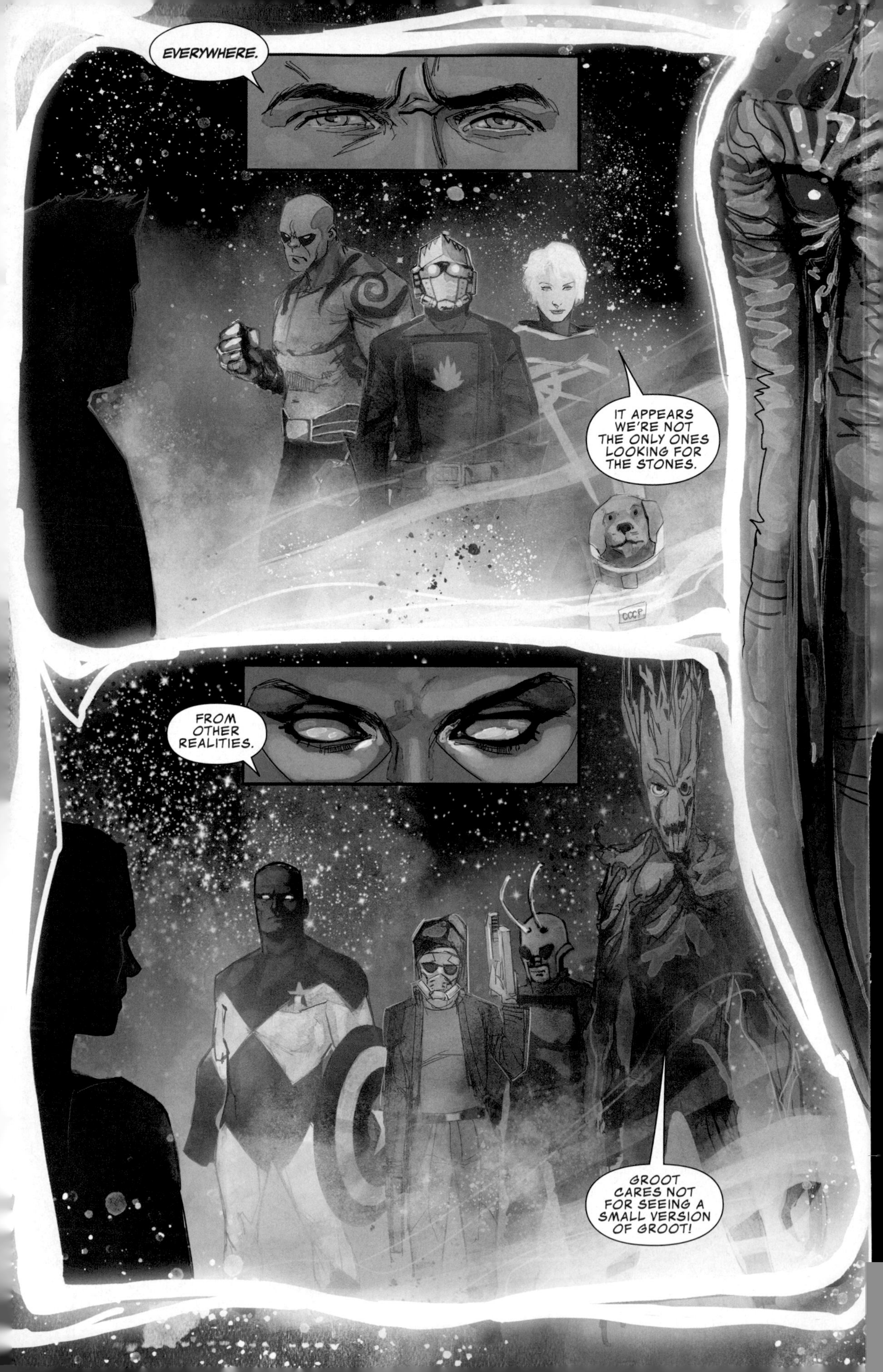
EVERYWHERE.
IT APPEARS WE'RE NOT THE ONLY ONES LOOKING FOR THE STONES.
CCCP
FROM OTHER REALITIES.
GROOT CARES NOT FOR SEEING A SMALL VERSION OF GROOT!

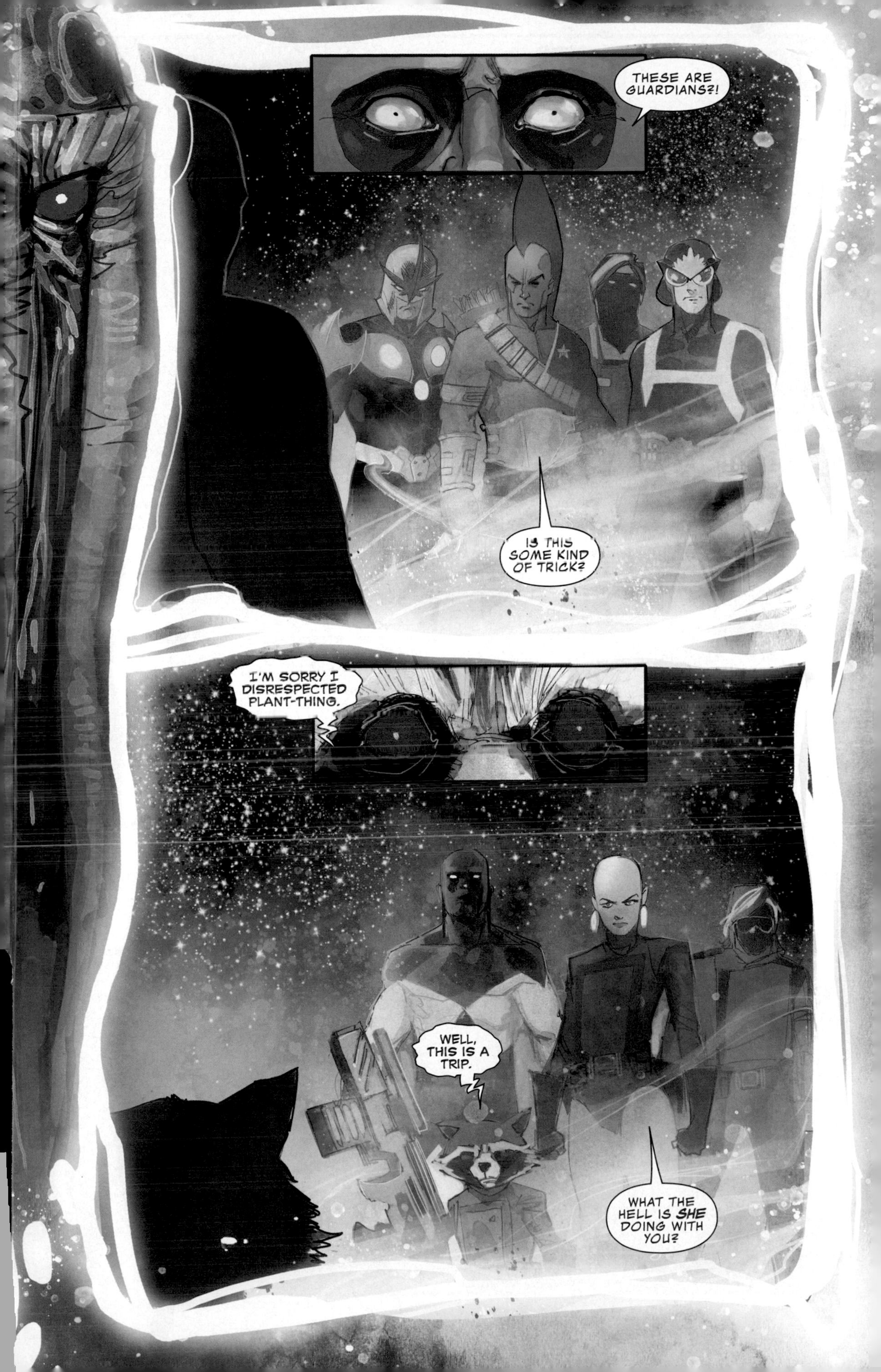
THESE ARE GUARDIANS?!
IS THIS SOME KIND OF TRICK?
I'M SORRY I DISRESPECTED PLANT-THING.
WELL, THIS IS A TRIP.
WHAT THE HELL IS SHE DOING WITH YOU?

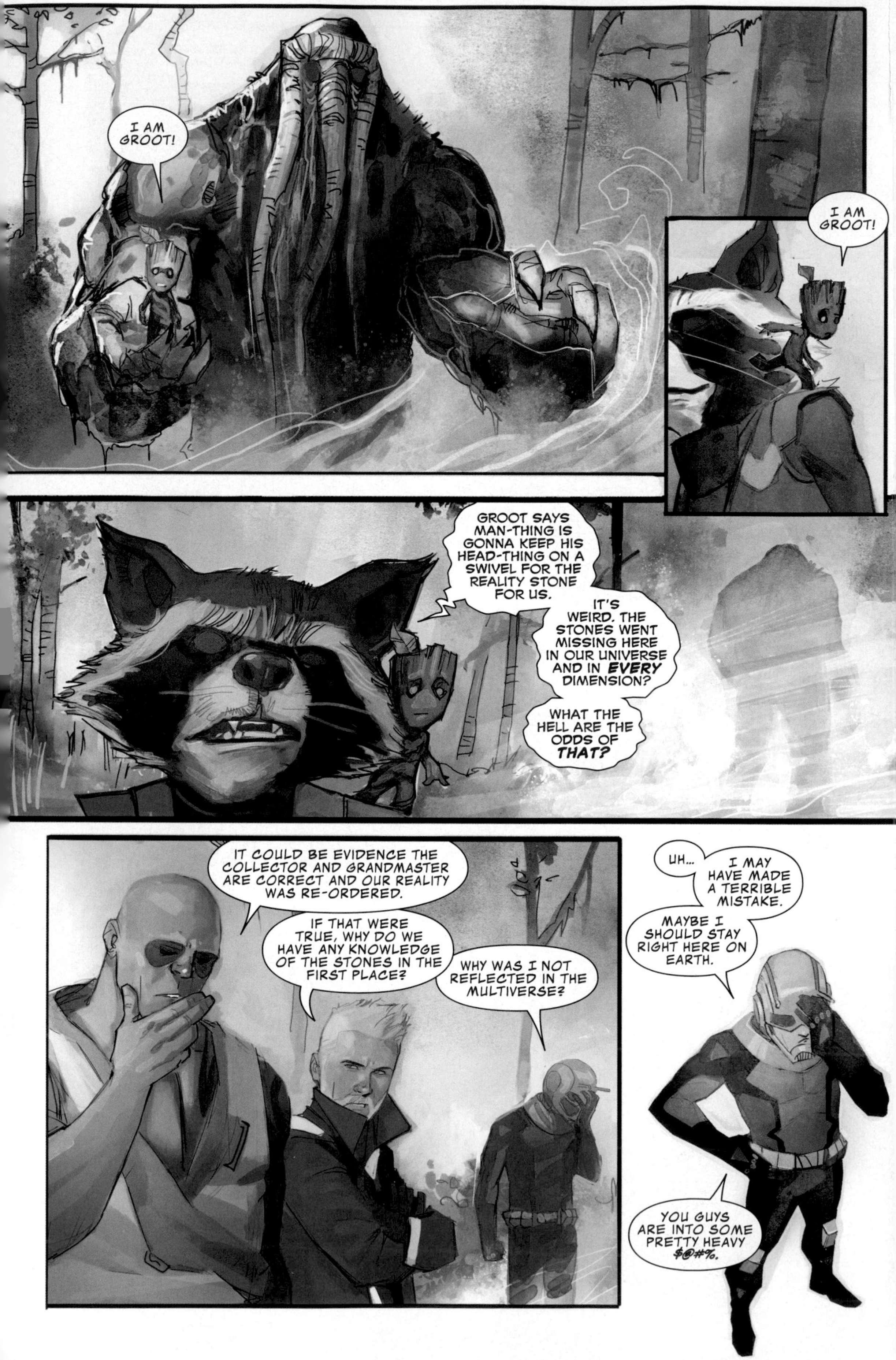
I AM GROOT!
I AM GROOT!
GROOT SAYS MAN-THING IS GONNA KEEP HIS HEAD-THING ON A SWIVEL FOR THE REALITY STONE FOR US.
IT'S WEIRD. THE STONES WENT MISSING HERE IN OUR UNIVERSE AND IN *EVERY* DIMENSION?
WHAT THE HELL ARE THE ODDS OF *THAT?*
IT COULD BE EVIDENCE THE COLLECTOR AND GRANDMASTER ARE CORRECT AND OUR REALITY WAS RE-ORDERED.
IF THAT WERE TRUE, WHY DO WE HAVE ANY KNOWLEDGE OF THE STONES IN THE FIRST PLACE?
WHY WAS I NOT REFLECTED IN THE MULTIVERSE?
UH...
I MAY HAVE MADE A TERRIBLE MISTAKE.
MAYBE I SHOULD STAY RIGHT HERE ON EARTH.
YOU GUYS ARE INTO SOME PRETTY HEAVY $@#%.

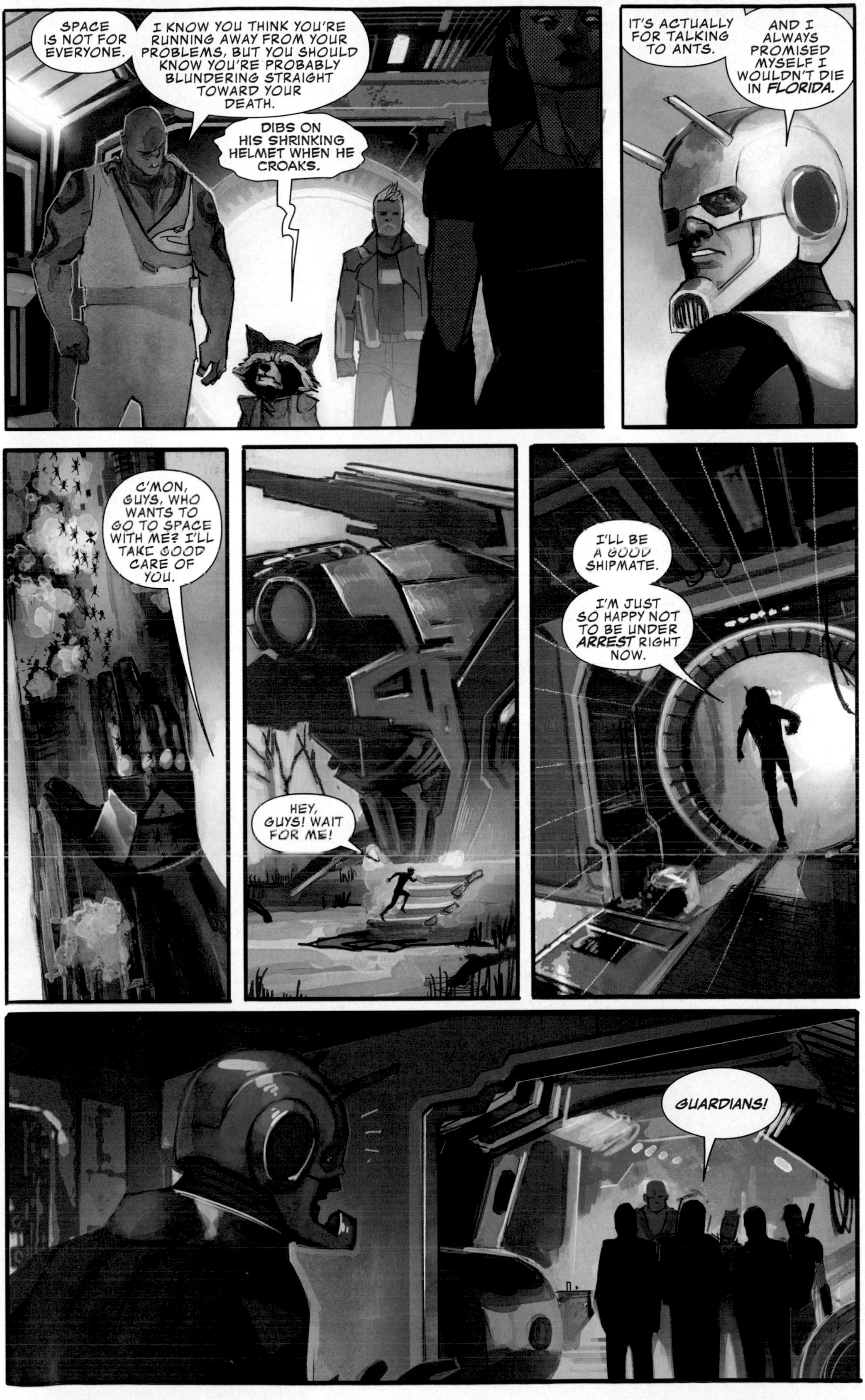
SPACE IS NOT FOR EVERYONE.
I KNOW YOU THINK YOU'RE RUNNING AWAY FROM YOUR PROBLEMS, BUT YOU SHOULD KNOW YOU'RE PROBABLY BLUNDERING STRAIGHT TOWARD YOUR DEATH.
DIBS ON HIS SHRINKING HELMET WHEN HE CROAKS.
IT'S ACTUALLY FOR TALKING TO ANTS.
AND I ALWAYS PROMISED MYSELF I WOULDN'T DIE IN FLORIDA.
C'MON, GUYS, WHO WANTS TO GO TO SPACE WITH ME? I'LL TAKE GOOD CARE OF YOU.
HEY, GUYS! WAIT FOR ME!
I'LL BE A GOOD SHIPMATE.
I'M JUST SO HAPPY NOT TO BE UNDER ARREST RIGHT NOW.
GUARDIANS!

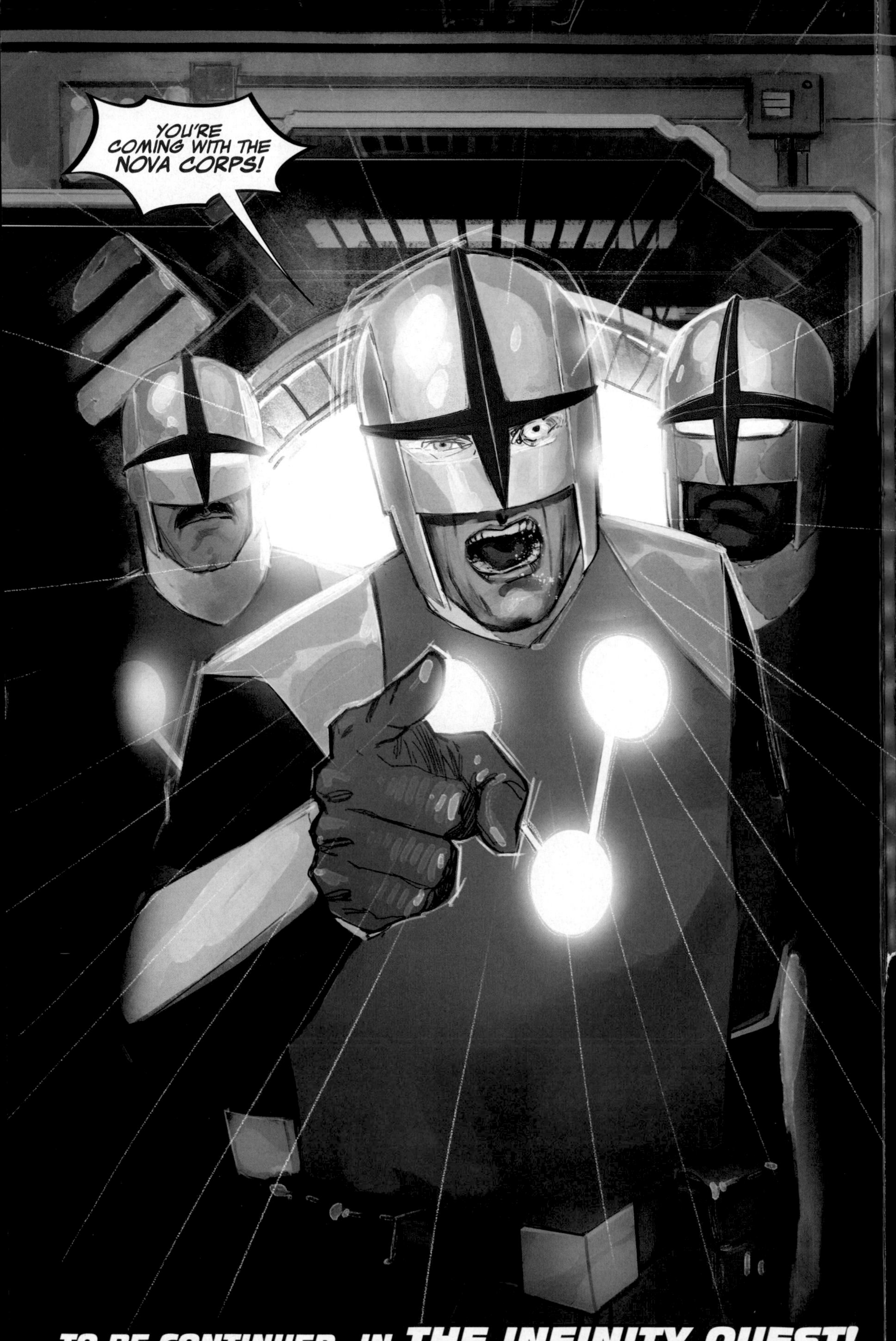

TO BE CONTINUED...IN THE INFINITY QUEST!

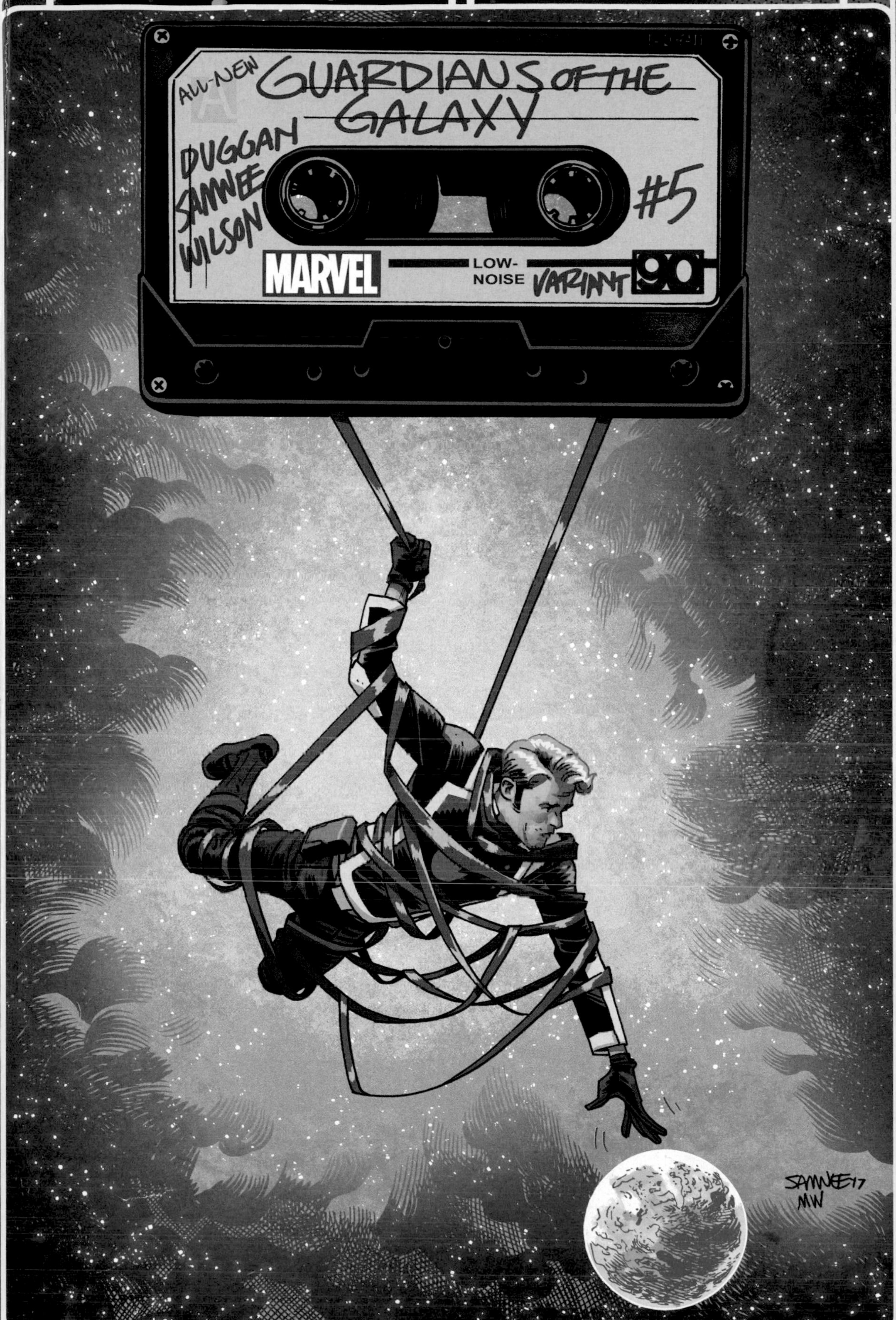
ALL-NEW
GUARDIANS OF THE GALAXY
DUGGAN
SAMNEE
WILSON
#5
MARVEL
LOW-NOISE
VARIANT
90
SAMNEE'17
MW

#5 VARIANT BY CHRIS SAMNEE & MATTHEW WILSON

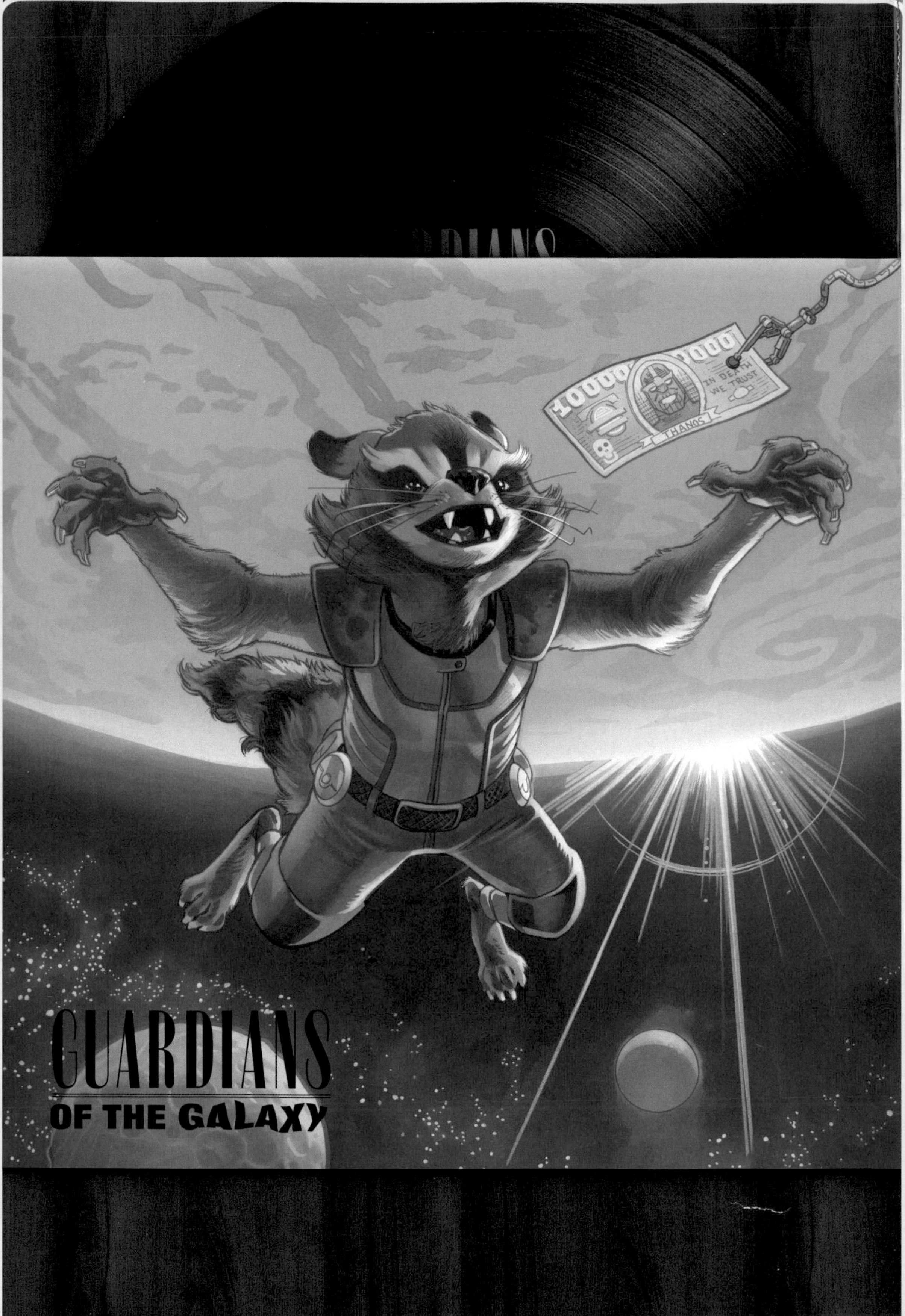
GUARDIANS
10000000
IN DEATH WE TRUST
THANOS
GUARDIANS
OF THE GALAXY

#9 ROCK-N-ROLL VARIANT BY MIKE HAWTHORNE & NATHAN FAIRBAIRN

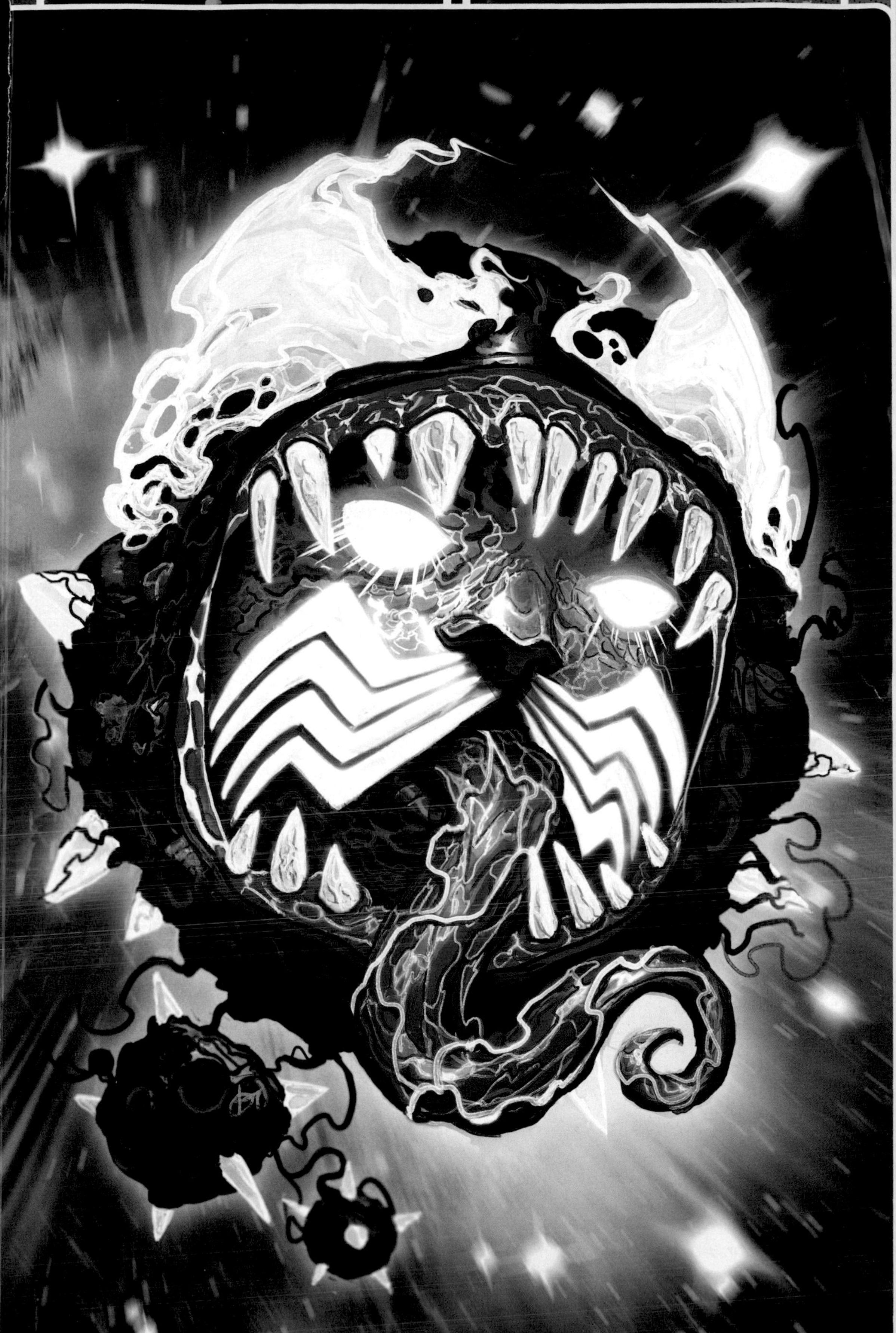

#9 VENOMIZED VILLAINS VARIANT BY **MIKE DEL MUNDO**

All-New GUARDIANS of the GALAXY

HOW TO DRAW GROOT
IN SIX EASY STEPS!
BY CHIP "I AM CHIP ZDARSKY" ZDARSKY

Wow! A "sketch variant cover"! Where comic companies make YOU do all the work! To prepare you to draw your very own GROOT, here's a fun and informative step-by-step guide!

1

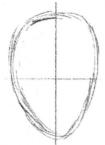

I am Groot.

2

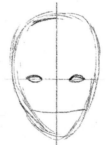

I am Groot.

3

I am Groot.

4

I am Groot.

5

I am—

6

—Groot.